RESURGENCE OF COUPS IN AFRICA

RESURGENCE OF COUPS IN AFRICA

REFLECTIONS FROM THE DIASPORA

UMARR ABU-DEEN

This book is dedicated to all Africans who have been compelled to leave their fatherland in search of a better life, driven away by the shadows of poor leadership. Your resilience, courage, and unwavering hope for a brighter future inspire this work. May this book serve as a testament to your struggles and a beacon for change.

If our leaders would channel but half the zeal
Spent chasing down minorities like LGBTQ,
To lifting their people from the depths of poverty,
Africa would rise, brighter, revitalized.

CONTENTS

INTRODUCTION

The migration crisis in Europe and America is an ever-growing concern. Countless young Africans are forced to leave their homelands each year, seeking refuge in foreign lands due to the inability of their governments to provide for their basic needs. This mass exodus is a testament to the deep-seated issues of poverty and political instability plaguing the continent.

The quiet villages and bustling cities of Africa represent places where dreams are born daily, only to be stifled by the harsh realities of life. These dreams, nurtured in the hearts of young men and women, often find no fertile ground to grow. The soil of their homelands, rich in culture and history, is impoverished by corruption and mismanagement. The seeds of ambition and hope struggle to take root amidst the drought of opportunity.

With each passing year, the numbers swell. Brave souls, driven by desperation and hope, embark on perilous journeys across deserts and seas. They face treacherous paths, risking everything for a chance at a better life. Their destinations are the lands of Europe and America, where they hope to find refuge, dignity, and the means to support their families back home. Governments, crippled by inefficiency and corruption, fail to provide the essentials—education, healthcare, employment. The very institutions meant to protect and nurture their citizens crumble under the weight of neglect. Political instability breeds fear and uncertainty, leaving many with no choice but to flee.

The migration crisis, then, is not merely a statistic. It is a living, breathing narrative of the African soul, yearning for the promise of a brighter tomorrow. It highlights the inability of governments to provide basic necessities and opportunities, leading to widespread dissatisfaction. This dissatisfaction weakens state institutions and creates a power vacuum that can be exploited by military factions or political rivals. The continuous outflow of young leaders and workforce further entrenches instability, increasing the likelihood of coups.

I am Umarr Abu-Deen Bakarr Sesay, from Sierra Leone, a Muslim, and a man whose path has taken unexpected turns. This is not my autobiography; it is the chronicle of countless young Africans like myself who are forced to flee their homelands each year, seeking refuge in Europe and America. Our numbers grow as we brave treacherous journeys to escape the grip of poverty and political instability.

In the United States, where I seek asylum, thousands of cases from Africa are processed every year. Many immigrants endure perilous crossings through South America and Mexico, risking their lives at the Southern border. I count myself among the fortunate ones who arrived through JFK International Airport, holding a visa I once obtained but had no opportunity to use due to my job. I never planned to live in another country other than as a tourist, but human rights abuses, economic hardship, and democratic backsliding have forced me and many others into exile to avoid confrontation with oppressive regimes.

My story is one among many. We all have different reasons for fleeing but our motives are largely not unconnected with poverty and bad leadership. Whether through an international airport, the Southern border, or precarious boats across the English Channel, we all share a common reason for not wanting to return home. From the internecine conflict in the DR Congo to the endless coups in the Sahel and terrorism in the Maghreb, the plight of young Africans is worsening amidst relentless political turmoil. This situation is worth brooding over and requires collective efforts by critical stakeholders, including the African Union, regional bodies, and the international community.

A notable concern is the resurgence of coups and the back-sliding of democracy. While many reasons are advanced for these unconstitutional changes of government, the common thread is leadership failure. This has inspired my work. I firmly believe that the only solution to reducing the surge of migrants, asylum seekers, and refugees from Africa is to address the root of the problem—Africa's bad leadership. It requires establishing democratic guardrails across the continent. My narrative emerges from a troubled mindset, one ill at ease with the reality that I cannot return home soon, and even as I reel from such thoughts, I share the concerns of Collier (2009). He notes that while democracy is a 'force for good,' the West is promoting its wrong features —"the façade rather than the essential infrastructure."

The incidence of coups in Africa is as intricate as it is multifaceted. It is a confluence of political, social, and economic factors. Data from various sources, including the United Nations and academic research, indicate that Africa has experienced over 100 coups since the 1950s, with a similar number of unsuccessful attempts. Corruption and economic mismanagement often serve as overarching rationales for these forceful takeovers, but deeper analysis reveals many motivations are externally induced and inherently self-serving. This work aims to delve into these antecedents and their impact, shedding light on how the masses' interests are often overlooked or exploited in the pursuit of power.

In West Africa, comprising 16 nations, military takeovers have been a recurring threat, with only Senegal managing to avoid such upheavals. Despite efforts to maintain stability, the region has not been immune to the specter of coups, as historical data and ongoing challenges indicate. The prevalence of coup attempts underscores a broader trend of political instability, with various factors contributing to the vulnerability of governments to such actions.

The concept of an autogolpe, or self-coup, adds another layer of complexity to understanding power struggles within African states. These occurrences, more commonplace than actual usurpations, often manifest in blatantly rigged elections and leaders seeking controversial third terms despite constitutional limitations and widespread protests. Even Senegal, the last bastion of democratic stability, has not been immune, as evidenced by President Macky Sall's unsuccessful attempt to extend his term.

It is, therefore, safe to infer that the increasing frequency of unconstitutional changes of government (UCGs) can be attributed, in part, to a declining trust in democracy among many Africans. Based on Afrobarometer findings, the preference for democracy over other forms of governance has declined from its 2012 level of around 75% to 66% in 2021/22 (AB Newsrelease, 2023). While this may seem like a substantial majority, it includes a significant number of individuals with uncertain opinions. Notably, 53% expressed the view that a coup could be deemed legitimate when civilian leaders abuse their power.

Examples of leaders who refuse to leave power after the expiration of their tenure abound. The late President Pierre Nkurunziza of Burundi in 2015, Alassane Ouattara of Côte d'Ivoire, and Alpha Condé of Guinea, both in 2020, are but a few. In response to the unrest caused by their actions, they declared states of emergency, suspended their countries' constitutions, and cracked down on protesters. These moves allowed them to maintain power and suppress opposition forces, highlighting the vulnerability of democratic processes to manipulation by incumbents seeking to prolong their rule. This underscores the challenges of democratic consolidation in Africa and the potential for leaders to subvert constitutional norms to cling to power.

The context in which usurpations occur has evolved over time, with globalization playing a pivotal role in reshaping Africa's political economy. The penetration of global forces across state boundaries has brought about significant changes, challenging existing power structures and creating new dynamics within African societies. Against this backdrop, the study of coups in Africa takes on added significance, offering insights into the broader forces shaping the continent's political landscape.

As we examine the varied manifestations of UCGs in our continent, it becomes evident that a deeper understanding of historical trends, contemporary challenges, and future trajectories is essential. This work seeks to contribute to this ongoing dialogue, providing a nuanced analysis of the resurgence of coups in Africa and their implications for the continent's future.

Definition

The term "coup" conjures different images depending on one's perspective. For someone from Burkina Faso, a coup is seen as nothing more than the intervention of people in military fatigues seizing political power. On the other hand, a person from Cameroon or Uganda, where dictatorships have used every means to perpetuate themselves in power, may view coups as part of a broader continuum of power struggles. Indeed, all these are coups in their motley manifestations.

The official definition of a coup, according to key regional instruments such as the Lomé Declaration of 2000 and the African Charter on Democracy, Elections, and Governance of 2007, refers to an unconstitutional change of government. These documents outline several scenarios that constitute such changes: military coups against democratically elected governments, interventions by mercenaries to replace elected administrations, the overthrow of elected governments by armed dissident groups or rebel movements, and the refusal of outgoing administrations to relinquish power after losing free, fair, and regular elections. These definitions underscore the importance of upholding democratic principles and processes in governance across Africa.

However, the reality on the ground is more complex. In countries where governments are not democratically elected, the legitimacy of power transitions is often in question. This situation presents a critical issue that regional bodies like the Economic Community of West African States (ECOWAS) and the African Union (AU) must address. Yet, finding an adequate response remains elusive. As Fonteh Akum et al. (2020) aptly captured, "...the focus on unconstitutional changes of government reflects simplistic approaches to governance crises."

Consider the situation in Zimbabwe, where Robert Mugabe's long rule ended not through an electoral process but a military intervention that many Zimbabweans welcomed. Immediately after, the ousted president sent in his resignation to parliament, but not before the House initiated impeachment proceedings against him. The ruling Zanu-PF party announced that former vice-president Emmerson Mnangagwa will succeed Mr. Mugabe. (BBC, 2017). By what alchemy would a leader who is already ousted resign? I am sure even Zimbabweans were perplexed about whether they should call the transition a coup, a voluntary resignation, or a resignation because of the impeachment proceedings. Or maybe it was time for the Zanu-PF to get a change of leader through their long-suspended but typical one-party parliamentary style. Whatever it was, many viewed it as a necessary correction. In Egypt, the military ousted President Mohamed Morsi, an elected leader, following mass protests against his rule. While some viewed this as a return to military dictatorship, others saw it as a necessary action to restore order and prevent further chaos.

The essence of democracy is increasingly being questioned globally, with emerging trends suggesting a shift from focusing solely on procedural aspects to emphasizing the outcomes of democratic processes. These evolving dynamics compel us to reconsider our understanding of democracy and its implications for governance. In Sudan, the ousting of Omar al-Bashir in 2019 followed months of civilian protests demanding his removal after three decades in power. It was followed by a fragile transition to civilian rule, and in 2023/24, a stalemate superintended by military factions who refuse to cede power to each other. This blurs the dichotomy between military and civilian leadership in the post-coup period.

The challenges are, therefore, manifold. How do we address the legitimacy of power when the initial election itself was flawed, such as in Sierra Leone? How do we ensure that interventions lead to positive outcomes rather than further instability? How do we reconcile the immediate need for change with the long-term goal of democratic consolidation?

As I reflect on these questions from my status as an asylee, I see the need for a deeper, more nuanced approach to understanding coups and their impact on African governance. Perhaps it is not enough to condemn or support these events based on their adherence to procedural norms since what constitutes norms in one instance may prove an exception in another, based on the mood of our Western benefactors. Perhaps we should consider the broader context—the socioeconomic conditions, the aspirations of the people, and the ultimate goals of peace, stability, and development.

In this narrative, the definition of a coup extends beyond the simplistic image of soldiers seizing power. It encompasses the struggles of ordinary people against autocratic regimes and façade democracies, the complex interaction of local and global forces, and the ongoing quest for a political system that truly represents the will of the people. This is the story of Africa's coups—intricate, multifaceted, and deeply intertwined with the continent's past, present, and future.

Purpose and Scope of the Book

This book is born from the urge to take an insightful look at the rationale behind forceful transitions of power, particularly as they come full circle at the beginning of the third decade of the millennium.After a period of relative stability, this third surge of coups signals a troubling reversal of progress toward democratic governance in Africa, highlighting the need for a nuanced approach of the problem and concerted efforts to address underlying issues and uphold democratic principles across the continent. The factors driving this resurgence vary, including political instability, socioeconomic challenges, ethnic tensions, and dissatisfaction with entrenched leadership. Also, external influences, such as geopolitical competition and interference, can exacerbate internal tensions and contribute to the erosion of democratic norms. An in-depth look at these factors and how they converge to motivate usurpations is what rivets me.

However, it bears mentioning that this book is not a historical account of coups, which indicates a departure from conventional approaches that focus solely on past events. It is also not intended to provide a sequential order of coup orchestration. The aim is to dissect the causes, dynamics, and implications of UCGs in our beloved continent, much like peeling the layers of an onion. Each peel is as revealing as the previous one. As we unpeel further, we aim to critique prevailing notions of democracy in the continent and reinvigorate the view that much of what Africans call democracy is a make-believe conception about what the political system is actually not. It is merely a façade, lacking in functionality and bereft of the integrity of true democratic systems. This is an attempt to set an objective standard for it, and examine it based on such western standards.

As Africans in the diaspora, we are profoundly affected by the level of democratic backsliding. Our ties to our home countries remain strong, and we feel the impact of political instability on our families, friends, and communities back home. The erosion of democratic norms and the resurgence of coups remind us of the fragility of progress and the need for robust, functional governance systems, which this work intends to highlight.

Additionally, we may seek to draw parallels with other governance systems in the globe, shedding light on areas of divergence and convergence. In attempting this, we will explore the policy implications of misconceptions about democracy in Africa, offering insights for policymakers and practitioners.

This work also aspires to contribute to academic discourse by challenging existing paradigms and offering alternative perspectives on democracy and coups in Africa. It aims to reinvigorate the discussion around what true democracy should entail and how it can be realized on the continent. In line with a pragmatist worldview, this book hopes to provide valuable insights for scholars, policymakers, activists, and regional bodies like the African Union, helping them to understand and address the political challenges facing Africa.

Significance of the Study

At no point in Africa's tumultuous history has the need to study the issues confronting our body politic been more justified than now. Examining recent coups provides valuable insights into the political dynamics within African countries, including power struggles, governance issues, and the role of the military in politics. Such analysis reveals how these usurpations often challenge democratic governance, highlighting the fragility of democratic institutions across the continent. By scrutinizing these events, we can better understand the state of democracy in Africa and identify critical areas for improvement.

Coups, as contagious as they can be, significantly impact regional security, necessitating a thorough understanding of regional dynamics. This study emphasizes the importance of policymakers appreciating the underlying issues that influence stability and peace. A proper grasp of these dynamics can help in crafting effective strategies to promote regional stability and prevent the spread of conflict.

Understanding the factors that contribute to coups is

crucial for shaping international responses and interventions. Coups invariably affect international relations, disrupting diplomacy and foreign policy. By identifying early warning signs and the general and specific motivations behind coups, this study can contribute to conflict prevention efforts. Addressing underlying grievances before they escalate into violence or political instability is essential for maintaining peace.

Moreover, this study aims to contribute to the broader discourse on democratic governance by providing a nuanced analysis of contemporary coups. It highlights the importance of robust democratic institutions and the need for reforms to enhance their resilience against undemocratic forces.

Also, knowing the motivations behind UCGs can help stem the mass exodus from the continent. Many Africans flee their home countries to escape the political instability, economic hardship, and human rights abuses often precipitated by coups. This mass migration exerts significant pressure on Europe and America, straining resources and complicating immigration policies.

The significance of this study extends beyond academic discourse. It seeks to provide actionable insights for policymakers, regional bodies, and international organizations. By promoting a deeper understanding of the causes and consequences of coups, the study aims to foster more effective interventions and support for democratic governance.

In conclusion, studying contemporary coups in Africa is essential for advancing our understanding of political developments, promoting democratic governance, enhancing regional stability, and fostering peaceful relations both within Africa and with the international community. This study not only seeks to unravel the complexities of coups but also to provide a roadmap for building a more stable and democratic Africa.

ONE

HISTORICAL CONTEXT

Parallels Between Post-Independence Coups and
Contemporary Usurpations

Our hearts remain tethered to the pulse of Africa, disheartened by the turmoil that has engulfed our homeland. The resurgence of coups in Africa and the varying of western democracy to fit different contexts cannot bear ignoring. Lately, the coup landscape has been shaped by factors beyond the motivations observed in the post-independence era. These factors serve to gloss the existing political, social, and economic undercurrents on the continent and, at the same time, provide additional reasoning for the seizure of power. Post-colonial Africa witnessed a surge in the incidence of coups, reflecting the nascent and rudimentary nature of our body politic, but also Africans' quest to improve their lot and get their governance architecture right.

Corruption, economic mismanagement, and poverty provided overarching rationale for the coups of yester years.

While these challenges still resonate across the continent, in recent times, justification for the usurpation of power has snowballed into nuanced political factors and, ironically, at times, democratic influences. Habitually, larger democracies now endorse certain segments of society to seize power through force, putting an end to the rule of so-called democratic governments. As witnessed in many countries like Egypt under Mohamed Morsi, governments elected through democratic processes are the ones that other stakeholders find themselves needing to safeguard democracy against.

The first decade of the millennium was a buffer between the old order and the second surge. A semblance of democratic stability prevailed. Militaries had grown weary of meddling in politics. Civil wars were being negotiated to peaceful settlements by international moral guarantors. That notwithstanding, the optimism that characterized the early years of independence was never met. Few nations like Ghana, Mauritius, and Senegal showed signs of economic stability, but the struggle of the masses never ended, accentuating the need for more desperate usurpations. Dictatorship in North Africa festered, leading to a second wave of power seizure, characterized by massive protests and overthrows, primarily led by civilians—the Arab spring.

Colonial influence in independent Africa, especially in the context of cold war superpower rivalry, was the common vice that ailed nations. Under the sobriquets of nationalism and Pan-Africanism our primogenotors nurtured high hopes in having their kith and kin assume the mantle of power. The vast wave of nationalism that swept the continent, therefore, provided a major catalyst to self-rule. The nascent nationalist movements in British and French colonies received significant momentum from the Second World War. Both colonial powers had enlisted their African subjects to join the war effort, and the response was remarkable: over one million Africans participated in conflicts across Europe, North Africa, and the Far East. They were consistently told that they were risking their lives in the name of freedom and democracy (BBC History Extra, 2021).

The euphoria of self-rule carried with it a specter of optimism that almost threw caution in the wind. The nationalists little envisioned the challenges that attend inheriting a governance monolith that Africans were never predisposed to. One that is out of kilter with their economic realities, and, above all, one that relied on the goodwill of the people they would wrest it from. The ethno-regional diversity of people living within the same national boundaries eventually compounded the problems of the new African states. In less than a quarter of a century after independence, the state system witnessed a growing indigenous character. These states, being among the world's newest, were characterized by a polity of strong regional, tribal, clan-based, and religious affiliations over and above national imperatives (Crocker, 2019).

Besides the ethno-regional factor, the nationalists' drive was on a collision course withAfrican institutions that they thought aided the white man to tarry. Bates (2010) maintains that a significant aspect of the nationalist movements was the extent to which they targeted the institution of chieftaincy, which was a major traditional structure the colonialists had mainstreamed in their governance arrangement.

Hence, European powers bequeathed a poisoned chalice in the form of weak democratic institutions and poor macroeconomic fundamentals, as well as bitter sub-national rivalries that only benefitted the west. They had made minimal efforts to foster the necessary conditions for the establishment and flourishing of democratic politics. Few nations had the opportunity of conducting multi-party elections, while some held them only on the eve of independence. In others, the colonial powers tried to manipulate elections to impose their allies, exposing the continent to the first bouts of election rigging. In Sierra Leone, the opposition leader who asked for earlier elections through an Elections Before Independence Movement (EBIM) was made to celebrate his country's independence in jail.

Therefore, the colonial legacy resulted in the establishment of governments marked by a form of 'fragile authoritarianism' (The Conversation, 2021). Liberation leaders who, after achieving independence, held political visions and ideological stances that conflicted with the interests of major colonial powers did not survive to recount their experiences. Political entrepreneurs took over, and they were more concerned with giving the white man what he wanted with the give-and-take of accumulating greater power. Their governance style only further stretched the gap between the state and society.

Few decades on dissatisfaction would turn towards the long spell of dictatorship of these political entrepreneurs that have nothing to show for it. This would occasion a new form of restlessness, leading to popular uprisings. With the belief that these dictatorships or façade democracies have the imperial nod of the former colonial powers, especially France, a new wave of anti-imperialist sentiments among the populace would permeate the continent.

The Cold War influence saw perhaps the most overbearing motivations to abrupt regime changes and the shaping of political dynamics. The major powers avoided direct confrontation but instead fueled conflicts between their allies in Africa (as well as in Asia), turning extensive portions of the continent into battlegrounds where primarily locally enlisted soldiers engaged in combat. In effect, Africans were the losers. Intelligence agencies in the United States and the Soviet Union acted as kingmakers, providing funds and orchestrating coups to install compliant rulers.

In 1945, Africa was predominantly under the influence of the United States' allies and clients, including Britain, France, Portugal, Belgium, and Spain. At that time, only four states were independent: Liberia, Egypt, Ethiopia, and South Africa. By the mid-1950s, the Cold War had a significant impact on North Africa, with the commencement of the Algerian War of independence against France in 1954 and Egypt adopting an assertive, independent foreign policy. Egypt's actions included challenging British influence in the Middle East, supporting Algerian rebels, and procuring weapons from the Soviet bloc (Gleijeses, 2021). In essence, what sets previous takeovers apart from contemporary times is the accumulation of factors that have lent force to the invisible western hand. While international influences still play a role, the nature of global geopolitics has evolved.

Against the backdrop of poverty that has persisted to contemporary times, the already distressing situation has been exacerbated by the impact of national emergencies like the coronavirus pandemic, which dealt a severe blow to Africa's vulnerable economies. To the extent that trade and aid from our global partners ground in one fell swoop, the macro-economic responses from the African side of the globe certainly spelled doom for our balance of trade, exchange rates, commodity exports, and our sovereign balance sheets altogether. Joblessness in Nigeria stood at 33.3% (1 in 3) by 2021. (The Guardian, 2021). More than half the continent's population was reckoned to be extremely poor in the wake of the pandemic.

Nations' overdependence on trade concessions, aid, and mining royalties was given a reality check. For the first time, governments got the jab to shake off from their slumber and utilize the abundance of domestic resources, both human and natural, to think and act independently of foreign aid. In essence, COVID-19 was meant to serve as a neutralizing agent to the Dutch disease that plagued Africa since independence.

However, African leaders' inability to draw an abiding lesson from the pandemic and build resilient economies was debilitating. All they saw was another opportunity to divert the nozzle of pandemic funds. This presented a strain on already weak governments and an even heavier burden on dictatorships. Some leaders exploited the crisis to consolidate power and extend their terms, citing the need for stability during uncertain times. States of Emergency were imposed without due process, while human rights violations assumed a new high in the midst of spiraling cost of living crises. In effect, the drag left by the pandemic and the trend towards increased authoritarianism led to resistance and created a new bold brew for opposition groups and civil society.

The impact of Covid-19 was just another peel to the multi-layered issues that revealed governance vulnerabilities and prepared the ground for some desperate and forceful takeover of power. As hinted earlier, the perversion of democratic processes and institutions is among the more overbearing motivations for forceful takeovers these days. While Africa grapples with the third surge of coups since 2019, nations are still dealing with nation-building in a manner reminiscent of the immediate post-colonial era, only this time, threatened by the devastation of democratic dictatorships. "Democratic" because most leaders have sculpted a way to go by the epithet.

Authoritarian and semi-authoritarian leaders, mindful of international perceptions, have adorned their regimes with democratic façades, including periodic but manipulated elections. Presidential term limits have often been bypassed through constitutional coups. Heads of state have skillfully exploited societal divisions and accentuated concerns about hostile foreign intervention to divert public scrutiny from their undemocratic governance. As a result, takeovers happen in nations that have made significant progress toward democratic governance, giving rise to concerns about the erosion of already established democratic institutions and practices.

This presents a notable shift in the way military coups are conceptualized and implemented. In the past, those in the defense department, mostly the mainstream military, were the perpetrators. Now, spurred by the groping and endorsement of non-state actors, we see the involvement of a new force of Presidential Guards as supposed do-gooders, giving rise to a phenomenon political commentators refer to as 'Feel Good' Militarism.

Elite presidential guard units are typically smaller, more tightly controlled, and more loyal to the sitting president than the broader military. Their involvement in coups suggests that discontent with the government may exist even within the inner circles of power, reliving the Shakespearean adage—security gives way to conspiracy. Moreover, elite units presuppose precision and control, much more than the broader military's potential for chaos and resistance. This trend underscores the complex relationships between political leaders, security forces, and the broader population, raising questions about governance, accountability, and the consolidation of democratic norms.

The dynamic interplay between technology and politics significantly influences the landscape of coup dynamics in the contemporary era. The Information Age and the internet play a crucial role in the orchestration of coups by facilitating rapid communication, anonymous planning, and the dissemination of information for propaganda and mobilization. These technologies also provide access to intelligence, support global networks, and expose coup attempts through public awareness. Additionally, governments leverage the internet for surveillance and countermeasures to detect and prevent coup activities.

Perhaps it could be argued that dictators and semi-autocrats that are falling prey to usurpations do not quite appreciate the power of media in the modern era. Their penchant for the perquisites of power has a deficit in their obliviousness of information and communication technology. Communication is no more the exclusive estate of traditional media institutions that can be easily gagged by the state. As a result, governing, vis-à-vis dealing with dissent, comes with a heavier burden in this era of citizen journalism. Previously, despots had to worry more about security than public scrutiny. Now, opposition and civil society fire on all cylinders, with the prying yet evasive media tools in ample supply. Specifically, the rise of social media has altered the communication landscape. Protests, mobilization, and information dissemination happen rapidly, influencing the speed and dynamics of political events. Coup plotters no longer have to wait to lay hold of the state broadcaster to announce their presence.

Early coups were sometimes met with limited public resistance, and popular participation was not as prominent. Now, civilian movements, protests, and social mobilization are more common. People often play a more active role in expressing dissatisfaction and shaping the outcomes of political transitions. While the military were the sole agents of abrupt change in the past, we later have instances when civilian-led movements and protests have played a crucial role in shaping political transitions on the continent. The Arab Spring uprisings that started in Tunisia and permeated across Arab North Africa led to the ousting of President Ben Ali, Hosni Mubarak and other leaders, including Colonel Muamar Qaddafi. Massive protests and demonstrations, primarily led by civilians, played a significant role in their ouster.

The irony is that while the influence of external players has not waned much, their democratic diktats on African nations do not seem to be able to stem the growing tide of coups. A phenomenon definitely worth brooding over and one which helped to ignite the flicker of inspiration for this work. There is an increased emphasis on diplomatic pressure, sanctions, and international condemnation of coups. Regional organizations and the African Union play more active roles in responding to political crises than deterrence. However, the occurrence of these coups in any given country does not spell the end of similar such occurrences in that country. It simply portends a chain reaction that is only waiting to ignite the next tinder box.

Mali's coup, and indeed Burkina Faso and Niger, were motivated by security considerations emanating from terrorist activities in the region. While some coups in the past may have been motivated by anti-colonial sentiments or grievances against authoritarian regimes, they were less directly linked to contemporary forms of terrorism, as seen today (ISS/PSC Report, 2023). In addition, unlike the post-independence era when the coup context was characterized by Cold War dynamics, most modern coups occur in regions where terrorism is already prevalent, such as in the Sahel where terrorist groups like Al-Qaeda in the Islamic Maghreb (AQIM), Islamic State in the Greater Sahara (ISGS) or Boko Haram operate. This can further exacerbate security challenges and complicate efforts to restore democratic governance.

References

1. Adebajo, A., & Rashid, I. (2004). West Africa's Security Challenges: Building Peace in a Troubled Region. Lynne Rienner Publishers.
2. Adekoya, R. (2021). Why are coups making a comeback in Africa? CNN.
3. Afrobarometer. (2019). Democracy in Africa: Demand, Supply, and the 'Dissatisfied Democrat.'
4. Afrobarometer Newsletter. (2023) Declining satisfaction of threatens African democracy, Afrobarometer CEO reveals. Afrobarometer.
5. African Union. (2021). African Peer Review Mechanism (APRM) Reports. Retrieved from https://au.int/en/organs/aprm
6. Akum, F., Djilo, F. and Handy, P. (2020). Governance in Africa: From Complexities to Realities. Institute for Security Studies.
7. Al Jazeera. (2019). Sudan: How Bashir Fell.
8. Bates, R. (2010). Democracy in Africa: A very Short History. Social Research.
9. BBC News. (2017). Zimbabwe's Robert Mugabe resigns, ending 37-year rule.
10. Bratton, M., & van de Walle, N. (1997). Democratic Experiments in Africa: Regime Transitions in Comparative Perspective. Cambridge University Press.
11. Cheeseman, N. (2015). Democracy in Africa: Successes, Failures, and the Struggle for Political Reform. Cambridge University Press.
12. CNN.com. (2021). France returns 26 looted artifacts and artworks to Benin.

13. Collier, P. (2009). Wars, Guns, and Votes: Democracy in Dangerous Places. HarperCollins.

14. Crocker, C. (2019). African Governance: Challenges and Their Implications. Hoover Institution.

15. Freedom House. (2021). Freedom in the World Report.

16. Gleijeses, P. (2021). Africa in the Cold War. Oxford Bibliographies.

17. Herbst, J. (2000). States and Power in Africa: Comparative Lessons in Authority and Control. Princeton University Press.

18. History Extra. (2021). Snuffed out democracies and poisoned toothpaste: how the Cold War wreaked havoc in post-colonial Africa. BBC Magazine.

19. International Crisis Group. (2020). Crisis Watch: Tracking Conflict Worldwide. Retrieved from https://www.crisisgroup.org/crisiswatch

20. Nwabueze, B. O. (1993). Democratization. Spectrum Books.

21. Organization of African Unity (OAU). (2000). Lomé Declaration on Unconstitutional Changes of Government.

22. The Conversation. (2021). How Colonial Rule Predisposed Africa to Fragile Authoritarianism.

23. The Guardian. (2020). Alassane Ouattara Wins Third Term in Côte d'Ivoire Elections.

24. The Guardian. (2021). Unemployment rises to 33.3%.

25. The World Bank. (2021). World Development Report.

26. Transparency International. (2021). Corruption Perceptions Index.

27. United Nations Development Programme (UNDP). (2020). Human Development Report.

28. van de Walle, N. (2001). African Economies and the Politics of Permanent Crisis, 1979-1999. Cambridge University Press.

TWO
GENERAL TRIGGERS 1: GOVERNANCE ISSUES

Comprehending the probable motives behind forceful takeovers as we know them today necessitates an examination of antecedents that culminate into desperation among citizens, ultimately resulting in a breakdown of state order. Such antecedents are of a diverse character and begin with governance issues, which encompass a range of challenges, including corruption, weak institutions, lack of accountability, and limited transparency. Together, these provide an appealing recipe for state capture.

Political stability vs Democracy

I explore this subject, mindful of the West's role in it. Western powers, with their selective application of democratic standards to Africa, stand as both observers and actors in the ongoing saga between stability and democracy. My realization is stark and clear: coups will remain a fixture of African politics as long as we continue to sacrifice democracy on the altar of political stability. States in contemporary Africa have mastered the craft of subverting democratic tenets and remain politically stable, but only so far. Stability is often associated with order, predictability, and the absence of political turmoil, which can be essential for economic development and social well-being. A politically stable environment provides a foundation for sustained growth and prosperity.

However, political turmoil becomes almost inevitable in the absence of foundational democratic principles such as the rule of law, justice, transparency, and accountability to the citizens. This makes political stability and democracy two aspects of state governance that reinforce each other. Military regimes often justify their rise to power in the absence of political stability and democratic backsliding (Price et al.), making both phenomena two complementary halves of the governance equation.

African nation-states have found a way to make the two concepts mutually exclusive, giving heightened regard to the imperative to stay stable, even in the absence of good governance credentials. Often and eventually, this comes with a price to pay. Rwanda, under Paul Kagame, represents a live bill board of a politically stable country that bears the hallmarks of democratic uncertainty. Freedom House, the globally-renowned evaluator of the degree of freedom enjoyed by citizens of various countries and specific territories, stated this about the Rwandan government in their 2022 Freedom in the World report:

"While the regime has maintained stability and economic growth, it has also suppressed political dissent through pervasive surveillance, intimidation, torture, and renditions or suspected assassinations of exiled dissidents."

Such a scenario obviously serves as a compelling incentive for seizing power. Despite winning international commendation for its low carbon footprint and a relatively successful economic model, Rwanda is only but a powder keg in the incendiary atmosphere of coups. There are extensive reports of opposition parties facing intimidation and harassment in the country, which has been under the continuous rule of the same party since 1994. Throughout his tenure as president, Kagame has effectively subdued the nation into a state of Pentecostal obedience, governing it with the precision and fervor reminiscent of an exemplary charismatic church.

The scenario where a country is liberated by a military hero or freedom fighter is given greater consideration by Andrew Friedman in an article captioned Kagame's Rwanda: Can an Authoritarian Development Model Be Squared with Democracy and Human Rights?He drewparallels with George Washington, a military leader of the American Revolution, and Nelson Mandela, a civilian figure of the apartheid struggle, both of whom emerged as leaders with "tremendous influence that eclipses the popularity and strength of the new government." Both individuals opted to surrender power in a manner that epitomizes democracy, but unfortunately, others like Robert Mugabe and Kagame himself clung to power through increasingly repressive measures.

"While some countries have been fortunate enough to have their transitions transformed and continued by a leader willing to peacefully and constitutionally step down from power, far more countries have been cursed with a revolutionary leader that opts against ceding power. It is an unfortunate occurrence that many more societies have found the process of democratization doomed by a Mugabe rather than sustained by a Mandela." (Friedman (2012) p 270 Vol. 14,253)

North Africa, before the Arab Spring, was marked by a significant democratic shortfall that sabotaged the foundations of stability. Tension built up and eventually led to an eruption.

Another illustration of a relatively prosperous and stable regime with a huge democratic deficit was Gabon before the ouster of the forty-years Bongo dynasty. A few hours after Alie Bongo was declared winner of the presidential elections, the military took over power, reinforcing the argument that stability is only skin-deep in the absence of democratic tenets. Equatorial Guinea also looms large among many others.

However, most African nations demonstrate hybrid regimes, blending democratic characteristics with prominent autocratic traits. Despite their outward portrayal of democracy, they frequently lack the essential elements necessary for genuine democratic governance. The Conversation (2017), in a publication titled 'What drives instability in Africa and what can be done about it,' highlights that these pseudo-democracies inherently pose a heightened risk of instability and are more vulnerable to disruptions compared to either fully democratic or fully autocratic systems. With all the forward momentum, it will not take long before the vulnerabilities revealed by despots catch up with them and the nations they lead.

Corruption and Nepotism

Dynastic rule is a decisive feature of African politics. It carries with it all the hallmarks of corruption and nepotism. Corruption is the most cited justification for usurpations, making the monstrosity the biggest canker to Africa's progress. The Washington Post aptly captured corruption as being 'as old as power and as current as the morning headlines, in Africa as in the rest of the world.'

By Afrobarometer studies in 2019/20, perceptions that

corruption was worsening were most widespread in Mali, Gabon, Ivory Coast, and Guinea. Three of these countries have witnessed usurpations, while Ivory Coast saw a dramatic change of constitution that has propelled the president into a controversial third term. Transparency International, 2023 chronicled a marked rise in corruption in Mali (28), Guinea (26), Niger (32) and Gabon (28). Every facet of public life is either a pervasion of due process or a drain of public funds.

The prevalence of corruption additionally undermines the rule of law by weakening the institutions responsible for upholding a country's legal system. KPMG, in a report on tackling corruption in South Africa, noted that regardless of the methods employed to scrutinize the immediate and indirect impacts of the menace, it implies a reduction in the state resources allocated to fulfill socio-economic rights. These rights encompass access to basic education, healthcare, food, water, social security, and housing. Usurpations generally thrive on these lacks.

Democracy was invented to do away with monarchies, but African dictators are more inclined to practice the latter in all but name. Republics exemplify imperial rule with a sense of grotesqueness that only typifies the middle ages. In Equatorial Guinea, President Teodoro Obiang Nguema Mbasogo, who deposed his uncle in a military putsch, appointed his son as Vice President and is on his sixth term in office since 1979.In states where public office is a family heirloom rather than earned based on merit and trust, there is a systematic waste of competencies and talents. Those who do not bequeath power to their sons have legacy candidates for succession as if missing out on the nepotistic drive would cost them their fame and fortune.

For us, citizens in the diaspora, the effects of corruption and nepotism are profound. These maladies have driven us to seek refuge in foreign lands, where we hope for better governance and opportunities. Corruption and nepotism have stripped our home countries of their potential, leaving behind a trail of poverty, instability, and disillusionment. We watch from afar, disheartened by the ongoing struggles yet hopeful that our stories and experiences can contribute to the call for change and a brighter future for Africa.

Weak Institutions

The continent faces significant losses in inadequacies and seepages in public institutions. From revenue collection to justice dispensation, the story does not get better. Customs and tax revenue are constantly being stymied for private gains. Tax avoidance and evasion, especially involving multinational companies, only add to the quandary. The Economic Development Report 2020 from UNCTAD indicated that Africa suffered a loss of $88.6 billion due to illicit financial flows in 2019, around the inception of the last surge.

Parks (et al. (2017)) in a Brooking publication, aptly describe the lip service paid by public institutions.

"Developing countries create anti-corruption commissions with no intention of ... recovering public funds; pass legislation that criminalizes human trafficking but fails to investigate ... egregious violations of the law; create "one-stop shops" to simplify ... registering a business without addressing ... challenges to operating a business; and establish courts and appoint judges that are nominally independent while tacitly endorsing interference in the affairs of the judiciary."

This palpability creates fertile ground for leaders to perpetuate themselves in office as well as nurtures the condition for usurpations. In the Democratic Republic of Congo (DRC), weak institutions have facilitated power grabs and prolonged political instability. The country, before 2019, experienced years of conflict and authoritarian rule, with successive leaders exploiting institutional weaknesses to cling to power. In the absence of strong democratic institutions, political elites have resorted to violence, corruption, and manipulation of the electoral process to maintain their grip on power.

Similarly, in South Sudan, weak institutions and entrenched ethnic divisions have fueled a protracted civil war and power struggle among political elites. The failure to build strong state institutions following independence in 2011 created an environment ripe for conflict, with competing factions vying for control over resources and power. As a result, the country has been mired in violence and instability, with devastating humanitarian consequences.

Invariably, democratic institutions are at their lowest ebb of functionality during national emergencies, as leaders exploit pandemics and security threats to subvert them to self-serving schemes. Campbell and Quinn (2021), in an article published by the Council on Foreign Relations, cite Covid-19 as a major culprit for the decline of democracy in sub-Saharan Africa.

Prior to the pandemic, a growing number of African heads of state were already taking steps to undermine term limits or manipulate elections to prolong their stay in power. The advent of COVID-19 afforded them increased leverage, offering a justification for delaying elections in Somalia and Ethiopia, suppressing opposition figures in Uganda and Tanzania, and imposing restrictions on media throughout the continent.

The Trifecta of Woes

As I reflect on the mainstreaming of lies, the blight of political parties, and the "party pikin" mentality that have shaped and often undermined our societies, I have come to understand that it is through the agency of the people that some of society's problems are perpetuated by bad leaders. At the same time, it is through their collective agency they are potentially remedied. The following explores how these factors play out in the political landscape of our continent, drawing attention to the intricate ways in which they influence governance and stability.

a) Mainstreaming Lies

Most governments are run not by agenda but by propaganda. In essence, lies are an essential ingredient of the African body politic. Leaders recruit lie entrepreneurs in the guise of civil society organizations and media outlets to promote their nefarious agenda. Consistently across the board, where constitutions are being bastardized to allow for an extension of term limits, it begins with personnel in the civil society engaging the media with concocted narratives to prepare the ground for the grand commission. All perverted government processes in Sierra Leone in recent times were induced by either the complicity of or active participation of civil society elements that were supposed to watch out for the people.

Governments have devised various tactics to mainstream lies, including control over traditional media, restrictions on freedom of the press, online censorship, propaganda through state-controlled outlets, and manipulation of state institutions. They use state resources to influence media coverage and state security to criminalize dissent and stifle information disclosure. Each day, politicians' engagement with the media involves generating a stream of lies and propaganda. Oftentimes, when they are caught in their web of lies, they either engage the services of lie entrepreneurs or scheme other lies to cover the initial set of falsehoods.

Regrettably, our public officials seldom resign for distorting the truth. This lack of accountability fosters a culture where misinformation and propaganda thrive, contributing to the pervasive corruption and instability that plague the continent. In stark contrast, my experience in the West has shown a different standard of accountability, where public officials often resign when caught in lies or to demonstrate candor. For example, in the United Kingdom, Damian Green, the First Secretary of State, resigned in 2017 after misleading the public about the presence of pornographic material on his office computers. Another instance is the resignation of General Michael Flynn in 2017 as National Security Advisor after it was revealed he had lied about his conversations with the Russian ambassador. In fact, the sacking of public officials mainly comes in the form of resignation, unlike in Africa, where deceitfulness is standard operating procedure.

Government strategies are regularly aimed to shape narratives, regulate information flow, and maintain political control by influencing public perception. The tactics employed may vary across countries, but they generally involve measures that restrict independent journalism, limit freedom of speech, and manipulate the dissemination of information to serve the government's agenda. But like the laws of nature, it often does not take long before the lies catch up with leaders and create a feeling of disenchantment that leads to unrest.

The provision of social services is one area where propaganda must not be made. Like the proverbial pudding, their proof lies in tangible results. The promise and eventual failure to deliver these has undone many a leader in the continent.

Much of the coups are premised on the failure of leaders to deliver on assurances and, eventually, the lack of basic social services, which worsen the condition of living of the people.

b) The Blight of Political Parties

The configuration and operations of political parties across the continent are not in line with modern democratic tenets. Many ruling parties in Africa have entrenched themselves in power through undemocratic means, such as electoral fraud, repression of opposition, and manipulation of legal frameworks. Once in power, these parties often prioritize their own interests over the welfare of citizens while neglecting to address pressing socio-economic challenges. They lack strong institutional structures and mechanisms for effective governance. In Zimbabwe, the ruling ZANU-PF party has centralized power around its leadership. Institutional checks and balances are weak, and efforts to promote accountability and transparency in governance are stymied by party leadership.

Party secretariats are often plagued by corruption and lack of accountability, while most officials engage in embezzlement, bribery, and other forms of malfeasance. The ruling MPLA party in Angola faced allegations of corruption and nepotism, with party elites enriching themselves at the expense of the country's development. Numerous reports and investigations by international organizations like Transparency International and Human Rights Watch, highlighted the prevalence of corruption within the MPLA-led government, with allegations of high-level officials enriching themselves at the expense of the country's development.

Additionally, the MPLA's control over key sectors of the economy, such as oil and diamonds, facilitated corrupt practices and limited accountability. While erstwhile President José

Eduardo dos Santos' successor, President João Lourenço, has pledged to tackle corruption and reform governance structures, allegations of corruption involving the MPLA party continue to surface, underscoring the persistent challenges facing Angola in combating corruption and promoting transparency.

When not in government, parties are mostly impoverished. While waiting to form governments, they are venture capitalist concerns, waiting to be buoyed by the funds of shady business dealers. In systems where quality assurance operates only in principle, where the one-stop-shop model for registering businesses is only in name and policy, and where the business climate is ferocious, the tendency for party executives to be compromised when they assume office is high. This provides room for clientelism and patronage.

Additionally, many of them in Africa lack clear political ideologies. They prioritize gaining power over articulating a coherent vision or set of principles to steer the country on. Hence, their performance is characterized by opportunism and unpredictability. They lack strong internal structures and mechanisms for accountability, which invariably results in weak governance and the inability to effectively represent the interests of the people. Above all, their focus is primarily on winning the next elections rather than engaging in sustained grassroots organizing and policy development. This election-centric focus can contribute to a lack of long-term development planning.

Moreover, the African political system often gives rise to leaders whose charisma surpasses their political parties. This phenomenon is exemplified by leaders like Yoweri Museveni in Uganda, who has maintained power for decades through a combination of charisma, patronage, and repression. Such concentration of power erodes democratic norms and poses challenges to peaceful leadership transitions, as seen in the protracted and contentious transitions in countries like the Democratic Republic of Congo during the post-Mobutu era in the late 1990s and early 2000s, as well as during the 2018 presidential election.

In Togo, the succession of Gnassingbé Eyadéma's son, Faure Gnassingbé, in 2005, was botched as much within the internal structures of the ruling party as it was on the national front. The transition was marred by national protests and violence due to concerns about the legitimacy of the electoral process and the continuation of dynastic rule. The culture of strongman politics represents the most inhibiting feature of the growth and democratization of political parties. This definitely undermines democratic principles and has led to myriad challenges in leadership transitions.

c) Party Pikin Mentality

The thinking that nothing bad could possibly come from one's own political party or its leaders is a big cancer in African politics. Such blind deference to leaders only makes the supporters vulnerable rather than solving their collective problems. Excessive loyalty has led to challenges such as the personalization of power, limited internal accountability, factionalism, and the promotion of clientelism and patronage systems. For much of it, the youth become the tools of manipulation by politicians, doggedly subverting their sense of patriotism for parochial partisan alignments. Where the party interest is at stake, the *party pikin* (child of the party), a Krio tag for a resolute operative, would rather have hell break loose. However, as Americans know, this isn't something restricted to the developing world. The events of the US Capitol storming on January 6, 2021, showed that *party pikin* phenomenon can occur even in a nation with supposedly strong democratic systems. But its prevalence in Africa is overwhelming.

Similarly, in Kenya, Nigeria, Sierra Leone, Zimbabwe, and in many other countries, the political landscape has been characterized by intense party loyalty, with supporters of ruling and opposition parties fiercely defending their leaders, often at the expense of constructive policy debates and accountability. This loyalty has contributed to the perpetuation of ethnic-based politics, patronage networks, and electoral violence, hindering efforts to foster inclusive governance and address socio-economic challenges. Through activities such as electoral fraud, voter intimidation, and divisive rhetoric, the *party pikin* contributes to political polarization and hinders efforts to foster inclusive governance and social cohesion.

Moreover, their prioritization of party loyalty over substantive policy debate stifles dissenting voices, diminishes citizen engagement in the political process, and erodes public trust in democratic institutions. Addressing these issues requires strengthening democratic institutions, promoting civic education, and fostering a culture of accountability to ensure that political parties serve as vehicles for inclusive governance and sustainable development across the continent.

The influence of loyalty extends to succession dynamics and the potential for populism in a way that impacts the overall governance landscape in African countries. Striking a balance between loyalty and internal democratic principles is often elusive, creating an unhealthy political environment.

References

1. Acemoglu, D. & Robinson, J. (2012) Why Nations Fail: The Origins of Power, Prosperity, and Poverty. Crown Publishing Group.

2. Afropop Worldwide. (2020) Afrobarometer Round 8 Survey: Public Perceptions of Corruption in Africa. Afrobarometer.

3. Campbell, J. & O'Neil, S. (2021) How Covid-19 Is Hastening Decline of Democracy. Council on Foreign Relations.

4. Diamond, L. (2008) The Spirit of Democracy: The Struggle to Build Free Societies Throughout the World. Times Books.

5. Freedom House. (2022) Freedom in the World 2022: Rwanda. Freedom House.

6. Freedom House. (2022). Freedom in the World Report. Freedom House.

7. Friedman, A. (2012). Kagame's Rwanda: Can an Authoritarian Development Model Be Squared with Democracy and Human Rights? African Studies Review.

8. Gleijeses, P. (2021) Africa in the Cold War. Oxford Bibliographies.

9. Human Rights Watch (2023) Country Summary: Zimbabwe. Human Rights Watch, 2023.

10. Katjomuise, K. (20023) Digitizing Africa: Key to Stronger Institutions. Global Issues.

11. KPMG South Africa. (2020) Tackling Corruption: A South African Perspective. KPMG.

12. Osei, Akwasi, & Tertsakian, C. (2017) Time for

Change: A New Political Landscape in Angola. Human Rights Watch.

13. Parks, T., et al. (2017) Improving Public Governance. Brookings Institution, 2017.

14. Transparency International. (2023) Corruption Perceptions Index 2023." Transparency International.

15. United Nations Conference on Trade and Development (UNCTAD). (2020) Economic Development Report 2020: Illicit Financial Flows and the Covid-19 Pandemic. UNCTAD.

16. Washington Post. (2021) Africans think their governments aren't fighting corruption hard enough. Washington Post.

17. The Conversation (2017) What drives instability in Africa and what can be done about it. The Conversation.

18. The Guardian (2017) Damian Green sacked as first secretary of state after porn allegations. The Guardian.

19. The Guardian (2017) Michael Flynn resigns as national security adviser. The Guardian.

THREE
GENERAL TRIGGERS 2:
SOCIOECONOMIC FACTORS

Primordial Economic Interests

AFRICANS HAVE BEEN INGRAINED WITH THE BELIEF THAT the primary concern of Western nations is the transfer of power between political classes, unaware that the central focus is, in fact, their economic policies. While there are efforts to promote democratic governance and the transfer of power, particularly through support for initiatives aimed at strengthening institutions and advocating for free and fair elections, these endeavors are but facades masking underlying economic motives. Western nations have sometimes been accused of prioritizing stability and strategic alliances over democratic principles, leading to partnerships with authoritarian regimes. This has led to accusations of hypocrisy and inconsistency in Western foreign policy. Despite rhetoric surrounding democracy promotion, the reality is often a complex interplay between economic imperatives and political values, necessitating a delicate balancing act in Western engagement with Africa.

Diktats such as Structural Adjustment Programs (SAPs), as

well as trade agreements, foreign aid and investment, and debt relief initiatives, mandated neoliberal reforms that had detrimental effects on domestic industries and social services in many African countries. Trade agreements, like the Economic Partnership Agreements (EPAs) with the European Union, have been criticized for favoring Western interests and limiting African policy autonomy.

In addition, foreign aid, investment, and debt relief often come with conditions that require adherence to donor priorities and governance standards. In her book "Dead Aid: Why Aid Is Not Working and How There Is a Better Way for Africa," Damisa Moyo contends that aid has failed to spur sustainable economic development in Africa and has instead fueled a cycle of poverty and underdevelopment. This underscores the extent to which Western powers shape economic policies in our continent, often at the expense of domestic development agendas.

While economic considerations alone may not trigger coups, their interaction with political and social dynamics plays a crucial role in shaping the conditions for political upheaval. High levels of economic inequality, coupled with widespread poverty and unemployment, create a sense of desperation and frustration among the population.

However, the agency of coup plotters in exacerbating economic woes is not to be exculpated. A common parameter about African coups is that the factors that lead to their orchestration invariably become the casualties they leave in their wake. Despite military regimes' citing of corruption and economic mismanagement as their motivation to seize power, they often end up leaving the people that hailed their arrival worse off than they met them, having pilfered enormous public funds themselves. The National Provisional Ruling Council (NPRC) staged a very popular coup in Sierra Leone in 1992, when a civil war had just started. As a boy, I remember seeing crowds of people in the streets cheering the arrival of the young freedom fighters. Most of them were in their twenties, with their leader, who was around 26 years old, being celebrated as the youngest head of state in the world. A small section of the country was affected by the war when they took power. The soldiers came with the promise of ending the war and closing the lid on massive corruption.

Nevertheless, when they handed over power to a democratic government four years later, the war had already consumed more than half of the country, presenting the newly elected President Ahmad Tejan Kabba with a battle on two fronts—combating the rebels and stabilizing an economy that has been pillaged by the former administration of Julius Maada Bio.

In a speech delivered on January 2, 1997, in Freetown, President Kabbah accused the erstwhile junta of trying to stage a return through another set of coups, which his government successfully thwarted. The loot had become addictive, and the junta desired a second shot at the power. President Kabbah emphasized that Bio and his cohort had relinquished power solely due to the determination and activism of the people, who were weary of military rule.

Furthermore, he accused Julius Bio of engaging in widespread corruption within the state apparatus. During a critical period when the nation was grappling with challenges and as the junta was stepping down, Bio and his associates were allegedly involved in negotiating questionable contracts and inflating contract prices. This, President Kabbah asserted, was a scheme to benefit themselves at the expense of the country (Politico SL, 2012). Such a decorated kleptocrat would later assume the presidency in a democratic arrangement two decades on.

Poverty and Inequality

Africa is currently falling short of achieving the Sustainable Development Goals (SDGs), holding the highest global rates of extreme poverty. Out of the world's 28 poorest countries, 23 are in Africa, each exhibiting extreme poverty rates surpassing 30%. The estimated extreme poverty rate in Africa, using the $1.90 per day poverty line, stands at approximately 35.5%. This figure is 6.8 times higher than the global average for the rest of the world (Outreach International, 2023). The biggest culprit to this problem is economic instability. Government policies fail to prioritize the needs of the most vulnerable citizens of society.

Emerging data indicates that inequality presents a pronounced challenge in Africa, surpassing levels observed in other developing regions. Despite the continent's youthful demographic and rapid population expansion, entrenched poverty and inequality persist. These challenges are exacerbated by inadequate investment in crucial sectors like healthcare, education, and social services, alongside significant macroeconomic imbalances. Furthermore, Africa grapples with deficient infrastructure and enduring structural trade deficits. For instance, countries like Nigeria and South Africa struggle with stark income disparities, hindering efforts to address poverty and promote inclusive growth.

A big thing about African economies is that economic growth does not positively impact income inequality and, therefore, does not reduce the level of poverty. A major case study is Nigeria, which boasts the biggest economy in the region while the lot of the average Nigerian is still deplorable. This situation only leads to restlessness among the populace. According to the United Nations, rural areas in Africa exhibit a poverty rate of 17.2%, which is over three times greater than the 5.3% rate observed in urban areas. Such disparity in wealth distribution across Africa may contribute to social unrest and instability, further complicating efforts for poverty alleviation (World Bank, 2021).

Youth Unemployment and Drug Abuse

Youth unemployment and drug abuse stand as twin challenges to governance in Africa. Together, they hinder progress across economic, social, and health domains. The severe youth unemployment situation in sub-Saharan Africa continues to persistently stifle their potential and threaten their financial stability. The African Development Bank (AfDB) estimates that, with 1.4 billion people, Africa has the world's largest proportion of unemployed and under-employed youth. More than 60% of the continent's population is under the age of 30. In an engagement with Prince's Trust International in November 2023, Akinwumi Adesina of the AfDB said, "Too often, way too much lip service is given to youth programs. That must change. Together, we have an opportunity to create youth wealth and eradicate poverty, which is not a tradable commodity."

This poignant estimate of unemployment in Africa points to a staggering loss of human potential and opportunity (AfDB, 2019). The enduring absence of job prospects not only hampers individual economic progress but also hinders the cultivation of a skilled workforce, thereby impeding overarching development objectives and extending cycles of impoverishment.

While Africa boasts a significant level of youth engagement in the informal sector, as per International Labor Organization (ILO) studies, many face underemployment or endure poverty despite their work, primarily due to low wages and the absence of a robust social safety net. In certain African countries, the informal sector provides employment for approximately 80% of the population, with the majority being women and youth, constituting around 9 in 10 workers. This poses a problem for the youth unemployment statistics since most of the young people engaged in the informal sector could pass for employed. It makes it challenging to draw direct comparisons between African countries and more advanced economies.

Also, myriad researches have emphasized disparities between the skills acquired by African students in school and those demanded by employers. Efforts made by the government to tackle this employment deficit are bereft of inclusion. Many other youths with different skill sets than those captured in youth empowerment schemes are left out of the loop, aggravating the problem further.

There has also been a historical emphasis on professions like medicine, law, and business, while creative fields such as writing, art, music, drama, and fashion are often considered as recreational pursuits, with little government support to bolster these sectors. YouthPower, an online platform for resources on positive youth development, noted this somber outlook with precision.

An Afrobarometer study spanning 34 countries from 2016 to 2018 (the inception period for the last surge) revealed that "unemployment" was identified as the most critical issue requiring attention by African governments. Both young individuals aged 18 to 25 years and those aged 26 to 35 years consistently highlighted unemployment as the predominant concern demanding governmental action across all 34 countries surveyed.

Simultaneously, drug abuse compounds these economic challenges by sapping individuals' productivity and straining already limited healthcare resources. The United Nations Office on Drugs and Crime (UNODC) has noted a concerning rise in drug abuse across Africa, driven in part by factors like poverty, unemployment, and social dislocation (UNODC, 2018). Communities afflicted by drug abuse experience heightened levels of crime, family breakdowns, and health problems, exacerbating the already complex landscape of development challenges.

A synthetic opioid known as Kush, a kind of "zombie drug," is wreaking havoc in West Africa, particularly Sierra Leone. It has been present for the past six years, undergoing occasional modifications in its formulation to heighten its potency. Frequently blended with various substances like acetone and formalin—commonly used in mortuaries for body preservation—Kush poses grave health risks to its predominantly youthful users. Its affordability ensures widespread availability, attracting unemployed young Sierra Leoneans seeking respite from their dire circumstances.

The most alarming aspect about its prevalence in Sierra Leone is the involvement of high-ranking government officials, who serve as its primary importers and sometimes even manufacturers, with their agents and retailers spread throughout the country. Dismantling the Kush cartel, therefore, presents a significant challenge for both law enforcement and civilian watchdogs. While targeted raids on distribution points are conducted, it is often the impoverished youth who suffer the consequences, while the kingpins, comfortably entrenched within government circles, evade justice. Consequently, any attempts to address the issue at its roots are thwarted by directives from above.

The disenchantment of the youth, therefore, becomes cannon fodder for revolutions. In countries where usurpations do not succeed, the youth are constantly at daggers drawn with security forces, only further putting such nations in the way of revolutions.

Ethnic and Religious Tensions

Ethnic and religious tensions in Africa contribute to coups through a vivid panoply of factors, including divisive politics, marginalization, resource competition, power struggles, election-related violence, military loyalties, and external influences. Examples include the North-South divide in Nigeria, the Darfur conflict in Sudan, the Hutu-Tutsi tensions in Rwanda, political crises in Ivory Coast, post-election violence in Kenya, and ethnic grievances in Mali. These tensions, often intertwined with other factors, create a complex backdrop for political instability and coup dynamics in various African countries.

The presence of religious tensions is exacerbated by weak states, according to Matthias Basedau, a German academic. Religious extremism gains more appeal when the government fails to deliver essential public services, and corruption prevails among politicians. Nevertheless, religion represents just one facet of these conflicts, which can also encompass ethnic, power, or resource-related disputes, for it is believed that no conflict arises solely from religious grounds.

The region between North Africa, with a predominantly Muslim population, and Southern Africa, which is mainly Christian, serves as a significant convergence point of the two faiths, and it spans a 4,000-mile stretch from Somalia in the east to Senegal in the west. This centralized region is the fault line of religious tensions, as most of such conflicts in Africa are located here. Notably recognized as the site of al-Qaeda's initial major terrorist attack — including bombings. Additionally, it has been the scene of recent ethnic and sectarian violence in Nigeria, resulting in the loss of hundreds of lives among Muslims and Christians (Pew Research, 2024).

As if religious tensions were inherently not bad enough, there is a new wave of politicization of religion that has superimposed the existing fissures. Pew Research Center (2024) notes that the urgent reliance on religious approaches to address socioeconomic and political issues has intensified social divisions, giving rise to extremist and violent insurgencies like the ongoing Boko Haram Islamist terrorist campaign. This campaign has resulted in casualties and injuries among both Christians and Muslims. Over the past thirty years, religious tensions in Ethiopia have intensified. In 2022, over 20 people lost their lives in attacks targeting Muslims in the northwestern city of Gondar.

Traditionally, African societies functioned within a complex framework that revolved around the family, lineage, clan, tribe, and, ultimately, a coalition of groups sharing ethnic, cultural, and linguistic similarities. These entities served as the fundamental units for social, economic, and political organization, fostering inter-communal relations. During the establishment of colonial states, groups were either divided or amalgamated with scant consideration for their shared characteristics or unique attributes. They found themselves integrated into new administrative structures governed by unfamiliar values, institutions, and operational principles. The formerly autonomous local perspectives of the old order gave way to the regulatory mechanisms of the state, wherein the ultimate authority rested in the hands of an outsider, a foreigner. Francis M Deng, in a Brookings publication in 1997, commented about the new African state that had been brought to superimpose the traditional political arrangement thus:

"This mechanism functioned through the centralization of power, which ultimately rested on police and military force, the tools of authoritarian rule."

Analysts have generally held one of two perspectives on the role of ethnicity in the conflicts in Africa. Some perceive ethnicity as a root cause of conflict, while others view it as a tool wielded by political entrepreneurs to advance their ambitions. Deng (1997) believes that, in reality, it encompasses both aspects.

In many African nations, the commitment to safeguard national unity after gaining independence served as the impetus for one-party rule, the concentration of power, authoritarian regimes, and the systematic infringement of human rights and fundamental liberties.

Independence leaders within the structure of the OAU consistently opposed secession movements, with examples including Katanga's unsuccessful attempt to break away from the Congo (which later became Zaire and is now the Democratic Republic of the Congo). Similarly, the secessionist Biafran war in Nigeria and Somalia's endeavor to acquire the Ogaden from Ethiopia were both resolutely thwarted. Southern Sudan, after struggling for 17 years to secede from the North, ultimately settled for autonomy in 1972. Subsequently, when hostilities resumed in 1983, the declared objective has persisted: the establishment of a new Sudan free from any form of discrimination based on race, ethnicity, culture, or religion. However, the journey to independence finally ended in 2011 after decades of civil war, primarily driven by religious, ethnic, and economic differences.

References

1. Acemoglu, D., & Robinson, J. A. (2012). Why Nations Fail: The Origins of Power, Prosperity, and Poverty. Crown Publishing Group.
2. African Development Bank Group. (2019). African Economic Outlook 2019: Macroeconomic

Performance and Prospects. African Development Bank.

3. Afrobarometer. (2018). Afrobarometer Survey Findings: Unemployment and Youth Employment in Africa. Afrobarometer Publications.

4. Alesina, A., & Dollar, D. (2000). Who Gives Foreign Aid to Whom and Why? Journal of Economic Growth, 5(1), 33-63.

5. Basedau, M. (Ed.). (2015). The Routledge Handbook of Religion and Security. Routledge.

6. Birdsall, N., & Nellis, J. (Eds.). (2003). Winners and Losers: Assessing the Distributional Impact of Privatization. Brookings Institution Press.

7. Deng, F. M. (1997). The Sudan Peace Process: Challenges and Future Prospects. Brookings Institution Press.

8. Easterly, W. (2006). The White Man's Burden: Why the West's Efforts to Aid the Rest Have Done So Much Ill and So Little Good. Penguin Books.

9. Herbst, J. (2000). States and Power in Africa: Comparative Lessons in Authority and Control. Princeton University Press.

10. Huntington, S. (1996). The Clash of Civilizations and the Remaking of World Order. Simon & Schuster.

11. International Labour Organization (ILO). (2020). World Employment and Social Outlook: Trends 2020. International Labour Organization.

12. Moyo, D. (2009). Dead Aid: Why Aid Is Not Working and How There Is a Better Way for Africa. Farrar, Straus and Giroux.

13. Nunn, N. (2008). The Long-Term Effects of

Africa's Slave Trades. The Quarterly Journal of Economics.

14. Outreach International. (2023). Outreach International Report on Poverty and Inequality in Africa. Outreach International.

15. Pew Research Center. (2024). Religion and Public Life in Africa: A Pew Research Center Report. Pew Research Center.

16. Sachs, J. D. (2005). The End of Poverty: Economic Possibilities for Our Time. Penguin Books.

17. Stewart, F., Brown, G. K., & Langer, A. (2015). Fragile States: Causes, Costs, and Responses. Oxford University Press.

18. Tilly, C. (1992). Coercion, Capital, and European States, AD 990-1992. Blackwell.

19. United Nations Office on Drugs and Crime (UNODC). (2018). World Drug Report 2018: Analysis of Drug Markets - Opiates, Cocaine, Cannabis, Synthetic Drugs. United Nations Publications.

20. United Nations Development Programme (2020). Human Development Report 2020: The Next Frontier, Human Development and the Anthropocene. United Nations Development Programme.

21. World Bank. (2021). World Development Indicators 2021. World Bank Publications.

FOUR

GENERAL TRIGGERS 3: EXTERNAL INFLUENCES

Security and National Stability

THERE EXIST DIVERSE AND EVOLVING SECURITY THREATS TO Africa. Numerous extremist groups persist in various countries within the region. The civil conflict in Ethiopia has resulted in the displacement of 2 million people, contributed to extensive human rights violations, and raised the risk of famine in the northern Tigray region. The Gulf of Guinea stands out as the global epicenter for piracy according to the International Maritime Bureau (IMB) map, 2022. Other concerns include drug trafficking in West/Central Africa, as well as in West/East Africa. Additionally, cybercriminals operate throughout the region. Lastly, U.S. adversaries are extending their influence on the continent by establishing naval bases, supplying surveillance technology and drones, and deploying mercenaries to conflict zones.

The situation in Mali highlights the imprudence and potential futility of emphasizing global-power competition on countering violent extremism while addressing democratic backsliding. There is a notable risk of intersecting and negative reinforcement, and it is crucial to remain vigilant about the interconnected nature of these three priorities (CSIS, 2021).

Russia is mentioned in connection with both the 2021 and 2020 coups in Mali and Burkina Faso in 2022. As I write, their direct involvement in the Mali usurpations is yet to be established. However, Russia does have some level of involvement in Mali's security and military affairs, primarily through arms sales and military training programs. What is remarkable, nonetheless, is the swiftness of Moscow to forge friendly ties with Mali ex-post. In 2020, through its ambassador to Mali, it started a fruitful engagement with delegates of the transitional government, the National Committee for the Salvation of the People (CNSP), after the coup in 2020.

Furthermore, Russia has been known to establish diplomatic and economic ties with various African countries, especially in the Sahel, as part of its broader geopolitical strategy to expand its influence in the region. Samuel Ramani (2020) predicted that while it's improbable that Russia will dispatch private military contractors (PMCs) to the Sahel region, it may capitalize on the instability triggered by the Mali coup to market arms and broaden the scope of its military cooperation pacts with Burkina Faso, Chad, Mali, Mauritania, and Niger, thereby enhancing its strategic influence in the region.

While he may not have foreseen the presence of operatives like the Wagner Group, it is crucial to note that the Russian mercenaries in the Sahel are largely on a frolic of their own and may not be under direct control of Moscow.

However, their involvement in the region is a little overbearing. Like their military counterpart and clients in the continent, they are both saviors and oppressors of the people in one fell swoop. Jessica Donati, in March 2024, highlighted human rights organizations' report that the Russian Wagner is aiding government forces in central and northern Mali by conducting raids and drone strikes resulting in the deaths of numerous civilians, including a significant number of children. These reports cover the period from December to March. That notwithstanding, the Russian group has come in handy in battling extremist groups in the region, and for this and a number of neocolonial considerations, governments in the Sahel opted to replace French military assistance with the Wagner Group, perceived as offering greater flexibility and potential effectiveness compared to the French forces (Broderick McDonald and Guy Fiennes, 2023).

Although Wagner Group cannot offer long-term solutions, the extended presence of the French military proved ineffective in achieving peace and stability in the region. Marred by a botched colonial legacy in North Africa and limited success in addressing the Sahel crisis since 2013, France faces mounting resistance and anti-French sentiment from both civilian populations and Sahel governments as it grapples with containing Salafi-jihadist insurgents operating in the area.

While terrorism has historically been prevalent in Africa, its incidence has recently increased. Depending on how one defines terrorism, it has been utilized as a tactic during decolonization and amid conflicts between competing armed groups. Powell (2021) suggests that in circumstances where the government is perceived as offering ineffective leadership or fails to equip the military adequately for successful counterinsurgency operations, a coup attempt may become an appealing option.

Recent trends in the continent, not least in relation to contemporary usurpations, have exposed the correlation between growing insecurity, democratic backsliding, and poor governance. Travis Adkins, Deputy Assistant Administrator in the Bureau of Africa at USAID, aptly put it in a video interview with the Center for Strategic International Studies (CSIS)

"...what is it to be free from kinetic violence if you don't have access to electricity? What is it to be free from kinetic violence when you don't have access to water and sanitation? What is it to be free from kinetic violence when you cannot overcome the burden of disease in your nation, when you cannot fight back against the erosive changes that come from climate change, and when you don't have the capacity to develop your latent possibilities? And all of these things, of course, lead to drivers of certainly instability and in the worst cases conflict."

The majority of African nations lack a comprehensive national security strategy, hindering their ability to prioritize security threats, coordinate effectively, and allocate resources. This absence results in a lack of consensus on the vision and objectives for national security, as well as a failure to establish a unified foundation for leveraging assistance from international partnerships. Consequently, security provision often fails to serve the common welfare in many African countries.

Despite the efforts of the Damiba government, the security situation in Burkina Faso did not significantly improved since the January coup. Jihadists continue to expand their influence in remote regions, causing economic disruptions through block-ades. While there is acknowledgment of progress in enhancing the army's capabilities, it was deemed insufficient by Gen. Ibrahim Traoré, an army captain who led Burkina Faso's second coup in 2022. Traoré ousted Damiba and assumed leadership of the junta in September, citing the deteriorating conditions on the front as justification for his actions.

Security challenges may force governments to make difficult decisions, potentially escalating the issue and increasing the likelihood of further upheavals.

Economic Dependence and Leverage

I have treated the issue of economic dependence on foreign aid, loans, or investments in other chapters of this work, but it bears emphasis that political dynamics in African countries can be greatly influenced by these variables. External actors wield considerable influence over our domestic affairs. One aspect of this influence is through the conditionality attached to aid and loans provided by donor countries or International Finance Institutions (IFIs). For instance, IFIs may require recipient nations to implement specific policy reforms, such as austerity measures or privatization of state-owned enterprises, in exchange for financial assistance. This conditionality gives external actors leverage over recipient governments, as failure to comply can result in the withholding of aid or the imposition of sanctions. The effect of foreign aid, loans, and investment, therefore, warrant separate handling under this subject.

a) Foreign Direct Investment (FDI)

Instances of investment agreements between African countries and foreign corporations or governments constitute a large scoop of FDI. In pursuit of economic development and growth, African nations often seek foreign investments in key sectors such as mining, agriculture, and infrastructure. However, these investments may come with strings attached, including preferential treatment for investors, exploitation of natural resources, or limited local participation in the economy. As a result, African governments may prioritize the interests of foreign investors over the needs and concerns of their own citizens, leading to tensions and conflicts within society. Zambia attracted significant foreign investment in its mining sector, particularly in copper production. In 2019, the Zambian government entered into a controversial investment agreement with a Chinese-owned mining company, allowing it to acquire a majority stake in a large copper mine. However, the agreement was criticized for its lack of transparency and for favoring the interests of the foreign investors over those of local communities. This led to tensions and protests among Zambian citizens who felt marginalized and exploited by the deal.

The influx of FDI has the potential to alter power dynamics, particularly when it targets strategic sectors or initiatives. Foreign investors may wield influence over government policies, and the government's rapport with these investors can emerge as a critical factor in garnering political backing. According to the United Nations Conference on Trade and Development (UNCTAD) World Investment Report 2022, the global economic downturn induced by the COVID-19 pandemic, coupled with measures enforced by African governments to curb the virus's transmission, resulted in significant declines in FDI and considerable economic downturns in 2020.

FDI increased dramatically in 2021, reaching a record $83 billion. However, this figure is not evenly distributed, as Central Africa, a region prone to more conflicts, trails far behind the other blocs. The overall figure for the continent was boosted by a sole intra-firm financial deal in South Africa during the latter part of 2021 (UNCTAD, 2022). Excluding this transaction, the rise in investment in Africa appears to be modest, aligning more closely with trends seen in other developing regions. Other regions save North and Central Africa registered increase in flows. Central Africa saw no significant change, largely due to instability, while North Africa experienced a decline. The principal holders of foreign assets in Africa continue to be European investors, with the United Kingdom leading at $65 billion and France following closely behind at $60 billion.

b) Trade Relations

Trade relations with foreigners have not always yielded positive outcomes for African economies. In many cases, these relationships have contributed to negative impacts such as economic instability and social disparities. Limited market access and economic isolation resulting from ineffective trade relations have hindered Africa's ability to diversify its economies and achieve sustainable growth. Dependence on a few key sectors for exports leaves African countries vulnerable to fluctuations in global commodity prices, leading to economic volatility and uncertainty.

Moreover, the lack of technological advancements and higher trade costs associated with inefficient trade relations further exacerbate economic challenges in Africa. Inadequate infrastructure and bureaucratic barriers often impede the flow of goods and services, stifling economic growth and development. Additionally, the absence of regional integration and collaboration among African countries undermines efforts to harness the continent's collective economic potential. Fragmented markets and disjointed policies contribute to social and economic disparities, exacerbating inequalities within and between countries.

For example, the dominance of extractive industries in many African economies, fueled by trade relations with foreign partners, has led to environmental degradation, social unrest, and economic instability. In countries heavily reliant on exporting raw materials, such as oil or minerals, the benefits of trade are often concentrated in the hands of a few elites, while the majority of the population struggles to access basic services and opportunities for economic advancement. In essence, while trade relations with foreigners offer opportunities for economic growth and development, they have significantly presented challenges and risks for African economies. Policies that promote diversification, technological innovation, and regional integration are given short shrift.

c) Debt and Economic Conditionality Imposed by Global Financial Institutions

African countries burdened with heavy debt loads from foreign lenders often find themselves subject to conditions attached to loans or debt relief programs. These conditions, typically imposed by IFIs, exert significant influence over economic policies, governance structures, and political decision-making within these nations. For instance, in exchange for financial assistance or debt relief, African governments may be required to implement austerity measures, privatize state-owned enterprises, or liberalize their economies, regardless of their suitability or impact on local populations.

Also, the current landscape presents a heightened risk of escalating debt distress and economic inequality across the African continent. The accumulation of unsustainable levels of debt, coupled with conditions that prioritize debt repayment over social spending and development initiatives, threatens to exacerbate existing economic challenges and widen disparities within society. As a result, our countries may experience restricted overall economic activity, hindered growth prospects, and increased vulnerability to external shocks.

Instances of the negative impact of debt and economic conditionality on African economies abound. Structural adjustment programs (SAPs) implemented by the International Monetary Fund (IMF) and World Bank in the 1980s and 1990s imposed strict austerity measures and market-oriented reforms on many African countries, leading to widespread social unrest, economic stagnation, and deepening poverty levels. Similarly, the debt crises faced by countries like Zambia and Mozambique in recent years have been exacerbated by onerous repayment obligations and stringent conditionality imposed by creditors, contributing to economic instability and social unrest.

Debt and economic conditionality imposed by foreign lenders and IFIs have had profound and far-reaching negative impacts on African economies, worsening economic instability, widening inequalities, and setting the stage for upheavals.

d) Global Economic Trends

Our economies are heavily imperiled by external economic shocks like global economic recessions or fluctuations in commodity prices. Our countries heavily rely on exports of commodities such as oil, minerals, and agricultural products. Therefore, when global demand for these commodities declines, or prices become volatile, African economies suffer. For example, a drop in oil prices can severely affect oil-exporting countries like Nigeria, Angola, and Algeria, leading to reduced government revenues, currency devaluation, and budget deficits. Similarly, fluctuations in agricultural commodity prices can impact the livelihoods of millions of small-scale farmers across the continent, contributing to poverty and food insecurity.

Moreover, external actors, including international organizations or individual countries, may impose economic sanctions or trade restrictions on African nations in response to political developments. Economic pressure, in the form of sanctions, can have detrimental effects on African economies by disrupting trade, investment, and financial flows. For instance, sanctions imposed on Sudan and Zimbabwe by Western countries have hindered their access to international markets, impeded economic growth, and exacerbated humanitarian crises. Similarly, recent sanctions imposed on African nations by other African organizations or regional bodies, such as the African Union, can further exacerbate economic challenges and hinder prospects for development.

Furthermore, the removal of subsidies dictated by IFIs, and poorly designed tax policies can hinder economic growth and investment in African countries. High corporate tax rates, coupled with unpredictable tax regimes, create disincentives for entrepreneurship and innovation. This deters both domestic and foreign investors, stifling private sector development and job creation. Also, the removal of subsidies on essential goods and services, such as fuel or food, can disproportionately affect low-income households, leading to social unrest and political instability. The removal of fuel subsidies in Nigeria in 2012 and now in 2024 led to widespread protests and contributed to inflationary pressures, negatively impacting the overall economy. Sadly, the continent as a whole remains underfunded by these institutions, with limited access to financial resources for critical sectors such as healthcare, education, and infrastructure.

Ultimately, global economic trends, including external shocks, sanctions, and policy prescriptions from IFIs, can have significant adverse effects on African economies. These trends often exacerbate existing vulnerabilities, hinder economic growth, and impede efforts to alleviate poverty and achieve sustainable development. Addressing these challenges requires coordinated efforts at both the domestic and international levels to build resilience, promote inclusive growth, and mitigate the negative impacts of external economic pressures on African nations.

e) Aid Reliance

In an article published on social media titled Covid-19, A Divine Medication to the Dutch Disease in Africa (2020), I maintained that while foreign aid serves as a catalyst for development, its prevalence in the continent has exacerbated the Dutch disease. Our leaders tend to view development as contingent on foreign assistance, resulting in national development agendas with funding gaps reliant on grants. Aid dependence takes on new names like "development assistance" to gain currency. African governments are steered away from socialist policies and encouraged to reduce government spending, fostering an environment for private businesses. Consequently, our governments find themselves entangled in a complex web of aid and regulations, rendering them susceptible to Western political influences. Notably, Egypt, Kenya, and South Sudan are the primary beneficiaries of the 20 percent of U.S. aid allocated to Africa.

Moyo (2009) argues with empirical evidence, suggesting that excessive reliance on aid can indeed have adverse effects on recipient countries. Aid dependency may weaken incentives for domestic resource mobilization, discourage entrepreneurship and innovation, and perpetuate a culture of dependency among both governments and citizens. Additionally, aid flows can distort local economies, create rent-seeking behavior, and undermine accountability mechanisms, particularly in countries with weak governance structures.

Despite economic growth in certain regions of the continent surpassing global standards, Africa still perceives aid as a lifeline essential to preventing economic collapse and state failure. Many other social commentators contend that foreign assistance may be a significant factor in Africa's underdevelopment, as the influx of billions of dollars since independence has not substantially altered the continent's development trajectory. The proverbial "he who pays the piper calls the tune" underscores how much assistance is shaped by donor-set targets rather than reflecting the realities of the people.

Livelihood interventions are often unsustainable and prone to exploitation for selfish gains. Such aid tends to neglect the establishment of robust local training and research facilities, hindering the development of a well-trained indigenous workforce. Recipients frequently fail to achieve self-reliance. For powerful nations, aid becomes a display of dominance, leading to boasts about who contributes more. However, this does not absolve African leaders of their responsibilities in establishing effective government systems and feedback mechanisms to ensure proper utilization of loans and foreign assistance by both donors and government agents. Therefore, development assistance has a direct impact on power dynamics and political stability. Donor countries may use aid to promote specific policy reforms, good governance, or human rights practices.

f) The Resource Curse

In the same article in 2020, I averred that Africa's abundance of resources extends beyond mineral deposits and includes various elements such as climate, land fertility, and strategic geographical positioning. The phenomenon known as the "resource curse" is not limited to mineral-rich nations; it also affects regions where the mining industry contributes minimally to the GDP. Kenya serves as a representative case, possessing strategic significance as a gateway to East and Central Africa and hosting the largest seaport in the Indian Ocean. However, these blessings do not shield it from the challenges associated with the resource curse. Countries with resource wealth, even those with diverse economies like Kenya, often grapple with issues such as war, famine, and ethnic violence linked to mining and business activities. These conflicts garnered international attention in the last decade, spanning from diamond-related issues in the Democratic Republic of Congo to land disputes in Zimbabwe, oil concerns in Nigeria, and water disputes in the Horn of Africa.

None of these conflicts can be divorced from the underpinnings of corruption and poor governance, which give rise to issues related to the ownership, management, and control of natural resources, consequently inviting external interventions. While these conflicts were primarily internal, they were largely driven by global motivations, leaving Africa's image as the new frontier for investors and economic experts amid a global economic downturn compromised.

Despite a growing middle class overcoming challenges and reshaping the continent's narrative with a new 'rags to riches' theme, our leaders are inherently prone to corruption and violence. A Ghanaian economist characterized young Africans as the 'cheetah generation,' reflecting their eagerness to change their circumstances. The Global Entrepreneurship Monitor highlighted sub-Saharan African nations leading the world in early-stage entrepreneurial activity, with Zambia and Nigeria at the forefront. However, our inclination toward corruption only affirmed our struggle to self-govern, justifying stringent diktats from institutions like the World Bank and IMF and paving the way for increased external influence.

The New Media and the Blogger Effect

The influence of new media and bloggers on political events in Africa is characterized by the rapid dissemination of information, increased citizen participation, and challenges to official narratives. Social media platforms play a crucial role in shaping public perceptions, mobilizing citizens, and providing alternative perspectives. It is easy for citizens to relate to trends in other places in the globe and wish to apply them to their context.

Diaspora citizens of Africa, like us, play a prominent role in the new media wave pervading the continent and influencing behaviors. Unfortunately for our leaders, they have been caught up in this smart web of citizen journalism. Living beyond the reach of our oppressive governments affords us the liberty to create and disseminate the most critical contents about our leaders and get away with it.

During political unrest, the new media enables the quick spread of news globally, attracting international attention and solidarity. However, it also brings challenges, including the potential for the rapid spread of fake news and disinformation, government manipulation of narratives, and the use of social media as a tool for both organizing dissent and suppressing opposition. The impact of new media on coups is complex and varies based on the specific context and the strategies employed by different actors in utilizing these platforms.

The End SARS protest in Nigeria was significantly impacted by the pervasive influence of social media, serving as a catalyst for unprecedented mobilization and global attention. Platforms like Twitter, Instagram, and Facebook became vital channels for amplifying the voices of protesters, providing a platform for sharing personal stories of police brutality and rallying support. Through social media, protesters efficiently organized demonstrations, disseminated crucial information about protest logistics, and documented instances of violence, creating widespread awareness of the systemic issues driving the movement. Internationally, the movement garnered solidarity and support, with images and videos shared online sparking outrage and prompting action from governments and organizations worldwide. However, the digital sphere also became a battleground for misinformation and propaganda, with both government supporters and detractors using social media to shape public opinion. In response to the movement's digital mobilization, the government imposed restrictions on social media and internet access to suppress dissent. Despite these challenges, the impact of social media on the End SARS protest underscored its power as a tool for grassroots activism, amplifying voices, galvanizing movements, and exposing injustices on a global scale.

The Resurfacing of Cold War Dynamics

In recent years, the resurfacing of Cold War dynamics in Africa has become increasingly evident, fueled by the competitive landscape between global powers like Russia and the United States. This resurgence is marked by various key factors that reflect both historical legacies and contemporary global dynamics. The competitive pursuit of access to Africa's abundant natural resources, geopolitical influence, economic interests, security and counter-terrorism efforts, and ideological influence characterizes the rivalry between Russia and the U.S. on the continent. Notably, instances reflecting Cold War dynamics include proxy conflicts, ideological polarization, competition for influence, economic rivalry, and security concerns.

While reminiscent of the Cold War era, the current geopolitical landscape in Africa is also influenced by the rise of China and the multipolar nature of global politics, underscoring the complexity of the situation and the agency of African nations in shaping their own destinies. Instances like the display of Russian flags by coup supporters in Niamey, Bamako, and Ouagadougou highlight the role of external actors in shaping African politics. While analysts caution against inferring direct Kremlin involvement in the coups, the display signifies Russia's emergence as a standard-bearer of anti-Western sentiment in parts of Africa, adding another layer to the intricate dynamics of global competition on the continent.

Unlike post-Independence Cold War era, a significant shift is observed in the methods employed, notably marked by the presence of boots on the ground and advanced technological interventions. This transformation is epitomized by entities like the Wagner Group, embodying a more direct and visible form of military involvement, and the utilization of American drones, symbolizing the infusion of cutting-edge technology into the conflict landscape. Declan Walsh, (2023). The involvement of private military contractors and the deployment of American drones highlights the increasing privatization of security operations and the growing significance of unmanned aerial vehicles in contemporary warfare. This juxtaposition illustrates the evolution of conflict dynamics in Africa, transitioning from Cold War-era proxy struggles to a more hybridized and technology-driven form of warfare.

In recent times, the competitive landscape between Russia and the United States, or between Western and Eastern influences in Africa, revolves around various key factors, reflecting both historical legacies and contemporary global dynamics.

a) Natural Resources

Russia, the U.S., and other actors like France and China actively seek access to Africa's abundant natural resources, including oil, gas, minerals, and strategic metals, as part of their economic and strategic interests. Uranium, a radioactive mineral, is Niger's primary export, but amid heightening anti-French sentiment in Niger, the military junta purportedly declared the suspension of its export to France. According to the Euratom Supply Agency (ESA), Niger was the EU's second-largest provider of natural uranium in 2022, accounting for 25.38 percent of the total supply. Therefore, these western powers that are heavily reliant on nuclear power are queuing for access to secure and reliable sources of uranium to fuel their reactors. Power dynamics have shifted based on the management and control of the precious mineral.

Changes in leadership or political regimes in Niger can influence how uranium resources are managed, leading to shifts in alliances or agreements with Western powers seeking access to these resources. This dynamic can impact geopolitical relations and regional stability as different actors compete for influence and control over Niger's uranium wealth. In the past, unreliable intelligence suggesting a potential Iraqi acquisition of 500 tons of Nigerien "yellowcake" uranium contributed to the American justification for the "preemptive" invasion of Iraq. Ishaan Tharoor (2023).

b) Geopolitical Influence

Currently, the competitive landscape between Russia and the United States in Africa has been shaped by various key factors, reflecting historical legacies and contemporary global dynamics. Under President Vladimir Putin, Russia has actively sought to reassert its global influence, extending its reach into Africa as part of its broader foreign policy objectives. This expansion involves cultivating diplomatic ties, providing military assistance, and pursuing economic interests across the continent. For instance, Russia supported the Libyan National Army (LNA), led by General Khalifa Haftar, in its conflict against the internationally recognized Government of National Accord (GNA). Russian mercenaries from the Wagner Group have been reported to operate in Libya, providing military assistance to the LNA.

Conversely, the United States has traditionally maintained robust political, economic, and military relationships with numerous African nations. The U.S. often approaches Africa through the lens of strategic interests, such as counterterrorism efforts, access to natural resources, and the promotion of democratic governance. However, the extent of U.S. engagement in Africa fluctuates over time due to domestic priorities, evolving international dynamics, and regional security considerations.

For asylees, the fear is palpable. The uncertainty surrounding U.S. engagement means that the fragile democracies in our home countries remain vulnerable. Without consistent international support, these democracies face the risk of backsliding into authoritarianism or being undermined by internal conflicts and external influences.

c) *Economic Interests*

The competition of global powers in Africa extends beyond geopolitical influence to economic realms, where nations actively vie for trade and investment opportunities on the continent. The emergence of China's Belt and Road Initiative further complicates this landscape, intensifying the competition for Africa's abundant natural resources and expanding markets. For instance, the United States has historically pursued economic partnerships with African countries through programs like the African Growth and Opportunity Act (AGOA) and the Prosper Africa initiative, aiming to foster economic growth and investment opportunities. Similarly, Russia seeks to strengthen its economic presence in Africa through trade agreements, investment projects, and partnerships with resource-rich nations. However, the competition between these global powers for economic dominance in Africa raises concerns about the impact on local economies, governance structures, and sustainable development efforts. Disenchanted with the rate of democratic backsliding on the continent, I am deeply concerned about how this economic competition may exacerbate existing challenges and undermine efforts to promote stability and prosperity in Africa.

d) *Security and Counter-terrorism:*

I find it imperative to analyze the complex dynamics of security and counter-terrorism in Africa, particularly considering the competing interests of these global powers. The U.S. has traditionally focused on counter-terrorism efforts in Africa, viewing the continent as a strategic battleground in the fight against terrorism and extremism. Through initiatives like the Trans-Sahara Counterterrorism Partnership (TSCTP) and the

Africa Center for Strategic Studies, the U.S. has provided military assistance, training, and intelligence support to African countries to combat terrorist threats. However, Russia has also emerged as a significant player in the security landscape of Africa, positioning itself as a security partner for African nations.

Drawing on its experiences in conflicts like Syria and Ukraine, Russia offers military support, expertise, and arms sales to African countries, presenting an alternative security narrative to that of the U.S. This competition for influence in Africa's security domain has implications for regional stability, as African countries navigate between competing offers of military assistance and partnership. Examples of this competition include Russia's military involvement in conflicts such as Libya and the Central African Republic, where it supports different factions from those backed by the U.S. These instances underscore the complexities of security dynamics in Africa and highlight the need for African nations to assert their agency in shaping their own security agendas, free from external interference and geopolitical rivalries.

e) Ideological Influence

We must be deeply troubled by the erosion of democratic values across the continent and the ideological dimensions of security and counter-terrorism efforts, particularly concerning the competing influences of global powers like Russia and the United States. Vladimir Putin has actively promoted a conservative and authoritarian model in Africa, aligning itself with regimes that prioritize stability and centralized control over democratic principles. This approach resonates with certain African leaders who prioritize security and order over political freedoms. In contrast, the United States champions democracy and human rights as core values in its engagement with Africa. Through initiatives like the National Endowment for Democracy and USAID programs, the U.S. supports civil society organizations, promotes electoral transparency, and advocates for the rule of law.

This ideological competition between Russia's authoritarian model and America's democratic values creates a tug-of-war across the continent, shaping political discourse and influencing policy decisions. Examples of this ideological influence can be observed in African countries where authoritarian leaders cozy up to Russia for military support and economic assistance, while civil society organizations and pro-democracy activists look to the U.S. for support in their struggle for political freedoms. This ideological divide complicates efforts to address security challenges and counter-terrorism in Africa, as competing visions of governance clash and influence regional dynamics. It underscores the importance of recognizing and navigating the ideological undercurrents that shape security partnerships and policies in Africa as nations seek to balance security imperatives with democratic aspirations in an increasingly complex geopolitical landscape.

While these dynamics bear similarities to the Cold War, it's crucial to acknowledge the complexity introduced by the multipolar nature of global politics, the rise of China, and the agency of African nations in shaping their own destinies.

References

1. Adkins, T., (2021) Africa's Security Challenges: A View from Congress, the Pentagon, and USAID;

Center for Strategic & International Studies (CSIS).

2. African Development Bank (AfDB). (2020). African Economic Outlook 2020: Developing Africa's Workforce for the Future.

3. Amnesty International, (2024) Mali: Drone Strikes Killed 13 civilians Including Seven Children in Amasrakad.

4. Besley, T., & Persson, T. (2013). Taxation and development. Handbook of Public Economics.

5. Council on Foreign Relations. (2018) "China in Africa: The New Colonialism?" Council on Foreign Relations.

6. Donati, J., (2024) In Mali, Russian Mercenaries are Helping the Army Kill Civilians, Rights Groups Say. Los Angeles Times.

7. Global Entrepreneurship Report. 2020/2021 Global Report. Global Entrepreneurship Report.

8. McDonald, B. and Fiennes, G., (2023) The Wagner Group's Growing Shadow in the Sahel: What Does It Mean for Counterterrorism in the Region? Modern War Institute.

9. Moyo, D. (2009). "Dead Aid: Why Aid Is Not Working and How There Is a Better Way for Africa." Farrar, Straus and Giroux.

10. Powell, Lalalli, St. Pierre and Zimmerman, (2021) Livestream Panel Discussion; Scoping the Threat: Do African Salafi-jihadi Groups Threaten the West? AEI.

11. Tharoor, I. (2023) The coup in Niger puts spotlight on nation's uranium. The Washington Post.

12. UN Conference on Trade and Development, (2022) World Investment Report.

13. United Nations Economic Commission for Africa (UNECA). (2021). Economic Report on Africa 2021: Financing Africa's Post-COVID-19 Development.

14. Walsh, D., (2023) Coast to Coast, a Corridor of Coups Brings Turmoil in Africa. The New York Times.

15. World Bank Group. (2019). Africa's Pulse, No. 21, April 2019: Africa's Integration in the Global Economy.

FIVE

CONSTITUTIONAL AND ELECTORAL MOTIVATIONS

Understanding the probable motives behind contemporary insurrections requires examining political antecedents that all together amount to recipes of desperation by citizens, invariably leading to a breakdown of state order and usurpations. The continent has witnessed over 40 coups and attempts since 2010, with approximately 20 occurring in West Africa and the Sahel. From 2019 onwards, there have been over 7 such occurrences, comprising five successful coups and a few unsuccessful attempts.

African nations share common governance patterns characterized by the abuse of power by political elites, and leaders clinging to power through undemocratic means, such as rigged elections, constitutional amendments to extend term limits, or outright repression of opposition voices. This erosion of democratic norms undermines the legitimacy of governments and fosters public disillusionment with the political process, creating fertile ground for coups and other forms of political upheaval.

Recent motivations of coups are influenced by a combination of domestic grievances eventuated by democratic backsliding. Glossing over case-specific motivations, therefore, requires contextualizing them within the broader phenomenon of democratic regression perpetrated by our leaders.

Autogolpe

A glaring feature looms large in the turbulent terrains of our politics—executive overreach. Here, leaders have mastered the art of manipulating legal frameworks, including constitutional provisions, to perpetuate their hold on power, extend term limits, and erode the very foundations of democratic governance. Sometimes, they brazenly cast aside legal procedures altogether, orchestrating what political scientists term as autogolpe, a Spanish derivative for self-coup. It's a sinister maneuver where leaders hijack the democratic process to seize another mandate, thus entrenching their rule. In our continent, such autogolpes are unfortunately very common, and they epitomize the erosion of democratic principles that plague many nations.

As a researcher, I am disheartened to witness how these self-coups undermine the aspirations of our people for genuine democracy. They subvert the will of the electorate, such as in Guinea in 2020, stifle political pluralism, as in Uganda, and perpetuate a cycle of authoritarianism disguised as democracy, like in Togo. These actions not only betray the trust placed in leaders by their citizens but also deal a severe blow to the progress of democratic governance in our continent.

In delving into the intricacies of autogolpes, it becomes evident that what often masquerades as a coup in Africa is, in fact, a counter-coup of sorts—a deft response to executive overreach. Regional bodies and international observers have, on numerous occasions, recognized the distinction between coups aimed at toppling authoritarian regimes and those aimed at thwarting autogolpes. The timeliness of their responses are often dubious, but they have been forthcoming nonetheless.

There are two prominent instances of autogolpe that serve as stark reminders of the perilous path of democratic backsliding. These cases, though unique in their specifics, share a common thread of leaders manipulating legal mechanisms to entrench their power and undermine democratic institutions. Such actions not only undermine the rule of law but also erode public trust in the democratic process, laying bare the fragility of democratic governance in our continent.

Constitutional Coups

Constitutional coups emerge as insidious threats to democratic governance, subtly undermining the very foundations of representative systems. These maneuvers, while not always marked by overt military intervention, seriously erode democratic principles and sow seeds of political turmoil. Myriad instances or attempts at constitutional subversion exist across the continent.

There were wide speculations that President Macky Sall of Senegal would extend his term to a third after amendments to the constitution. The president's ambivalence about the issue reinvigorated the rumor, leading to massive protests that claimed lives. He later stated his intention not to run again despite insisting that the constitution would have allowed him another term. Aljazeera (Jul. 4 2023). But, as if to compensate for missing out on the polls, Sall encouraged the National Assembly to defer the election until December 15, extending the polling period by almost 10 months. Violent protests ensued anew, and the West African regional block, ECOWAS, called on the authorities to hold the elections on the scheduled date. Their call yielded compliance, and the people of Senegal voted for their President in March instead of December. By a slender margin, Senegal, the last bastion of unaltered democracy in sub-SaharanAfrica, teetered on the brink of undergoing an autogolpe, which would have challenged the mettle of one of the most proficient militaries in the region.

The Democratic Republic of Congo faced concerns of a constitutional coup as President Joseph Kabila delayed elections, citing logistical challenges. The postponement raised suspicions of an attempt to extend Kabila's rule beyond constitutional limits. Elections eventually took place in 2018, leading to a change in leadership.

Another glaring instance of such constitutional subversion unfolded in Guinea in 2020 under the tenure of President Alpha Condé, who had held power since 2010. He chose to defy constitutional norms by seeking a third term in office in 2020. His decision catalyzed a cascade of dissent, with citizens and opposition factions vehemently opposing the move. Despite facing widespread opposition and protests, Condé pressed forward with his agenda, leveraging controversial constitutional amendments to justify his bid for reelection. Through a contentious referendum, the constitution was revised to reset presidential term limits, effectively paving the way for Condé's extended stay in power. The subsequent presidential election held in October 2020 was mired in controversy, with allegations of electoral irregularities and voter suppression tarnishing its legitimacy.

The discontent simmering within Guinean society reached a boiling point in September 2021 when elements within the military, led by Colonel Mamady Doumbouya, orchestrated a coup d'état, culminating in the arrest of President Condé. The military coup, ostensibly driven by grievances over rampant corruption, human rights abuses, and economic mismanagement under Condé's rule, underscored the fragility of democratic institutions in Guinea.

The swift condemnation of the coup by the AU and the ECOWAS highlighted the collective commitment to upholding democratic norms and constitutional order in Africa. However, criticism often attends the response of regional bodies to constitutional coups. Such response often lacks the necessary vigor to effectively deter or reverse unconstitutional power grabs by sitting heads of state. Several factors contribute to this criticism and are exhaustively dealt with later in this work. The challenges in effectively addressing constitutional coups underscore the mixture of hypocrisy and limitations faced by African leaders in safeguarding democratic governance.

My frustration mounts as I realize that expressions of disapproval by regional bodies are not backed by punitive measures to deter future violations by incumbents. I am amazed by the energy they channel into reacting to coups instead of directing the same oomph towards preventing their potential occurrence. While political considerations take precedence over the preservation of democratic principles, there is a relentless assault on civil liberties and the suppression of dissent, prompting me to delve deeper into the underlying motivations and repercussions of these political upheavals.

In a strikingly similar fashion, the leaders seem to draw from the same playbook, utilizing a shared rationale to prolong their tenure—namely, that the time served prior to the constitutional amendment should not be considered as part of their official term. In 2015, the decision of President Pierre Nkurunziza of Burundi to pursue a third term sparked extensive protests. Notwithstanding condemnation both domestically and internationally, he justified his decision by asserting that his initial term, which was sanctioned by parliament rather than the populace, did not constitute a full term. Nkurunziza's eventual triumph in securing a third term was broadly perceived as a breach of constitutional principles. In August 2020, a military junta ousted President Ibrahim Boubacar Keïta, citing governance issues and corruption. While this event had elements of a traditional coup, it was triggered by a political crisis and dissatisfaction with Keïta's rule, including calls for constitutional reforms.

The justification takes a different form for leaders who have enjoyed a prolonged stay in power. Their strategy entails continually amending the constitution and readying measures to quell protests. Eventually, when amendments have become one too many, they merely introduce a clause to eliminate term limits altogether. President Yoweri Museveni, in power since 1986, faced accusations of constitutional manipulation to prolong his rule. In 2005, presidential term limits were removed, and in 2017, age limits were lifted, enabling Museveni to seek another term in the 2021 elections.

These instances illustrate the diverse ways in which leaders have manipulated constitutional provisions to stay in power or consolidate authority, often undermining democratic norms and triggering political instability.

Electoral Coups

Constitutional coups frequently pave the way for electoral coups, intertwining these two phenomena. However, there are cases where electoral coups occur independently of prior constitutional amendments aimed at extending term limits. Instead, other legal provisions are violated in the lead-up to elections or sometimes in the period between elections and the announcement of the winner. Sierra Leone stands out in this regard, serving as a prominent example of an electoral coup due to its blatant flouting of constitutional or legal provisions.

The implementation of the Proportional Representation electoral system, merely six months prior to the June 2023 elections, cast a slur on the application of constitutional provisions to the electoral process and introduced unexpected hurdles to Sierra Leone's democratic journey. The 1991 constitution expressly provides conditions for the application of the PR system. It had only been used during the civil war when some areas of the country were inaccessible due to security concerns. The extant electoral system was the "First Past the Post/Constituency-based" arrangement. This electoral framework was employed in the past three elections (Dubawa.org). Despite the PR system's reputation for fostering inclusive representation, its abrupt adoption caught the nation's electoral management system off guard and disrupted peace and stability. The ensuing confusion, coupled with inconsistencies in the election outcomes, sparked concerns regarding the suitability of such a significant alteration within an already fragile political environment. The abrupt departure from the conventional constituency-based system further exacerbated suspicions about the incumbent's motives and the electoral commission's complicity.

As if the irregularities following the alteration of the electoral system were not sufficient, the premature announcement of the results of the June 24, 2023 elections by the Chairman of the Electoral Commission for Sierra Leone (ECSL), made even before the tally process was completed, tarnished the credibility of the entire process. National and international observers, known for their credibility, decried the results as illegitimate. Their concerns span from the lack of transparency in the tabulation process to the failure to disclose disaggregated results from individual polling stations. What sets this process apart and marks a departure from previous elections is the unprecedented action by the Chief Electoral Commissioner, who disregarded the actual votes cast by the people and fabricated figures for the announcement. This breach of protocol was why the ECSL was hesitant to release the results.

The main opposition party, APC, rejected the results but refrained from seeking legal recourse for two main reasons. Firstly, they expressed a loss of trust in the judiciary, making them hesitant to engage in legal proceedings. Secondly, they dismissed the legitimacy of the announcement, as it lacked support from the results database. In essence, they were still waiting for the proper announcement, even as a committee brokered by the international community was set up to review the contested results.

In Cameroon, President Paul Biya secured a predictable victory, purportedly obtaining 71.28 percent of the vote. Numerous opposition candidates and ordinary Cameroonians raised concerns about extensive fraud. Furthermore, the election faced challenges with elevated insecurity and violent extremism in at least three of the country's 10 regions—the Far North, Northwest, and Southwest regions. The presidential election in Malawi in 2019 faced legal challenges and accusations of irregularities. The Constitutional Court of Malawi nullified the results, citing widespread irregularities, leading to a rerun of the election.

The 2016 presidential election in Uganda faced criticism for lack of transparency, restrictions on opposition activities, and claims of voter intimidation. Yoweri Museveni, who had been in power for decades, was declared the winner amidst accusations of irregularities. The presidential election in Zimbabwe in 2008, pitting Robert Mugabe against Morgan Tsvangirai, was marred by allegations of irregularities and violence. Tsvangirai withdrew from the runoff, citing violence against his supporters. Despite international criticism, Mugabe claimed victory.

i) Secrecy and Lack of Transparency in the Tabulation Process

One of the key issues arising from the 2023 elections in Sierra Leone is the perceived lack of transparency in the tabulation process and its associated secrecy. Traditionally, the tabulation of election results in Sierra Leone has been marked by transparency, involving the presence of observers, party agents, and Electoral Commissioners.

In past elections, the tabulation process included a thorough verification of results, enabling prompt resolution of disputes in cases of irregularities, tampered envelopes, or discrepancies in figures. However, the criticism from both local and international observers regarding the secrecy surrounding the tabulation process in June 2023, along with statistically questionable outcomes, cannot be easily disregarded. The Electoral Commission for Sierra Leone's (ECSL) argument against releasing the results seems unconvincing when considering the precedent set in the 2018 and previous elections, where results were disclosed at the polling station level. These concerns cast doubt on the results and contributed to the erosion of public trust in the election management body. Publishing results at the polling station level could have enhanced the institution's credibility.

ii) Setting Aside Votes and Announcing the Winner

The premature announcement of the June 24, 2023, election results by the Chairman of the ECSL, even before the completion of the tally process, raised doubts about the credibility of the outcome. Credible national and international observers criticized the results as dubious, citing concerns ranging from the lack of transparency in the tabulation process to the failure to publish detailed results by polling stations. A distinctive aspect of this process, deviating from past elections, is the Chief Electoral Commissioner's complete disregard for the voters' choice, fabricating figures solely for the announcement. This explains the ECSL's reluctance to release the results. Although the main opposition, All Peoples Congress (APC), rejected the results, it refrained from seeking legal recourse for the two main reasons provided above.

In expressing their protest to the abuse of due process, the APC opted to boycott parliamentary and local government activities, resulting in a government deadlock. The declared winner of the elections, the incumbent President Julius Maada Bio of the Sierra Leone Peoples Party (SLPP), faced a legitimacy crisis, exacerbated by skepticism from credible observers such as the National Elections Watch (NEW), the European Union, the Carter Center, and western governments regarding the credibility of the announced results. The resolution involved a diplomatic intervention orchestrated by the AU, ECOWAS, and the Commonwealth, culminating in a national peace dialogue. The dialogue provided the opposition with some assurances of addressing their electoral grievances, but only partially.

It is hence reasonable to assert that this, and other scenarios, might have coincided to motivate an attempted coup in Freetown on November 26. This perspective aligns with the African Union's stance in 2014, as articulated by the Peace and Security Council (PSC). The PSC noted in a press statement titled 'Unconstitutional Changes of Governments and Popular Uprisings in Africa' that coups in Africa were primarily propelled by issues such as inadequate diversity management, human rights violations, Corruption, resistance to accepting electoral defeat, quality of electoral processes, manipulation of constitutions to serve narrow interests, etc. (AU PSC, 2014).

References

1. Adkins, T. (2021). Africa's Security Challenges: A View from Congress, the Pentagon, and USAID. Center for Strategic & International Studies (CSIS).
2. African Development Bank (AfDB). (2020). African Economic Outlook 2020: Developing Africa's Workforce for the Future.
3. Africanews. (2019). Peter Mutharika wins Malawi's presidential election: official.
4. Amnesty International. (2024). Mali: Drone Strikes Killed 13 civilians Including Seven Children in Amasrakad.
5. Baltoi, D. (2023). A Deeper Look into the West African Coup Wave. Foreign Policy Research Institute.
6. Besley, T., & Persson, T. (2013). Taxation and development. Handbook of Public Economics.
7. CGTN Africa (2018). Biya wins Cameroon Presidential Elections.
8. Center for Strategic and International Studies (CSIS). (2021). Africa's Security Challenges: A View from Congress, the Pentagon, and USAID.
9. Chitofiri, K., & Nkomo, L. (2022). Violence, Victimhood and Retaliation: The 2008 Elections and the Cyclic Nature of Political Violence in

Norton, Zimbabwe. Journal of Asian and African Studies.

10. Council on Foreign Relations. (2018). "China in Africa: The New Colonialism?" Council on Foreign Relations.

11. Donati, J. (2024). In Mali, Russian Mercenaries are Helping the Army Kill Civilians, Rights Groups Say. Los Angeles Times.

12. European Union Election Observation Mission Sierra Leone (2023). Final Report of General Elections 2023. https://www.eeas.europa.eu/eom-sierra-leone-2023/sierra-leone-2023-final-report-general-elections-june-2023_en?s=410315.

13. Global Entrepreneurship Report. (2020/2021). Global Report. Global Entrepreneurship Report.

14. Karimi, F., Ntale, S., & Botelho, G. (2016). Uganda leader Museveni declared winner – despite issues, tensions. CNN.

15. McDonald, B., & Fiennes, G. (2023). The Wagner Group's Growing Shadow in the Sahel: What Does It Mean for Counterterrorism in the Region? Modern War Institute.

16. Moseray, F., & Koroma, J. (2023). The controversial proportional representation system in Sierra Leone and matters arising; Dubawa.org.

17. Powell, Lalalli, St. Pierre, & Zimmerman. (2021). Livestream Panel Discussion; Scoping the Threat: Do African Salafi-jihadi Groups Threaten the West? AEI.

18. Tharoor, I. (2023). The coup in Niger puts spotlight on nation's uranium. The Washington Post.

19. The Carter Center. (2023). Final Report General Elections in Sierra Leone.
20. UN Conference on Trade and Development. (2022). World Investment Report.
21. United Nations Economic Commission for Africa (UNECA). (2021). Economic Report on Africa 2021: Financing Africa's Post-COVID-19 Development.

SIX

UNRESOLVED HISTORICAL ISSUES

Legacy of Colonialism

HISTORICAL ISSUES, INCLUDING THE ENDURING EFFECTS of colonialism, play a significant role in perpetuating political instability, prompting some to view coups as a means of rectifying past grievances. The arbitrary demarcation of colonial borders, undertaken without regard for the complex ethnic, linguistic, or cultural realities of African societies, has left deep-seated imprints on governance and stability in the region.

Such haphazard division of territory has left a legacy of unresolved territorial disputes, ethnic tensions, and governance challenges that continue to fuel instability. For example, the delineation of borders splits ethnic groups, creating artificial nations with diverse populations and competing interests. It has often resulted in internal conflicts, secessionist movements, and power struggles among rival factions vying for control. Additionally, colonial-era boundaries failed to account for natural resources, leading to disputes over resource-rich territories and exacerbating regional tensions.

During the late 19th and early 20th centuries, European colonial powers scrambled to establish territorial control over various parts of Africa. The process often involved the arbitrary drawing of borders to suit colonial interests rather than reflecting the cultural or historical realities of the African peoples. For instance, the borders of present-day Democratic Republic of Congo were drawn without consideration for the diverse ethnic groups inhabiting the region, contributing to later conflicts.

At the Berlin Conference in 1884/85, European powers gathered to partition Africa among themselves without any African representation. This led to the arbitrary drawing of borders that often cut across ethnic, linguistic, and cultural lines. The border between present-day Nigeria and Cameroon was drawn without regard for the indigenous peoples living in the region, leading to tensions and conflicts.

Agreements between Britain and France, such as the Anglo-French Convention of 1890, delineated spheres of influence in Africa. These conventions resulted in the arbitrary partitioning of territories between the two colonial powers, leading to the creation of artificial borders that divided ethnic groups and communities. One notable example is the border between Mali and Niger, which separates the Tuareg people, leading to decades of conflict over identity and resource control.

Moreover, the imposition of colonial rule disrupted traditional governance structures and undermined indigenous systems of authority, further contributing to governance deficits and social unrest.

a) Divide and Rule

Colonial policies of divide and rule entrenched inequalities and fostered distrust among different ethnic and social groups, making it challenging to build cohesive and inclusive governance systems post-independence. During Sierra Leone's independence, the British colonial administration implemented policies that favored certain ethnic groups over others, leading to the promotion of groups from the protectorate region while marginalizing the Krios, who were descendants of freed slaves and had historically occupied positions of influence.

One instance of this phenomenon was the introduction of the protectorate system, which divided Sierra Leone into a colony and a protectorate. The British administration granted greater autonomy and political representation to indigenous groups in the protectorate, while the Krios, who were predominantly concentrated in the colony of Freetown, saw their influence diminished.

The British favored the recruitment of indigenous chiefs and leaders from the protectorate into administrative and political positions, effectively sidelining the Krios from positions of power. This policy was intended to co-opt indigenous elites into the colonial administration while undermining the influence of the Krios, who were perceived as culturally distinct and less compliant with colonial rule.

Furthermore, educational opportunities and access to government positions were often limited for the Krios, crystalizing the epoch in Sierra Leone's political history described as the Rise and Fall of the Krios. The British administration prioritized the education and advancement of indigenous groups from the protectorate. This systematic marginalization contributed to tensions between the Krios and other ethnic groups, especially the Mendes, and laid the groundwork for social and political divisions that persisted after independence. Decades on, the Krios, who dominated the civil service, developed a cavalier attitude in government and, due to their historical privilege and entrenched positions in the civil service, enabled or turned a blind eye to corruption among political leaders from other ethnic groups. This could have been driven by factors such as deep-seated colonial grievance, perceived arrogance or elitism, patronage networks, or a shared interest in maintaining the status quo.

Additionally, systemic issues within the government bureaucracy, such as weak oversight mechanisms, lack of transparency, and inadequate anti-corruption measures, may have contributed to a culture of corruption and a decline in the quality of governance and public administration.

In Rwanda, the Belgian colonial administration favored the Tutsi minority over the majority Hutu population, granting them privileged positions in society. Such discriminatory practice intensified existing ethnic tensions and sowed the seeds of resentment between the Hutu and Tutsi communities. When Rwanda gained independence in 1962, these deep-rooted divisions erupted into violence, culminating in the tragic genocide of 1994, where extremist Hutu militias slaughtered hundreds of thousands of Tutsis and moderate Hutus.

Similarly, in Burundi, the Belgians also favored the Tutsi minority, heightening tensions between the Tutsi elite and the majority Hutu population. This policy of favoritism and marginalization led to decades of ethnic conflict and power struggles following Burundi's independence in 1962. The assassination of the Hutu prime minister in 1965 sparked waves of violence, leading to cycles of ethnic reprisals and political instability. The legacy of colonial manipulation of ethnic identities continues to influence politics in both Rwanda and

Burundi, fueling social divisions and contributing to periodic outbreaks of violence and unrest.

These examples highlight how the colonial "divide and rule" strategy exploited ethnic differences to maintain control, ultimately laying the groundwork for the internal conflicts and instability that plague the continent to this day. Addressing these deep-seated divisions and promoting inclusive governance structures is essential for fostering lasting peace and stability in the region.

b) Resource Distribution Disparities

The partitioning of Africa frequently led to nations facing unequal access to resources. This imbalance has sparked internal conflicts in countries like the Democratic Republic of Congo and Sudan, where resource-rich areas cross borders. Such conflicts are often fueled by competition for valuable commodities such as minerals, oil, and agricultural land. For instance, in the Democratic Republic of Congo, the control and exploitation of mineral resources in the eastern provinces have been central to the prolonged conflict in the region. Similarly, in Sudan, the quest for dominance over oil resources in areas like South Sudan was a significant instigator of conflict and instability. These instances underscore the lasting repercussions of colonial-era resource disparities on governance and stability in Africa, emphasizing the urgent need for fair resource management and inclusive governance structures.

c) Arbitrary Border Designs and Inherited Border Disputes

In examining the impact of colonialism on Africa, the arbitrary border designs imposed by colonial powers emerge as a critical factor contributing to governance challenges and internal conflicts. The borders, often drawn without consideration for natural geographical features or existing social structures, resulted in administrative complexities and tensions within affected nations. Mali and Niger bear witness to the repercussions of such arbitrary border delineations, with straight-line boundaries disrupting traditional nomadic routes and fueling disputes over resources.

The colonial borders disrupted age-old patterns of migration, trade, and cultural exchange, fragmenting cohesive ethnic groups and creating artificial divides. As Mamdani (1996) highlights in Citizen and Subject: Contemporary Africa and the Legacy of Late Colonialism, these imposed borders led to fragmented societies, with tensions over issues such as resource access, grazing rights, and political representation, fueling conflicts both within and between nations. For example, the Somali-speaking communities, including the Somali, Oromo, and Borana peoples, have recurrently clashed over grazing land and water sources along the borders of Somalia, Ethiopia, and Kenya. This enduring legacy of colonial border demarcations continues to shape interethnic dynamics and regional geopolitics in Africa. It underscores the need for inclusive governance frameworks and cross-border cooperation to address these complex challenges.

Similar to Mali, Niger's borders were arbitrarily drawn by colonial powers, dividing ethnic groups and disrupting traditional migration patterns. The country's northern regions, inhabited by Tuareg and other nomadic groups, have experienced tensions over resource access and political representation. Herbst (2000) discusses how the imposition of borders by colonial powers has complicated governance and resource management in areas such as the Air Mountains, which straddle the border between Niger and Algeria. The regions have historically been home to Tuareg communities, but the artificial borders have contributed to periodic unrest and conflicts.

Another prominent instance of inherited border disputes is the conflict between Eritrea and Ethiopia. The colonial partition of the Horn of Africa by European powers led to the incorporation of Eritrea into Ethiopia in 1952. However, Eritrea's desire for independence sparked a prolonged struggle, culminating in a 30-year war for liberation. Despite gaining independence in 1993, tensions over border demarcation persisted, ultimately erupting into full-scale conflict between Eritrea and Ethiopia in 1998. The war claimed tens of thousands of lives and resulted in significant displacement and economic devastation. Even after a peace agreement in 2000 and subsequent international arbitration, the precise delineation of the border remains contested, fueling ongoing tensions between the two nations.

These examples underscore the enduring legacy of colonial border demarcations and their profound implications for governance and stability in Africa. Ioanes (2023), in his article "What's behind Africa's recent coups" on Vox, highlights how these historical border issues contribute to contemporary conflicts and coups. The urgent need for equitable and contextually sensitive approaches to border management is evident in addressing the root causes of these disputes.

d) Imposition of Colonial Structures

The imposition of administrative structures during the colonial era has had enduring effects on governance and stability. Colonial powers often enforced centralized governance systems that disregarded pre-existing traditional structures, leading to governance challenges and social unrest. Mamdani

(1996) discusses how these imposed systems disrupted indigenous governance, creating lasting problems.

The legacy of centralized governance in regions with historically decentralized systems is evident in countries like Cameroon and Nigeria. In Cameroon, the British and French colonial administrations merged diverse ethnic groups and territories into a single administrative unit. This imposed administrative structure marginalized certain ethnic groups and fueled grievances, contributing to secessionist movements such as the Anglophone crisis in the northwest and southwest regions (Fanso, 2017).

Similarly, Nigeria's amalgamation of diverse ethnic entities by the British colonial government led to a deeply divided nation with underlying tensions along ethnic and religious lines. Herbst (2000) explores how the imposition of centralized governance exacerbated internal conflicts, including the Biafran War, and laid the groundwork for subsequent governance challenges and political instability.

In the 2023 Nigerian Presidential Elections, ethnicity played a significant role, resulting in heightened tensions and violence. Among the 18 presidential contenders, four emerged as frontrunners, representing the country's major ethnic groups —the Hausa/Fulani, Yoruba, and Igbo (Adibe, 2023). The electorate predominantly voted for candidates from their own ethnic backgrounds. Notably, all four leading candidates secured victories in their respective states of origin, except for the APC Candidate, Bola Ahmed Tinubu. Peter Obi's endorsement by Ohanaeze Ndigbo, the pan-Igbo socio-political organization, further emphasized the ethnic polarization within the country's political landscape. This scenario is not unique to Nigeria but is observed across the continent.

In summary, colonial boundary delimitations in Africa have significantly shaped governance and stability, creating complex challenges that persist to this day. The legacies of artificial borders, ethnic tensions, and resource disparities continue to influence political dynamics and contribute to conflicts across the continent. Englebert (2009) underscores how these historical divisions continue to affect contemporary African politics.

The Foumban Conference and the Ambazonian Crisis

One of the most protracted debacles of the colonial legacy is the conflict between English-speaking Cameroon and French Cameroon. Issues of governance and security in the country trace back to the 1960s. The Foumban ConferenJust a day later, Lansana's junior officers toppled him and established the National Reformation Council (NRC), headed by Lt.-Col. Andrew Juxon-Smith.ce held in a city of the same name in Western Cameroon in 1961 was a crucial moment in Cameroon's history, aiming to negotiate the reunification of the British-administered Southern Cameroons with the French-administered Republic of Cameroon. The conference brought together the leader of the Republic of Cameroon, President Ahmadou Ahidjo, and the Prime Minister of the Southern Cameroons, John Ngu Foncha. Against the backdrop of Cameroon's divided territories, with Southern Cameroons under British rule, as well as aspirations for independence, the conference sought to establish the framework for a unified, independent nation. Participants included representatives from both regions, resulting in the signing of the Foumban Accord, which outlined provisions for a federal state structure, a transitional government, and guarantees for the rights of Anglophone minorities in West Cameroon.

Despite paving the way for reunification, the Accord also laid the groundwork for later tensions, notably the Anglophone

Crisis, driven by grievances over marginalization. The legacy of the Foumban Conference underscores Cameroon's struggle with unity and diversity management. Prior to the unification, during a conference in London from July 30 to August 22, 1953, the Southern Cameroons delegation had sought a distinct region. The British consented, and Southern Cameroons gained autonomy. Its capital was established in Buea.

During the decolonization period, when French Cameroon and Nigeria were moving towards independence, Southern Cameroonians were confronted with three choices—joining Cameroon, joining Nigeria, or opting for complete independence. However, only the first two alternatives were presented to them in the plebiscite, while the third option of independence was inexplicably omitted, limiting the choices for the people. Ultimately, votes in favor of joining Cameroon prevailed, leading to Southern Cameroons becoming part of the Federal Republic of Cameroon on October 1, 1961. It was meant to be a partnership of equals, a concept strengthened by bilateral discussions that commenced prior to the vote and endorsed by a UN resolution in April 1961. The UN recognized the joining of the two former territories as a federation comprising two states, each with equal status and autonomy.

The Foumban Conference resulted in the signing of the Foumban Accord on July 21, 1961. Key provisions of the agreement included, a) the establishment of a federal state structure with two autonomous regions: East Cameroon (formerly French Cameroon) and West Cameroon (formerly Southern Cameroons); a transitional government to oversee the reunification process; and guarantees for the protection of the cultural and linguistic rights of the Anglophone minority in West Cameroon.

Thus, the new federation came into existence, yet it was

never a harmonious alliance. Although the regions were governed centrally, the Anglophone region missed out on much of the perquisites of power. The two presidents since the unification are from the French side. In fact, the popular notion following the unification conference was that the delegation from French Cameroon or the Republic achieved nearly all their objectives. Meanwhile, the Anglophones, who did not receive the support pledged by the British or the UN, found themselves marginalized, Fanso, (2017). They felt unjustly treated by the predominantly French-speaking government, constituting 80% of the country.

Since then, Anglophone activists have been protesting what they perceive as forced assimilation into the dominant Francophone society. Reliable sources reveal that the origin of the conflict has long been attributed to such unfair domination of French-speaking politicians in government. About 20% of the country's population of 29.02 million people are Anglophone. The majority are Francophone. The Anglophones did not believe that they were fairly treated by the French-speaking government of the country. Indeed, the agreement uniting the two states had been abandoned by the leaders of the French side with criminal intent. Following a French Cameroon unilateral referendum on 20th May 1972, and fearing that the Anglophones may one day seek a secession, a new constitution was adopted in Cameroon, replacing the federal state with a unitary state and giving more power to the francophone president Ahmadou Ahidjo, with no deference to the Anglophones.

Southern Cameroons forfeited its autonomous status and was transformed into the Northwest Region and the Southwest Region of the Republic of Cameroon. The representation and participation of Anglophones in various societal levels decreased after the Federal Republic of Cameroon transitioned into the United Republic of Cameroon that year. Consequently, UN Resolution 1608, issued on April 21, 1961, which mandated the UK, the Government of Southern Cameroons, and the Republic of Cameroon to engage in discussions to establish measures for the union of the two countries, was never executed. Pro-independence groups argue that the United Kingdom was negligent in terminating its trusteeship of the territory without ensuring proper arrangements. They assert that Cameroun's adoption of a federal constitution on September 1, 1961, amounted to the annexation of Southern Cameroons. Subsequently, there has been a growing demand for the Anglophone region to separate from Cameroon.

In a memorandum dated March 20, 1985, Fon Gorji Dinka, an Anglophone lawyer and President of the Cameroon Bar Association, declared the Paul Biya dictatorship as unconstitutional and proclaimed the independence of the former Southern Cameroons, naming it the Republic of Ambazonia. Dinka was subsequently detained without trial, and he managed to escape to Nigeria three years later. This marked the initiation of a full-fledged separatist struggle, with continuous appeals for the restoration of the once-autonomous Southern Cameroons, now referred to as the Republic of Ambazonia.

The political developments that followed the Foumban Conference in Cameroon reached a climax when nationalists from British Southern Cameroons proclaimed "the reinstatement of independence and sovereignty" for the region on December 31, 1999 (Ebong, 1999).

However, despite the increasing dissent, Cameroon's conflict has historically received limited international attention. It has now taken various turns, resulting in numerous atrocities and human rights violations. Both Cameroonian forces and separatists have been accused of serious abuses in the conflict, which initially began as a demand for English-speaking officials in the regions' schools and courts but escalated into a full-blown rebellion after the government violently suppressed peaceful protesters. The elections in October 2018, securing President Paul Biya's seventh political term, have only worsened the conflict situation. The conflict has created instability, leading to violence, displacement of populations, and disruption of normal life. The presence of armed groups and government security forces escalates tensions and undermines trust in political institutions. This instability hampers economic development and social cohesion.

Resolving the conflict in Cameroon requires addressing the underlying grievances while ensuring national unity and stability. More recommendations are addressed in Chapters 14 and 15, but in a 2018 speech, former Ghanaian President Jerry Rawlins emphasized that addressing the conflict in Cameroon, particularly concerning the English-speaking population, requires more than superficial solutions. He urged a thorough examination of the issue by the African Union (AU) and the United Nations (UN), emphasizing the importance of involving France, the main supporter of French Cameroon, in the resolution process. Rawlins highlighted the need for comprehensive and inclusive approaches to effectively resolve the conflict in Cameroon.

Unresolved historical issues like this create fertile ground for coups and political upheavals as different factions strive to assert their rights and reclaim their historical heritage. The legacy of colonialism continues to shape Africa's political landscape, perpetuating instability and providing fertile ground for coups and political upheavals as various groups seek to assert their rights and reclaim their historical heritage. It underscores the importance of addressing historical injustices and promoting inclusive governance frameworks that accommodate the diverse interests and aspirations of African societies.

Underrated Acts of Aggression

The unlawful occupation of territory or oppression of communities by Africans against fellow Africans is often downplayed and not classified as an act of aggression. This is a phenomenon that pervades the continent, and it is demonstrated through a spectrum of deeds, including land grabbing, forced displacement, suppression of minority groups, and ethnic discrimination. It undermines international norms and principles of sovereignty and human rights. Instances of such actions abound throughout our post-colonial history, often leading to conflict, instability, and humanitarian crises.

One prominent example is the situation in Western Sahara, where Morocco has occupied the territory since 1975 despite international condemnation and calls for self-determination for the Sahrawi people. Morocco's occupation has been characterized by human rights abuses, including restrictions on freedom of expression and association, arbitrary arrests, and the suppression of peaceful protests.

Similarly, it's worth restating that the ongoing conflict in the Anglophone regions of Cameroon illustrates how the oppression of minority populations within a country's borders can lead to violence and unrest. The Cameroonian government's heavy-handed response to protests and demands for greater autonomy has resulted in widespread human rights violations, displacement of civilians, and a full-blown rebellion.

Furthermore, in Sudan, the Darfur conflict saw the government accused of committing genocide and crimes against humanity against non-Arab ethnic groups, resulting in widespread displacement and loss of life. Despite the severity of the situation, the international response was relatively muted, with limited efforts to hold perpetrators accountable.

However, acts of aggression are not only meted to black

minority communities. In Zimbabwe, the Mugabe regime's land reform policies initiated in the early 2000s resulted in the forced displacement of thousands of white farmers, a significant portion of the country's agricultural sector. This action had profound repercussions, contributing to economic instability and widespread food insecurity throughout the nation. While ostensibly portrayed as a necessary measure to rectify historical injustices stemming from colonial-era land ownership disparities, the implementation of these policies was characterized by widespread violence, human rights violations, and political manipulation.

The land reform program, purportedly aimed at redistributing land to historically marginalized black Zimbabweans, often led to the seizure of productive farmland without due process or compensation. The chaotic and often violent manner in which these land seizures occurred disrupted agricultural production, causing a sharp decline in food output and exacerbating existing food shortages. Moreover, the lack of expertise among many of the new landowners, coupled with inadequate government support, further hampered agricultural productivity and food security.

The land reform program was also frequently exploited as a tool for political patronage, with well-connected individuals and ruling party loyalists receiving preferential treatment in the allocation of seized land. This politicization of land distribution fostered corruption and undermined the legitimacy of the reform process. It further created tensions and fostered a climate of uncertainty and fear among both black and white Zimbabweans.

The repercussions of Zimbabwe's land reform policies continue to reverberate, with the country grappling with the long-term consequences of disrupted agricultural production, economic decline, and persistent food insecurity. The experience serves as a cautionary tale highlighting the complexities and challenges inherent in attempts to address historical injustices while ensuring sustainable development and social cohesion.

Without meaningful accountability for acts of aggression and oppression, the cycle of violence and injustice will continue to spread instability and suffering across the continent.

Precedents

Coups can be both addictive and contagious and have a tendency to perpetuate themselves to normalcy. Instances of precedent setting the stage for future coup attempts can be found throughout history, serving as a cautionary tale for countries facing similar challenges. The normalization of military intervention in politics and the series of coups that took place in Sierra Leone in 1967 and 1968 continued to influence Sierra Leone's political landscape in the decades that followed and serves as a poignant example of how precedent can shape political instability and influence future coup attempts in a country.

In April 1967, Siaka Stevens' All People's Congress (APC) party won the general elections, but dissatisfaction with the results by the incumbent Prime Minister, Albert Margai, led to a military coup by his right-hand man in the military. Brigadier David Lansana. Lansana's coup, though short-lived, set a dangerous precedent by demonstrating that the military could intervene in politics to address perceived grievances.

Just a day later, Lansana's junior officers toppled him and established the National Reformation Council (NRC), headed by Lt.-Col. Andrew Juxon-Smith. Juxon-Smith's coup highlighted the fragility of Sierra Leone's democratic institutions and further entrenched the notion that the military could seize power as a means of political change.

Yet another putsch, dubbed as the Sergeant's Coup, was carried out in 1968 by junior army officers led by Brigadier John Amadu Bangura. They overthrew the government of Juxon-Smith, who was not enamored with the thought of handing over power to a civilian government. Bangura arrested every high-ranking officer in the army and police so that he could restore the constitution and democracy to Sierra Leone. He brought Siaka Stevens from exile in Guinea and handed over power to him as rightful winner of the elections. The coup was motivated by various factors, including the desire by Brigadier Bangura to return the country to democratic rule.

These coups, occurring within such a short timeframe, created an environment of uncertainty and instability in Sierra Leone. They set a precedent that military intervention could be a viable means of addressing political grievances, ultimately paving the way for future coup attempts in the country.

In Mali, the 2012 coup led by Captain Amadou Sanogo against President Amadou Toumani Touré opened the door to subsequent military interventions, with coup plotters citing grievances similar to those of their predecessors. The persistence of political instability and security concerns in Mali has made it fertile ground for further coup attempts, with the most recent one occurring in May 2021, led by Colonel Assimi Goïta.

Similarly, in Burkina Faso, the ousting of President Blaise Compaoré in 2014 by a popular uprising followed by a failed coup attempt in 2015 created an atmosphere of political uncertainty and volatility. The tumultuous period paved the way for additional coup plots, such as the 2022 coup led by Lieutenant Colonel Paul-Henri Sandaogo Damiba and later by Captain

Ibrahim Traore, highlighting the enduring influence of precedent in shaping the political landscape.

In Niger, despite progress made under the democratically elected President Mohamed Bazoum, the specter of past coups looms large. The history of military interventions, including the most recent coup in July led by General Abdourahamane Tchiani, underscores the persistent fragility of democratic institutions and the potential for coups to recur. The pretext of citing security concerns as justification for seizing power echoes past justifications used by coup plotters, demonstrating how coups can be both addictive and contagious in countries where they have become normalized.

These instances serve as stark reminders of the role precedent plays in shaping political dynamics and the susceptibility of nations to repeat patterns of instability. As long as the specter of past coups looms large, the threat of future political upheaval remains a looming concern for countries across the African continent and beyond. The resolve of Senegal's military was tested by Macky Sall's bravado to attempt a third term, but being the only country that has not experienced a putsch, the democratic imperative ultimately restored normalcy.

References

1. Abbink, J. (2019). Ethnicity and Conflict in the Horn of Africa. Oxford Research Encyclopedia of African History.
2. Abdullah, I. (2016). Sierra Leone: Conflict, Coups, and Corruption. African Conflict and Peacebuilding Review.

3. Adibe, J. (2023). Nigeria's 2023 presidential election: 10 factors that could affect the outcome.

4. Adekunle, J. (2010). Colonialism and Violence in Nigeria. Indiana University Press.

5. Autesserre, S. (2010). The trouble with the Congo: Local violence and the failure of international peacebuilding. Cambridge University Press.

6. Barasa, L. W. (2019). Ethnic Conflicts and Political Instability in Africa: A Case Study of Kenya's Post-Independence Ethnic Conflicts. Journal of African Studies and Development.

7. Chrétien, J. P. (2003). The Great Lakes of Africa: Two Thousand Years of History. MIT Press.

8. Cole, G. F. (1982). Sierra Leone's Post-Colonial Government: The Politics of Disillusionment. African Affairs.

9. Cole, T. (2014). The Krio of Sierra Leone: An Interpretive History. C. Hurst & Co. Publishers.

10. De Waal, A. (2017). The Real Politics of the Horn of Africa: Money, War and the Business of Power. Polity.

11. Englebert, P. (2009). Africa: Unity, Sovereignty, and Sorrow. Lynne Rienner Publishers.

12. Fanso, V. (2017). History explains why Cameroon is at war with itself over language and culture. The Conversation.

13. Herbst, J. (2000). States and Power in Africa: Comparative Lessons in Authority and Control. Princeton University Press.

14. Ioanes, E. (2023). What's behind Africa's recent coups. Vox.

15. Lemarchand, R. (1996). Burundi: Ethnic Conflict and Genocide. Cambridge University Press.

16. Mamdani, M. (1996). Citizen and Subject: Contemporary Africa and the Legacy of Late Colonialism. Princeton University Press.

17. Mamdani, M. (2001). When victims become killers: Colonialism, nativism, and the genocide in Rwanda. Princeton University Press.

18. Menkhaus, K. (2007). Somalia: State Collapse and the Threat of Terrorism. Oxford University Press.

19. Prunier, G. (1995). The Rwanda Crisis: History of a Genocide. Columbia University Press.

20. Reno, W. (1995). Corruption and State Politics in Sierra Leone. Cambridge University Press.

21. Richards, P. (1996). Fighting for the Rain Forest: War, Youth, and Resources in Sierra Leone. James Currey Publishers.

22. Sheriff, A. (1989). Slaves, Spices, and Ivory in Zanzibar: Integration of an East African Commercial Empire into the World Economy, 1770-1873. Ohio University Press.

SEVEN

LEADERSHIP DEFICIT AND THE AFRICAN PSYCHE

Historical Leadership Dynamics

To grasp leadership in Africa, one must first comprehend followership, as political leadership often emerges as a sum of the collective aspirations of a people. However, this notion invariably reflects leadership in a democratic context. Steven Friedman broods over the pertinent question, "If leadership is African democracy's problem, what made it a problem?" Suggesting a reply to this inquiry requires one to divest leadership in a democratic context from dictatorship or pseudo-democratic leadership. It also bears looking at historical perspectives relating to a consistent presence of leadership, typically personified in an individual, although exceptions exist, Bryman et al (2011). Nonetheless, the achievements and setbacks of individual leaders have been closely intertwined with the success of organizations (Karikari, 2013).

Our approach involves examining a broad sweep of historical contexts, cultural nuances, social dynamics, and contemporary challenges. It also encompasses the interplay between political, social, and economic factors that shape leadership dynamics in our continent. There is certainly universal applicability to this sweeping approach, but Africa has seen a motley manifestation of leadership that is as unique as it is diverse. Ours is one that has pushed the frontiers of human comprehension in a way, not least that it has stunted growth and hindered the continent's potential.

A common variable of authoritarian regimes is their suppression of civil liberties, political freedoms, and accountability, but often, leadership elsewhere compensates for that with rapid development and swift implementation of policies. Under authoritarian rule, China witnessed the implementation of long-term economic plans, prioritized social order, and spearheaded state-led development initiatives. Communist leaders since Mao have facilitated strategic investments in infrastructure, technology, and trade partnerships, propelling China to become a global economic powerhouse.

Controlled by dictatorial authority, several Arab countries have also implemented long-term economic plans and prioritized social order to varying degrees. One notable example is the United Arab Emirates (UAE), particularly its development model in Dubai. The UAE has strategically invested in infrastructure, technology, and trade partnerships to drive economic growth and diversification. Dubai stands out as a global economic hub and a symbol of rapid development in the Arab world.

These instances tend to mute the emphasis on democracy as the safest wager for development, but beyond that, they only expose the ill-motivations of African dictatorship. Leadership in the dictatorial mode in Africa is best remembered for exacerbating social cleavages and undermining national cohesion. By prioritizing the interests of the ruling elite or a particular ethnic group, authoritarian leaders sow seeds of resentment and inequality among different segments of society. However, it bears mentioning that the promotion of ethnic interests often proves to be more rhetoric than reality, as frequently only a privileged few within an ethnic group benefit from the perquisites of power. No single ethnic community has been raised from poverty by any nepotistic arrangement. In other parts of the world, dictatorships have succeeded in elevating nations out of poverty.

Therefore, dictatorial leadership in our continent only fuels ethnic tensions, sectarian violence, or even civil conflict, further destabilizing our countries and impeding development efforts. It has hampered economic growth and investment by creating an uncertain and hostile business environment. Investors, both domestic and foreign, are wary of committing resources to countries where property rights are insecure, the rule of law is weak, and corruption is rampant. The lack of transparency, accountability, and respect for contracts under dictatorship undermines business confidence, stifles entrepreneurship, and hampers innovation and technological advancement. We live with all these traits in Africa. As a result, economic opportunities have remained limited, unemployment rates have soared, and poverty persists, perpetuating a cycle of underdevelopment and dependency. Essentially, there is a deficiency both in development and in governance. The same holds for pseudo-democracies.

Yet, democratic leadership has received massive promotion as a placebo for Africa's afflictions. Since independence, our body politic has gravitated towards it, albeit in varied tempo and motley fashion. It stands as the central axis of contemporary governance. I am riveted by this import of leadership to reveal its abuses and subsequent motivations for UCGs in contemporary times. Therefore, understanding followership dynamics is essential for a better grasp of this type of leadership, for political leaders often rely on grassroots support and community networks for a wide spectrum of mobilization efforts, requiring an understanding of local dynamics and preferences.

Leadership in the Traditional Mode

It is fair to say that Africans' appreciation of democratic leadership is rooted in their worldview about the concept in a traditional way. In many African societies, leadership is deeply intertwined with the expectations, beliefs, and behaviors of followers. Traditional African cultures often emphasize collectivism, where the interests of the group supersede those of the individual. In such societies, leaders are expected to serve the collective good and uphold communal values. This collectivist mindset shapes followers' perceptions of leadership and influences their expectations of leaders. Respect for authority is deeply ingrained in the society. Traditional leaders, such as chiefs and village elders, command respect and authority based on factors such as age, wisdom, or social status. Conversely, leaders are expected to demonstrate wisdom, integrity, and benevolence in their decisions to maintain the trust and confidence of their followers. Leadership styles vary widely, with some cultures valuing charisma and assertiveness in leaders while others prioritize humility and modesty. Effective leaders must navigate these cultural nuances to establish rapport and credibility with their followers. They must understand the cultural values and expectations of their constituents to effectively lead and serve their communities.

In Ghanaian culture, traditional leadership structures such as chieftaincies play a central role in governance and community affairs. Chiefs are revered figures who are expected to uphold communal values and promote the welfare of their communities. Their authority is derived from a combination of hereditary lineage, wisdom, and moral standing within the community. Abanyie, Ampofo, and Boateng (2016) explore the role of traditional leaders in local governance in Ghana, highlighting the intertwining of leadership with communal expectations and beliefs.

Nigeria boasts a diverse array of ethnic groups, each with its own traditions and leadership structures. For example, among the Yoruba people of southwestern Nigeria, traditional rulers known as obas hold significant sway over their subjects. These rulers are expected to embody wisdom, integrity, and benevolence in their governance, drawing on cultural norms that prioritize communal welfare over individual interests (Ogunleye, 2013).

In South Africa, the concept of Ubuntu, which emphasizes interconnectedness and mutual obligation within communities, shapes leadership expectations and behaviors. Leaders are expected to demonstrate humility, empathy, and a commitment to collective well-being. The consultative leadership style is prevalent, with leaders engaging in dialogue and consensus-building to address community issues. Mbigi and Maree (1995) explore the principles of Ubuntu and their implications for leadership in South African organizations, highlighting the importance of cultural context in shaping leadership practices.

The commonality among the above cultural milieu lies in the deep intertwining of leadership with the expectations, beliefs, and behaviors of followers within African societies. Across Ghana, Nigeria, South Africa, and many other territories, traditional leadership structures emphasize collectivism, respect for authority, and participatory decision-making, reflecting cultural values that prioritize the welfare of the community over individual interests. In each context, leaders are expected to serve the collective good and uphold communal values, drawing on cultural norms that shape followers' perceptions of leadership and influence their expectations of leaders. This attitude towards traditional leadership segues to democratic leadership, presenting a perfect synthesis between the two and an equal applicability of opportunities and challenges for development.

While these values promote social cohesion and community resilience, they also risk fostering authoritarianism, resistance to change, and limited accountability in governance. The expectation for leaders to prioritize the collective good may marginalize minority voices and lead to slow decision-making processes, hindering timely responses to development challenges. This is not to say there is an inherent flaw in the African psyche towards leadership. If at all, it highlights the abusiveness of self-serving leadership in the face of absolute deference. By exploiting trust and deference, leaders undermine democratic norms, erode public confidence, and perpetuate inequality within societies. Such abuses of respect erode the foundation of effective governance, impeding progress and development while fostering environments of injustice and oppression. Evidenced by numerous instances across the continent's history and contemporary political landscape, the strong man syndrome in African leadership has been used not only as an instrument of abuse but also as a stunting mechanism of democracy and economic growth.

Charismatic Leadership in Post-colonial Africa

In African politics, the concept of charismatic leadership faces significant constraints (Sishuwa, 2020). Post-independence charismatic leaders often fell short in their efforts to bring about transformative change in their countries. This could be attributed to diverse reasons, ranging from moral decadence in the character of the leadership figure, as in the case of Mobutu Sese Seko of Zaire (the DRC), to external fetters, as exemplified by Kwame Nkrumah of Ghana. Either way, it underscores the fact that charismatic leadership in Africa has wielded profound influence over governance, shaping the trajectory of nations through periods of upheaval and transition. Rooted in the tradition of leaders possessing supernatural gifts, the concept was broadened by Max Weber to encompass individuals perceived as possessing extraordinary qualities, such as heroism and exceptional oratory skills.

When a society experiences significant social upheaval or oppression, resulting in distress and dissatisfaction among certain segments of the population, it creates an environment conducive to the rise of a charismatic leader (Friedland, 1964; Willner & Willner, 1965). This notion of charisma found fertile ground in Africa, where leaders like Kwame Nkrumah, Nelson Mandela, and Julius Nyerere emerged as iconic figures embodying the aspirations and struggles of their people (Karikari, 2013).

Weber (1978) suggests that followers of charismatic leaders often demonstrate unwavering personal allegiance to either the leader or their authority, which is rooted in the leader's convictions, bravery, or idealized vision of the future. Sishuwa (2020) notes that this profound loyalty has, in some cases, resulted in followers attributing messianic or savior-like qualities to charismatic leaders.

Nkrumah and a select few exemplified charismatic qualities, leveraging their powers of persuasion, vision, and personal magnetism to galvanize movements for independence and social change. Kenneth Kaunda, who led Zambia from independence in 1964 until 1991, was indeed revered by many of his supporters, and his leadership style often incorporated elements of charisma. The comparison of Kaunda to "God on earth" underscores the extent to which his leadership was idolized and elevated to almost divine status by some segments of the population (Sishuwa, 2020). Patrice Lumumba, the first Prime Minister of the Democratic Republic of Congo, possessed a charismatic aura that inspired many during the struggle for independence. His impassioned speeches and commitment to Pan-Africanism made him a symbol of resistance against colonialism and oppression.

Nelson Mandela's leadership during South Africa's transition from apartheid to democracy captivated not only his own nation but the entire world, earning him global admiration and respect for his unwavering commitment to reconciliation and forgiveness, coupled with his personal charisma. Similarly, as the first President of Tanzania, Julius Nyerere was renowned for his socialist ideology, simplicity, and moral integrity, resonating strongly with many Tanzanians and Africans across the continent through his vision of Ujamaa (African socialism) and emphasis on self-reliance.

As mentioned earlier, the social and historical contexts within which these leaders ascended to prominence played a pivotal role in shaping their charismatic appeal. Emerging amid the tumult of decolonization and nationalist fervor, they embodied the aspirations of their people for dignity, self-determination, and progress. Their ability to articulate a compelling vision of the future, coupled with a personal aura of authority and authenticity, engendered widespread admiration and loyalty. The effectiveness and satisfaction of followership under this leadership construct are underscored by the tangible achievements of these leaders in securing political freedom and laying the foundations for nation-building. The liberation movements they spearheaded not only dismantled colonial regimes but also inspired a sense of national identity and solidarity among diverse populations (Karikari, 2013).

However, the limitations mentioned at the outset run deep despite the charisma that post-independence leadership evinced. Some of the factors behind the failure of charismatic leadership are mentioned in this work as motivations of sorts for UCGs. These factors span from external constraints limiting the potential of these leaders to inherent internal and structural weaknesses within their administrations.

To start with, at the cusp of rolling out their post-independence African agenda, African leaders had to look over their shoulders for colonial operatives who lurked in the shadows, poised to influence every facet of political and public life. Their aim was to protect imperial interests, even if it meant toppling the leadership. Patrice Lumumba's fate lingers as a vivid reminder of imperial overreach. He faced opposition from Belgium and the United States due to his nationalist and anti-colonial stance. In June 1960, upon achieving independence, his impromptu speech during the official ceremonies in Kinshasa garnered a standing ovation, elevating him to hero status among millions. Within months, he fell victim to a conspiracy. He was apprehended, subjected to torture, and ultimately assassinated (De Witte, 2003).

In Ghana, Kwame Nkrumah's administration faced covert CIA involvement aimed at undermining his socialist policies and Pan-African agenda. The CIA supported opposition groups and funded efforts to orchestrate a coup, which eventually led to Nkrumah's ousting in 1966, (Stockwell, 1978).

Furthermore, the continued influence of former colonial powers, such as France's "Françafrique" system, imposed significant constraints on the performance of charismatic leadership in Africa after independence. In the case of Côte d'Ivoire, under the leadership of Félix Houphouët-Boigny, France wielded considerable influence over the country's political and economic affairs through close ties established during the colonial era. French companies dominated key sectors of the Ivorian economy, and Houphouët-Boigny's government relied heavily on France for military support and economic assistance. This close relationship also meant that Côte d'Ivoire remained dependent on France, and Houphouët-Boigny's regime faced criticism for its lack of true independence and for perpetuating neo-colonial relations.

Ahmed Sékou Touré, the first President of Guinea, a vociferous critic of French imperialism and an avid advocate for Pan-Africanism and socialism, was made to suffer a dire fate. Aside from his strong stance against imperialism, his leadership was characterized by his efforts to establish Guinea as a sovereign and self-reliant nation. Under his leadership, Guinea became the first French colony in Africa to gain independence in 1958. Touré's defiance of French colonial rule led to a rupture in Guinea's relationship with France. In response to the country's declaration of independence, France withdrew its technical assistance, including infrastructure and administrative support, and actively worked to undermine Guinea's economy and isolate it diplomatically.

Moreover, charismatic leadership was put to test in the 1970s. The decade saw a global economic downturn and a sharp decline in commodity prices, particularly for African countries heavily reliant on exports such as oil, copper, and cocoa. The economic shock severely impacted national economies and hindered development efforts. This grim outlook continued into the 80s and 90s when the Bretton Woods emerged with their anti-socialist conditionalities that only contributed to social unrest and economic hardships.

On the flip side, charismatic leadership in the post-colonial order perpetrated some of the most heinous instances of abuse, moral decadence, and corruption. There was a palpable tendency to prioritize personal authority over institutional development, often leading to authoritarianism, instability, and economic mismanagement. The continent had no shortage of leaders who relied heavily on charisma, centralized power, weakened democratic institutions, and perpetuated cults of personality, hindering accountability and fostering corruption. One notable instance is Mobutu Sese Seko. His charismatic leadership, coupled with his promotion of "Mobutism," led to the consolidation of power in his hands, extensive corruption, and economic decline that ultimately contributed to the country's instability and impoverishment.

Mobutu initiated the establishment of a single, formidable political party known as the Popular Revolutionary Movement, mandating membership for all Zairians. Initially, he endeavored to attract the most talented individuals from Zaire's university community, actively seeking their counsel. However, over time, the allure of flattery and an increasing thirst for power began to dominate, resulting in the president's governance becoming secluded and dictatorial. Those perceived as challengers, whether real or perceived, often met dire consequences (French, 1997).

Similarly, Idi Amin's charismatic rule in Uganda was marked by brutality, human rights abuses, and economic collapse. Amin's personalized and erratic style of governance, characterized by arbitrary decision-making and violence, undermined the rule of law and exacerbated ethnic tensions, leading to widespread suffering. These leaders justified the grim prejudice that the departure of colonial administrators often created a leadership vacuum, as there were few Indigenous leaders with experience in governance and administration. The vacuum was sometimes filled by political entrepreneurs who prioritized their own interests over those of the nation.

These examples highlight how charismatic leadership

alone may not be sufficient to lift countries from poverty. External factors such as global economic trends, debt burdens, and geopolitical dynamics, as well as internal challenges, including corruption, political instability, and ineffective governance, often hinder efforts towards poverty alleviation.

Leadership Incompetence

After independence in the mid-20th century, African nations faced the task of nation-building despite lacking the necessary experience and institutional infrastructure. Leadership incompetence emerges as the primary contributor to the challenges of this transitional phase, albeit not the sole determinant. Over time, the lack of effective leadership in numerous African nations has led to similar developmental outcomes. Put differently, the issue cannot be solely attributed to individuals holding governmental positions; rather, it reflects a prevailing culture of ineffective leadership. This pattern extends beyond the realm of government to encompass organizations and families, highlighting a significant power disparity between leaders and citizens. Within this context, leaders are not servants of their constituents; instead, they are served, as their positions grant them a sense of superiority and impunity. To tackle these challenges, Africa needs robust systems for developing leadership, underscoring the importance for development partners and global leaders to recognize the impact of cultural differences on these dynamics.

A stark indictment of leadership incompetence is our inability to convert the four-comma figure of foreign aid that has showered the continent since independence into any meaningful transformation of African lives (Moyo, 2009). Many African leaders perceive their countries primarily as recipients of aid, grants, and loans rather than as drivers of their own development. Donald Duke, former governor of Cross River State in Nigeria, likens African leaders to pilots who did not go to flying school, (Adeyemi, 2017).

Leadership incompetence has manifested in various detrimental ways, profoundly impacting governance, the economy, social services, and overall development. Corruption and nepotism have thrived under incompetent leadership, creating environments ripe for the misappropriation of public resources, as seen in the corruption scandals that plagued former South African President Jacob Zuma's tenure. Additionally, poor infrastructure and inadequate service delivery are stark indicators of ineffective leadership, exemplified by the collapse of essential services in Zimbabwe due to years of mismanagement under President Robert Mugabe.

Political instability and conflict have resulted from leadership failures, as evidenced by ongoing civil wars in South Sudan and Somalia, which displace millions and hinder development efforts. Economic mismanagement exacerbates poverty, with instances of hyperinflation and currency devaluation, such as those experienced in Zimbabwe under Mugabe's rule, leading to widespread suffering. Furthermore, human rights abuses are facilitated by incompetent leadership, with authoritarian tactics and crackdowns on dissent observed in countries like Cameroon and the Democratic Republic of Congo.

Accordingly, corruption and income disparities perpetuated by selfish leadership hinder progress, rendering foreign aid ineffective. Sam Adeyemi (2017) highlights globalization's adverse effects on Africa, escalated by corruption and a culture of dependency instilled by leaders. He stresses the need for development partners to engage in meaningful dialogue rather than superficial interventions. These examples underscore the urgent need for competent leadership and institutional reforms to foster sustainable development in Africa. Addressing the leadership deficit requires a shift towards servant leadership, recognizing the transformative impact of inclusive governance and ethical stewardship on the continent's future.

Cosmopolitan Leadership and Traditional African Values

A cogent vista of leadership in the wake of independence encompasses the conflict between traditional African values and a cosmopolitan worldview. The latter requires an embrace of diversity stemming from minority groups, gender, orientation, and cultural background, which serve as beneficial catalysts for growth and well-being (Makeka, 2016). The traditional African ethos often emphasizes communal harmony, respect for elders, and cultural preservation. However, in a rapidly globalizing world, leaders must navigate a complex landscape that demands inclusivity, diversity, and recognition of the rights and contributions of minority groups, individuals of diverse gender identities and orientations, and those from varied cultural backgrounds. Embracing this cosmopolitan perspective offers numerous benefits, serving as a catalyst for societal growth, prosperity, and overall well-being. Yet, African nations have encountered challenges in fully embracing this globalized outlook, often due to such factors as deep-rooted cultural traditions, political instability, and socio-economic disparities.

Despite efforts to promote gender equality, for instance, women continue to face significant barriers to political participation, economic empowerment, and access to education and healthcare in many of our countries. In places like Somalia, where traditional gender roles are deeply entrenched, women's representation in political leadership remains disproportionately low, hindering progress towards gender parity and inclusivity. However, the state of affairs is not entirely bleak. Rwanda's efforts to promote gender equality in political representation have led to significant advancements in women's rights and contributed to the country's overall stability and development.

Furthermore, traditional leaders in many countries hold significant influence within their communities based on customary authority. However, the introduction of Western-style democratic systems often challenges the legitimacy of these traditional leaders. In Nigeria, the clash between elected officials and traditional rulers over issues such as resource control, land rights, and political representation highlights the tension between traditional and modern governance structures.

Rapid urbanization provides another confluence. It has led to the emergence of cosmopolitan identities among urban elites, who may adopt Western lifestyles, values, and modes of governance. This can create tensions with traditional rural communities, where customary practices and social hierarchies remain dominant. For instance, in countries like Kenya and South Africa, urban elites have persistently advocated for progressive social policies and human rights, while rural areas adhere to traditional norms that may be more conservative and patriarchal.

Similarly, our nations have struggled to effectively address the modern menace of migration. The rights and needs of refugees and migrants, in keeping with global protocols, have not been adequately protected. In South Africa, xenophobic violence targeting foreign nationals has highlighted underlying tensions and discrimination against immigrants, underscoring the challenges of fostering inclusive and cosmopolitan societies.

Additionally, the pursuit of economic development and globalization often requires countries to adapt to international norms and standards. However, this has clashed with traditional values and practices, particularly in sectors such as agriculture, where communal land ownership and traditional farming methods may conflict with modernization efforts. In Ethiopia and Uganda, large-scale agricultural projects funded by international investors have sometimes displaced rural communities and disrupted traditional livelihoods, leading to social unrest and conflict.

Makeka (2016) underscores the challenge of reconciling youth-driven change with entrenched power structures in Africa, emphasizing the need for adaptive leadership in the face of evolving societal demands. Several African leaders have exhibited authoritarian tendencies, stifling political freedoms and suppressing youth-led protests and opposition to maintain power. But this has come with a huge cost to their reputation and international ratings, thanks to the preponderance of ICT tools and perception surveys. Leaders who have lost the trust of their people often resort to diverting attention by appealing to cultural sentiments. They exaggerate minority issues, such as LGBTQ+ rights, to fabricate a sense of preserving their heritage. In many of these countries, even their language remains under the influence of colonialism, unredeemed from its grasp.

Contemporary Leadership Failures Leading to Coup Attempts

Recent coups across Africa share common motivations rooted in grievances related to leadership failures, political instability, economic challenges, and security concerns. In Mali, for example, the 2020 coup led by Colonel Assimi Goïta was driven by widespread dissatisfaction with President Ibrahim Boubacar Keïta's administration, marked by allegations of corruption, economic mismanagement, and human rights abuses, as well as escalating security threats posed by jihadist insurgency. Similarly, the 2019 coup in Sudan, which ousted longtime President Omar al-Bashir, was fueled by public anger over economic hardship, political repression, and corruption, culminating in months of mass protests demanding regime change.

The 2021 coup in Guinea, orchestrated by Colonel Mamady Doumbouya, reflected popular discontent with President Alpha Condé's controversial third-term bid and perceived authoritarianism, compounded by economic stagnation and social inequality. In 2022, Burkina Faso experienced two coups in 9 months. A 34-year-old commander of an artillery unit in the Armed Forces, Captain Ibrahim Traoré, toppled Lieutenant Colonel Paul-Henri Sandaogo Damiba and cited Burkina Faso's worsening security conditions as the rationale behind his assumption of power. Damiba had previously orchestrated a coup in January 2022, also pledging to tackle the nation's security challenges (Africa Centre for Strategic Studies, 2022). Niger's President Mohamed Bazoum suffered the same fate under General Abdourahamane Tchiani, who, in a televised speech, outlined his roadmap, proposing a transition period lasting no longer than three years and emphasizing the importance of inclusive national dialogue.

These coups underscore a shared pattern of citizens mobilizing against entrenched leadership marred by corruption, repression, and failure to address pressing socio-economic issues, ultimately leading to military intervention. They also indicate a comeback of uniformed leadership and a new era of the military in politics. Such instances highlight the recurring themes of popular disillusionment with governance and the fragility of democratic institutions across the African continent. But these attempts pale in the face more desperate attempts by people who are not in active military service. Their bravado is best understood when one considers the dire circumstances in their country—Sierra Leone. The attempt at upending the establishment was unsuccessful, but the situation bears reliving.

Leadership Failure and an Attempted Coup in Sierra Leone

On the morning of Sunday, November 26, 2023, Freetown, the capital city, was rattled by gunshots. Initially dismissed as a minor security breach, the government later labeled it a coup attempt. Armed individuals breached an armory at the Wilberforce military barracks near the president's residence, followed by assaults on the Pademba Road Correctional Centre and the Special Court premises that house female prisoners, all resulting in the release of inmates. The army reported at least 19 casualties in the immediate aftermath, including 13 soldiers. Subsequently, the government announced the arrest of military officers and civilians. Some senior opposition politicians were detained, and others have experienced unannounced searches and harassment at their homes. Former President Ernest Bai Koroma was placed under house arrest, charged with treason, and later relocated to Nigeria with ECOWAS intervention.

Several explanations have been put forward by political and governance commentators regarding the incident. While acknowledging the potential influence of partisan motives, my objective is to offer a comparative analysis of the insurrection in relation to similar actions in ECOWAS sister countries, considering Sierra Leone's unique leadership challenges. I have chosen to use the term "insurrection" interchangeably with "attempted coup" to maintain a balanced stance of neither endorsing political propaganda nor undermining established state authority.

- *Antecedents to the November 26 Insurrection*

Understanding the likely motivations behind such an insurrection necessitates an exploration of political antecedents stemming directly from failed leadership. These factors collectively contribute to a sense of desperation among citizens, ultimately culminating in the breakdown of state order.

a) Parliamentary Coup and the Ousting of Opposition MPs

In 2018, the newly elected government of Julius Maada Bio assumed office, initiating a series of controversial decisions that plunged the country into a state of uncertainty. Prior to the opening of the 5th parliament, armed police officers forcibly entered the parliamentary chamber to assist in the imposition of a speaker by the ruling SLPP, despite lacking the parliamentary majority to do so legitimately. The main opposition APC, which clearly held the majority and the right to elect a speaker, intended to vehemently oppose this parliamentary maneuver, but their MPs were bludgeoned with police batons and evicted out of the well of parliament. The imposition of the Speaker marked a pivotal moment in Sierra Leone's political trajectory, triggering a cascade of events that would resonate throughout the nation. This incident had profound consequences, significantly impacting the nation's political landscape for the remainder of the 5-year term leading up to the 2023 elections.

Adding to the tension, ten APC MPs were petitioned through the courts and subsequently removed from their seats, resulting in a shift of parliamentary majority status from the opposition to the ruling party. Conversely, APC petitions against ruling party MPs were dismissed by the same court. Civil society groups, including the media, expressed discomfort and condemnation regarding this issue, with some citing it as a criminal act. Kandeh Yumkella, parliamentary leader of one of the minor parties, labeled the action as an enactment of 'junta democracy'. Activists and members of the media who dared to investigate these matters became targets of state persecution and harassment.

b) Controversial Commissions of Inquiry (COI)

With a pretext to fight graft and transition to a new dispensation of transparency and accountability, the Bio administration set up three commissions of inquiries to look into corruption and mismanagement of the previous APC government. The outcome was perceived as a non-procedural move to hound opposition politicians. Throughout the 5-year tenure of President Bio, tensions abound about the fairness of the process and the veracity of the findings that culminated in a government White Paper. The opposition party contended, among other points, that the instruments establishing the Commissions were not in harmony with the provisions outlined in the relevant constitutional clauses that prescribe the rules governing the practice and procedure of all Commissions of Inquiry. Popular concern about the failure of the government to establish Rules of Evidence in the proceedings of the COI also provided another damper to the people's trust in due process and shore up worries about political witch hunts.

c) Targeted Sackings of Civil Servants, Police and Military Personnel

During the 2018 campaigns, the SLPP (then in opposition) alleged that security personnel harbored intentions to assassinate their presidential candidate, Julius Maada Bio. Although they later retracted this assertion, it served as a pretext for the marginalization of military and police personnel based on tribal and regional affiliations.

The termination of civil servants with security of tenure, selective reassignment, and forced leave imposed on public servants by the Bio-led government raised concerns. The dismissal of public officials with North/Western surnames was widespread despite contravening the civil service code of practice and other legal statutes. Individuals with such surnames felt constantly threatened across various sectors of public life. While it is within the president's constitutional prerogative to "hire and fire," adherence to statutory provisions and the spirit of unity was crucial, particularly in the aftermath of a divisive electoral process

d) The Pademba Road Prison Massacre

On April 29, 2019, a fire erupted at the Pademba Road Correctional Center, a male prison located in the heart of Freetown. The state responded to extinguish the fire using unconventional methods beyond traditional fire engines. State security personnel, including Presidential Guards, arrived at the scene as if confronting armed assailants, resulting in the firing of live rounds. The subsequent onslaught resulted in a high number of casualties, noted as one of the deadliest incidents on a single day since the war. According to the government report, the violence unfolded between 07:30 am and 11:00 am, attributed to a response by security forces against an attack by a group of gangs on the facility. However, this explanation contradicts assertions made by Ms. Fatmata Sawaneh, the chairman of the SLPP women's wing, in a widely circulated audio recording before or during the event. Ms. Sawaneh claimed they were present at the scene before the incident occurred, having arrived to address an issue they themselves had created.

Sierraloaded, an online newsletter, indicated the findings of the incident and raised concerns about crucial records regarding the legal status of inmates, which have not only been lost and remain unrecovered but also appear to be a lack of efforts to rectify the situation. Auditor Report of the incident stated thus, "We also noted that following the April 2019 incident at the Correctional Center, important inmate records such as warrants of release were destroyed in the fire. Consequently, numerous inmates are still detained in prison as their warrants of release cannot be located." Speculations abound that even the records of deaths were lost in the fire. It is evident why inmates who should have been released are still confined.

The official government position stated that prior to the alleged attack by the gang, a significant number of senior government officials, including political leaders from the ruling party, were present at the location. These political figures appeared to have no direct involvement in security matters. Unconfirmed sources state that the operatives were present in the prison premises to get their share of a huge quantity of rice supply meant for the prison department. The fire may have been deliberately ignited to mask the massive depletion caused on the ration for inmates. Social media analysts raised probing inquiries, questioning why a party executive was present to manage a security situation when she was not a government representative. Moreover, there was intrigue surrounding the presence of government representatives, including political leaders from the ruling party, at the scene hours before the massacre began.

e) Suppression of Protests

State authorities resorted to employing extreme violence to quell the wave of protests that have swept the country since 2019. With police clearance consistently denied, Sierra Leonean citizens took to the streets to express their grievances regarding the severe economic challenges, blatant political intimidation, human rights abuses, and widespread corruption. Their concerns also encompass the selective enforcement of the rule of law and the lack of access to justice. Major towns and cities, particularly in opposition strongholds, including the capital, have witnessed significant instances of police brutality during these protests.

One of the most notable protests resulting in fatalities occurred on August 10, 2022, in Freetown and other northern towns. Sierra Leoneans, frustrated by the escalating costs of essential goods and other socio-economic challenges, had long been discontented. They marched through the main streets of Freetown and other urban centers chanting slogans such as 'Maada must go,' expressing their frustration with the president's leadership style and the state of the economy. In many instances, clashes erupted with the police, who responded with tear gas and live ammunition. Videos captured and verified by Reuters and other news agencies depicted police officers firing guns into crowds of people in Freetown.

The government established a Special Investigation Committee, which released its findings in March 2023. An Amnesty International article titled Sierra Leone: Still no Justice for Victims of August 2022 Protests More than One Year On, and published on their web on October 17, 2023, was not very pleased about the Special Investigation Committee Report. "Despite recommending training of police officers in avoiding heavy-handedness, the report falls short of recommending an investigation into excessive use of force during the protests. To date, none of the civilian deaths have been investigated." Family members of protesters and bystanders who lost their lives during the protests were denied the chance to identify their loved ones or say their farewells according to their customary rites and preferences. The victims were interred in a collective burial, in a manner reminiscent only of the mass graves used by the government for deceased youth who succumb to an opioid substance called Kush, which is ravaging Sierra Leone in 2024.

f) Cost of Living Crisis

Increase in the cost of living generated mounting dissatisfaction in the nation. By June 2023, the inflation rate surged to 44.81%, a significant rise from the 27.95% recorded in June 2022. According to a World Bank Press Release titled Tough Macroeconomic Policies Needed to Stabilize Sierra Leone's Economy, in 2022, the economy faced simultaneous challenges as external shocks compounded domestic macroeconomic vulnerabilities, leading to a swift accumulation of debt, escalating inflation, and heightened food insecurity. GDP growth decelerated from 4.1% in 2021 to 3.5% in 2022, while inflation surged from 12% in 2021 to 27% in 2022, reaching over 40% by May 2023, posing a threat to household well-being and exacerbating issues of food insecurity and poverty.

The fiscal deficit expanded from 7.6% of GDP in 2021 to 9.6% in 2022, influenced by a combination of macroeconomic challenges and policy lapses. The public debt-to-GDP ratio also rose from 84.7% at the close of 2021 to 96.3% at the close of 2022. The report emphasizes that, although external factors will influence the economic outlook, domestic policies are crucial and should prioritize the restoration of macroeconomic stability. (World Bank Press Release, 27th October 2023; Mayeni Jones of the BBC, in an interview to ferret potential reasons for the insurrection, stumbled into analyses that link it to high unemployment rate and a 'bleak economic outlook' for the country.

These challenges are certainly not unconnected with the leadership deficit leading to government mismanagement of the economy. The media was replete with reports about reckless spending practices on the country's finances, leading to budget deficits and economic instability. Excessive presidential travels and the high costs associated with them were no less palpable. Such trips definitely divert resources away from essential services and contribute to budgetary strains. Also, the problem of a bloated public sector wage bill was noted as a factor of fiscal vulnerabilities. Instances of the government failing to declare austerity measures during economic downturns have been documented, with analysts highlighting the detrimental impact on fiscal stability and the cost of living for citizens. Regarding business contracts, reports from reputable news agencies highlighted cases of the government dishonoring agreements, particularly in the mining sector, leading to reduced investment and economic growth. These instances and reports collectively underscore the significant role played by leadership deficiency in contributing to Sierra Leone's cost of living crisis.

g) *Low Confidence in State Structures and the Leadership*

In the lead-up to the June 24, 2023, elections, Sierra Leone experienced an alarming decline in trust in its court system and law enforcement agencies. The delayed handling and resolution of opposition-related cases, along with a lack of investigations into election-related violence, fueled doubts among the populace regarding the accessibility and efficacy of justice in the nation. Incidents of APC party representatives being expelled from SLPP strongholds added to the pre-election complexities, hindering their ability to participate and represent their interests in those areas during the electoral process.

The erosion of public trust was further exacerbated by the president and First Lady's reckless statements and uncontrolled spending of state funds. The First Lady made divisive political remarks against opposition party members and occasionally derogatory comments about the people of Sierra Leone on various platforms. These remarks have sparked numerous controversies in both local and international media. In one instance, she implicated other First Ladies in Africa, prompting citizens to question the spending habits of presidential spouses. Africanist Press, a prominent regional website known for exposing financial impropriety within the government, intensified its scrutiny of the president and the Office of the First Lady. Media outlets were flooded with headlines about the Presidency, while journalists delved into every detail to uncover information about the First Lady's activities. "I'm not receiving even a fraction of what other African first ladies are getting in the region," Madam Fatima Maada Bio lashed out in defense, admitting that her office received funds from the consolidated fund but denying any wasteful spending.

The persistent allegations by the Africanist Press against the Presidency and its consistent feature in the Auditor General's Report for unaccountable spending resulted in the Auditor General being indefinitely suspended without due process. The audit report uncovered financial and procurement irregularities in the President's travel expenses and the expenditure of the Office of the First Lady for the financial year 2020. It was reported that the President's Office had provided numerous falsified documents, such as forged hotel receipts and invoices, to the Audit Service as part of the president's travel expenses.

The combination of these instances of leadership shortcomings and oversight failures ultimately resulted in the widespread disillusionment that manifested in the November 26 insurrection.

Patterns and Trends in Leadership Changes Through UCGs

Leadership transitions in Africa consistently draw significant attention, characterized by their inherent unpredictability. Typically speaking, the only constant in African polity is that the seat of power will be occupied by all means. Attempts to discern a pattern or impute consistency in transitions, particularly in relation to democratic tenets, are neutered by rude awakenings. The vagaries of random transfers are one too many. Various methods of leadership change, including democratic elections, civil unrest, constitutional successions, negotiated settlements, or military coups, have manifested across the continent, spanning from Senegal to Somalia. However, these modes of power transfer are frequently marred by violations of constitutional norms or the agency of forces that directly or indirectly subvert the will of the people. With few exceptions, our electoral processes may be called many things but "democratic." Therefore, patterns and trends in leadership changes through coups in Africa have undergone evolution over the years, influenced by complex interactions of political, economic, and social factors. While there is no one-size-fits-all explanation, certain common themes and instances emerge.

Military Intervention as a Recurring Theme

Military coups have been the most common method of effecting leadership changes in Africa beyond the popular mandate. As noted throughout the book, they have been largely influenced by factors such as weak post-colonial institutions, massive corruption, and mismanagement, Cold War rivalries, socio-economic grievances, ethnic tensions, etc. These coups have often led to prolonged periods of authoritarian rule, human rights abuses, and economic mismanagement. While their frequency has decreased since the 1990s, their resurgence in the 2020s is alarming and reminiscent of weak governance structures.

From the recent coups in Mali to the ousting of Kwame Nkrumah in Ghana in 1966 and the 1983 coup in Burkina Faso led by Thomas Sankara, military interventions in politics have not ceased to be a constant presence. This recurring theme in Africa manifests in diverse forms, spanning from coups d'état orchestrated by personnel within the mainstream military to actions by elite presidential guards and even external military interventions like those conducted by NATO.

In recent years, we have witnessed a notable trend of elite presidential guards overthrowing our leaders. These elite units, often highly trained and well-equipped and tasked with the special role of protecting the head of state, have also become instruments of political power. President Alpha Condé of Guinea was overthrown in a military coup led by the Special Forces Group (Groupement des Forces Spéciales), an elite unit within the Guinean armed forces, led by the president's close confidant, Colonel Mamady Doumbouya. Following the coup, Colonel Doumbouya announced the dissolution of the government and the suspension of the constitution, effectively taking control of the country. General Abdourahamane Tchiani, head of Niger's influential presidential guard, assumed control following a military coup in the Sahel country. Tchiani proclaimed himself leader following a seizure of power that occurred in July 2023, during which his presidential guards detained President Mohamed Bazoum and confined him within the presidential palace (VOA, July, 2023). It did not take long before Gabon followed in Niger's wake.

In some cases, like in the case of mainstream military officers, the elite presidential guards have seized control of the government to protect their own interests or to prevent perceived threats to their influence. This pattern complicates the assessment of whether the motivations behind such takeovers truly aligned with the interests of the people.

Furthermore, external military interventions, exemplified by NATO's involvement in Libya in 2011 and now the Russian Wagner Group's involvement in the Sahel, constitute another dimension of military interference in African political affairs. Such interventions, often presented as noble endeavors aimed at protecting civilians, upholding global norms, or fostering stability, seldom deliver the promised outcomes. Instead, they unfurl into convoluted and unforeseen consequences, leaving behind a wake of chaos and instability.

NATO's foray into Libya, initially portrayed as a mission to shield civilians from the repressive grip of Muammar Gaddafi's regime during the Arab Spring uprisings, ultimately resulted in the ousting of Gaddafi himself. However, far from ushering in a new era of peace and prosperity, this intervention plunged Libya into deeper turmoil, exacerbating the nation's instability and fracturing its social fabric. The Wagner Group's involvement in Libya adds another layer of complexity to the dynamics of external intervention and further complicates efforts to resolve the conflict. The mercenary group has been accused of supporting the forces of Khalifa Haftar, a military commander who has been involved in a protracted conflict against the internationally recognized Government of National Accord (GNA).

I am compelled to question the legitimacy and sovereignty of such interventions. Do they truly serve the interests of African people, or are they driven by ulterior motives? And perhaps most importantly, what unintended repercussions lurk beneath the surface of these interventions, waiting to emerge and further destabilize our continent? The complexities inherent in them demand our scrutiny and vigilance. As I document these events from afar, I am reminded of the urgent need for African nations to assert their sovereignty, reclaim agency over their destinies, and chart a course toward a future free from external manipulation and interventions.

Civil Unrest

UCGs frequently occur amidst widespread discontent, social upheaval, and political instability. Observing the chaotic landscape of Africa, one cannot help but feel a profound sadness at the recurring incidences of civil unrest leading to changes of government. These upheavals, marked by mass protests, civil unrest, and sometimes violence, reflect the deep-seated frustrations and grievances of ordinary citizens who have long been marginalized and oppressed by their leaders.

One poignant example is the fall of President Hosni Mubarak in Egypt during the Arab Spring in 2011. The Egyptian people, tired of decades of authoritarian rule, took to the streets in massive protests, demanding political reform, economic justice, and an end to corruption. The sustained pressure from these protests eventually forced Mubarak to step down, ushering in a new era of uncertainty and transition in Egypt.

Similarly, the ousting of President Omar al-Bashir in Sudan in 2019 stands as a testament to the power of popular uprising. Sudanese citizens, weary of economic hardship, government corruption, and human rights abuses, staged months-long protests calling for Bashir's resignation. Despite brutal crackdowns by security forces, the protesters remained unwavering in their demands until Bashir was ultimately removed from power. It's even more disheartening that neither civilian nor junta-led administrations succeeding his government have managed to bring peace to the country. The most recent setback occurred with the outbreak of violent confrontations on April 15th, 2023, between the Sudanese Armed Forces (SAF) and the paramilitary Rapid Support Forces (RSF), resulting in the displacement of over 8.6 million individuals, including internally displaced people (IDPs), asylum seekers, and refugees. This conflict has further exacerbated Sudan's existing challenges, including ongoing conflicts, disease outbreaks, economic and political instability, and climate emergencies*.

In 2014, Burkina Faso was rocked by mass protests against President Blaise Compaoré's attempts to extend his 27-year rule. The people's outcry against Compaoré's bid for a constitutional amendment culminated in his resignation and the subsequent establishment of a transitional government.

These instances underscore the resilience and determination of African people to demand accountability, justice, and democratic governance from their leaders, even in the face of adversity. However, they also reveal the high human cost and uncertainty that often accompany such social upheavals. As I recount these events with a heavy heart, citizens of my country, Sierra Leone, have been subjected to such severe repression and have tragically succumbed during various encounters with security forces that they now exhibit a 'Bio syndrome', a morbid and pathological fear of protests or expression of free will (courtesy of the President Julius Maada Bio). It is a complete state of societal inhibition and suppression, one that should have no place in a modern democracy.

Leadership Consolidation and Authoritarian Rule

Throughout the pages of this work, I have delved into numerous instances where the concentration of power in the hands of one man or a select few has sowed the seeds of discontent and rebellion among the populace. One does not have to be entrenched in the narratives of Africa to attest to the fact that leaders consolidating power and establishing authoritarian rule often pave the path to heightened vulnerability to coups. One glaring example is the case of President Mobutu Sese Seko in the Democratic Republic of Congo. Through his decades-long reign marked by authoritarianism and corruption, Mobutu amassed immense power and wealth, suppressing dissent and subverting democratic institutions. However, his iron-fisted rule created fertile ground for opposition movements and ultimately led to his ouster in the First Congo War in 1997.

However, one would think that almost three decades after the fall of Mobutu, our continent would be free from a Mobutu-like leadership. Instead, autocrats of three decades standing are the ones heading the African Union, with their voices carrying a louder decibel than their more democratic peers. Most recently, a dynasty of the said magnitude was toppled in Gabon. President Ali Bongo Ondimba's prolonged rule was marked by allegations of authoritarianism, electoral fraud, and political instability. His father, Omar Bongo, governed Gabon from 1967 until his passing in 2009 when Ali Bongo was elected to assume his position. Ali Bongo's elections in 2009, re-election in 2016, and his recent re-election in 2023 were all tarnished by notable irregularities. Bongo faced criticism for entrenching his dynastic rule and suppressing opposition voices.

Teodoro Obiang Nguema Mbasogo, who assumed power in Equatorial Guinea in 1979 following his uncle's overthrow, is apparently grooming his son, Vice-President Teodorin Obiang Nguema, as his successor. The president's clan continues to dominate most positions of influence within the country, forming both a familial network and a central hub of state power (Yates, 2024). Dissatisfaction with the entrenched power of the ruling family; their perceived mismanagement of the country's affairs, and unequal distribution of wealth and resources, despite the country's significant oil revenues, may prompt the military and political factions to mobilize against the regime in pursuit of economic redistribution or reform. Therefore, coups may be seen as a means to overthrow dynastic leadership and usher in a new era of governance that is more inclusive and responsive to the needs of the population.

Regional Instability and Civil Conflicts

Regional instability and civil conflicts allow for the breakdown of governance and security systems, which indeed creates a fertile ground for coup attempts. They weaken the authority of existing leaders and institutions. The coup in Sierra Leone in 1997 occurred against the backdrop of a brutal civil war that ravaged the country, leading to widespread chaos and insecurity. Similarly, the coups in Mali in 2012 and 2021 occurred amidst escalating regional instability, exacerbated by the influx of weapons and fighters from neighboring conflicts, such as the Libyan civil war. Beneath what U.N. Secretary-General António Guterres labeled as a "spike in coups" lies a fundamental crisis of state legitimacy, worsened by Western security aid that overly prioritizes immediate counterterrorism victories (Dion and Sany, 2021).

The Central African Republic (CAR) stands as a stark example of a nation plagued by recurrent coups and protracted armed conflicts perpetuated by deep-seated ethnic tensions and intense competition for control over power and resources. The history of the CAR is marked by a series of coups and coup attempts, each exacerbating the already fragile socio-political landscape. In 2003, François Bozizé seized power in a coup, overthrowing President Ange-Félix Patassé. This coup unleashed a wave of violence and instability that engulfed the country, setting the stage for further turmoil.

The year 2013 witnessed another devastating coup, as the Séléka rebel coalition toppled Bozizé's regime, leading to widespread chaos and sectarian violence. The ensuing conflict between the predominantly Muslim Séléka rebels and Christian anti-balaka militias plunged the CAR into a humanitarian crisis characterized by atrocities, displacement, and humanitarian suffering.

Despite efforts to restore stability, including the deployment of international peacekeeping forces, the CAR continued to grapple with political instability and violence. In 2021, another coup d'état orchestrated by rebels led to the ousting of President Faustin-Archange Touadéra's government, further deepening the country's crisis. The recurring coups and armed conflicts have exacted a heavy toll on the people of the CAR, worsening poverty, displacement, and humanitarian suffering. The cycle of violence fueled by ethnic rivalries and struggles for power has perpetuated a sense of insecurity and instability, hindering the country's prospects for peace, development, and reconciliation.

These crises don't just disrupt governance and security systems; they actively dismantle them, leaving behind a vacuum of authority that ambitious individuals or factions are all too eager to exploit. They underscore the correlation between regional instability and coup attempts in Africa.

Intervention Against Perceived Corruption

Virtually all coups occur under the pretext of addressing corruption and mismanagement, but I am impassioned to recount the extent to which African leadership indulge in graft and the rate at which such indulgence has provided motivations for takeovers. The Ghanaian coup of 1981 orchestrated by Flight Lieutenant Jerry Rawlings. Rawlings seized power under the banner of rooting out corruption and mismanagement within the government. He accused the ruling elites of embezzling public funds and exploiting the masses, positioning himself as a champion of the people's struggle against corruption. Despite the initial bloodshed and authoritarian rule that followed, Rawlings' regime did make strides in combating corruption and implementing economic reforms, albeit through controversial means.

In March 2009, Madagascar plunged into turmoil as opposition leader Andry Rajoelina seized control with the backing of the military, ousting President Marc Ravalomanana. Rajoelina's rise to power was driven by accusations of corruption and authoritarianism against Ravalomanana's government. Presenting himself as a champion of democracy and good governance, Rajoelina pledged to bring about a new era of transparency and accountability.

The removal of Ravalomanana marked a pivotal moment in Madagascar's political journey, revealing the fragility of democratic institutions and the vulnerability of power struggles to descend into violence. Despite Rajoelina's claims to uphold democratic principles, his seizure of power through military intervention raised concerns about the erosion of democratic norms and the rule of law. The events in the island nation underscore the complexities of Africa's pursuit of democracy and effective governance. While the allegations against Ravalomanana may have been valid, the manner in which power changed hands highlights the difficulties in achieving peaceful and democratic transitions of power.

Reflecting on Madagascar's political upheaval, I am struck by the resilience of the Malagasy people and their enduring commitment to democratic values. I remain hopeful that, through dialogue, reconciliation, and a steadfast adherence to democratic principles, Madagascar can overcome its turbulent history and chart a course toward a brighter future for all its citizens.

Presidential Successions

Growing up, I was keenly attuned to presidential successions on the continent. Whether constitutional or otherwise, they have hardly occurred without someone lodging a protest. That is to say, they often serve as motivations for chaos due to the perceived vulnerabilities and power vacuums created during these transitions. I've observed a spectrum of succession types, each with its own implications for stability and governance.

Constitutional successions, where power is transferred through democratic elections or established legal procedures, are intended to ensure a smooth transition of power. However, in many of our countries, these processes can be marred by irregularities, allegations of fraud, or contentious outcomes, leading to political tensions and dissatisfaction among the populace. Disputed election results in countries like Kenya sparked protests and unrest, creating opportunities for a disruption of the political order. In December 2007, over 1,200 individuals lost their lives in the East African nation due to post-election violence. The lack of confidence in the courts by the defeated candidate at that time was seen as a contributing factor to the unrest. (Reuters).

Meanwhile, presidential successions in Africa through constitutional abuse manifest in various forms, including manipulation of legal provisions, term limit circumventions, or electoral process exploitation. Leaders may amend constitutions to extend their tenures, flout term limits outlined in legal frameworks, or manipulate elections to secure victory. Such actions undermine democratic principles, bolster authoritarian regimes, and sow seeds of instability and unrest. Notable examples include leaders like Yoweri Museveni in Uganda and Faure Gnassingbe in Togo. These types of successions yield far-reaching consequences, intensifying existing challenges and hindering progress towards democratic governance.

It's important to note that such patterns are not exhaustive, and each coup attempt is influenced by unique circumstances.

Out-of-court Settlements of Electoral Disputes

It is disheartening to witness the challenges surrounding out-of-court settlements of electoral disputes back home. These disputes, which often reflect deeper political tensions and power struggles, have significant implications for the future of democracy and stability in the continent.

The fact that out-of-court settlements sometimes emerge as a response to perceived failures of the judiciary hits particularly close to home. Trust in the judicial system is crucial for upholding the rule of law and ensuring that electoral disputes are resolved fairly and transparently. When the judiciary falls short, whether due to delays, allegations of bias, or inadequacies in the legal framework, it erodes confidence in the entire democratic process.

While such settlements may offer a temporary respite from the chaos of prolonged legal battles, they often skirt around the underlying issues that fuel electoral disputes in the first place. Success in such settlements hinges on several factors, including the political context, legal frameworks, and the willingness of parties to engage in dialogue and compromise.

Assessing the extent of success in effecting power change through out-of-court settlements requires examining specific cases where such settlements occurred and resulted in significant political outcomes. Kenya, Zimbabwe, and Liberia demonstrate instances where out-of-court settlements contributed to power-sharing agreements, peaceful transitions, or resolutions to electoral disputes without resorting to prolonged legal battles.

In 2013, Kenya's presidential election was challenged in court by the opposition leader Raila Odinga. The Supreme Court of Kenya ruled in favor of the incumbent president, Uhuru Kenyatta. Despite the court's decision, both parties engaged in negotiations, leading to the creation of a power-sharing agreement known as the "Handshake" between Kenyatta and Odinga in 2018. This agreement aimed to foster national unity and address electoral disputes outside of the courtroom.

In the 2017 presidential election in Liberia, the opposition candidate, George Weah, challenged the election results, alleging irregularities. However, before the Supreme Court of Liberia could rule on the matter, the two candidates, Weah and his opponent Joseph Boakai, engaged in talks facilitated by international mediators. This led to a peaceful resolution, with Weah emerging as the president-elect and Boakai accepting the results, thereby avoiding prolonged legal disputes.

A unique case of out-of-court settlement of electoral disputes has emerged in Sierra Leone. Vivid and visceral portrayals of democratic backsliding were witnessed in a country that is still convalescing from the setbacks of a decade-long civil war. Democratic institutions and processes dropped in standards precipitously, leading to a naked and unabashed action of the Chief Electoral Commissioner. Based on the opposition's boycott of parliament and local government, as a result of accusations of massive mischief and irregularities in the June 2023 elections, the newly elected president found himself in a bind and could not effectively administer the affairs of the state. This stalemate only shores up the notion that a government in a democratic arrangement is as strong as its weakest opposition. The president, therefore, sued for peace. Through a negotiated settlement facilitated by multilateral partners like the AU and the Commonwealth, a joint communique was signed with eight resolutions.

One of the resolutions involves the establishment of a tripartite investigation body. The provision states, "The President, in consultation with the APC party, will constitute a cross-party Committee on Electoral Systems and Management Bodies Review with a three-way leadership nominated by the Government of Sierra Leone; the APC party and Development Partners...to examine the electoral systems, structures, and processes of the June 2023 multi-tier electoral cycle." The investigation is underway as of the time of writing, but its success in reversing the blatant electoral theft will serve as a testament to the sincerity of Western interest in Africa's democracy and a litmus test to international resolve on good governance.

The Role of Personality Cults

In a continent that is becoming increasingly youthful and urbanized, with mounting expectations for change, one would think that the cult of personalities would be a relic of bygone times. However, as one leader bows out of the political limelight, another one steps up to occupy the stage with a larger-than-life portrayal of themselves. It is in this respect that followership becomes a tool to perpetuate the dominance of self-serving leadership. The role of personality cults in African politics refers to the elevation and glorification of a political leader to an almost deity-like status, often involving excessive loyalty and adulation from the public. Their posture on the national stage has projected them as "sovereigns" over the nation (Eze, 2010). This phenomenon can have significant implications for governance, democracy, and political stability. The leaders command unwavering loyalty and adoration from their supporters, who view them as almost infallible and irreplaceable. Such cults are built around the leader's charisma, often fueled by propaganda, and are characterized by the suppression of dissenting voices and the concentration of power in the hands of the leader.

By any measure, ordinary citizens are adversely affected by the operationalization of these personality cults. The glorification of the leader often comes at the expense of accountability and transparency in government. Economic resources may be squandered on projects that serve to bolster the leader's image rather than address the needs of the population. Ultimately, the cult of personality perpetuates a cycle of autocratic rule, leaving ordinary citizens disenfranchised and marginalized.

Cults of personality are in no short supply in our continent. Paul Biya, President of Cameroon since 1982, has fostered a personality cult, portraying himself as the embodiment of

Cameroonian nationalism and stability. State-controlled media depicts him as a unifier, even though the internecine conflict in Southern Cameroon is mainly due to his failure to make the English-speaking people feel part of governance despite the abundance of natural resources in the region. His image is omnipresent in public spaces, and his ruling party, the Cameroon People's Democratic Movement (CPDM), has elevated him to a near-mythical status. His extensive tenure, spanning as long as my four-decade lifetime, has only resulted in the idolization of his leadership. Here's an analysis of the motley manifestations of personality cults in our continent:

Consolidation of Power:

For the everyday African, such cults mean living under the shadow of an omnipotent leader, where individual freedoms are sacrificed at the altar of loyalty, and dissent is met with harsh reprisals. These cults serve as a tool for leaders to solidify their authority, fostering unwavering loyalty and dependence among the populace. Take the case of Muammar Gaddafi in Libya, whose decades-long rule was upheld by a pervasive personality cult. Through state-controlled media and a formidable security apparatus, Gaddafi ensured that his image as a unifying figure was ingrained in the minds of the people, suppressing dissent and maintaining his grip on power.

Political Stability or Instability:

Personality cults can be a double-edged sword, either providing stability through perceived strong leadership or contributing to instability if the leader becomes a focal point for dissent. They thrive on the perceived connection between autocracy and stability, (Spotlight 2023). However, extended periods of rule are actually correlated with increased instability, as well as hindered democratic and institutional progress. Mobutu's cultish rule initially provided stability but ultimately contributed to the country's decline.

Erosion of Institutions:

The danger of having power increasingly concentrated in the hands of a single leader is that even after the removal of such leaders, the systematic undermining of independent governance institutions by them ensures the survival of their legacies, hindering the progress of democratic transitions (Spotlight, 2023). Robert Mugabe's lengthy rule and the development of a personality cult undermined democratic institutions and led to economic and political crises.

Suppression of Dissent:

It is a common trend in the continent for leaders with entrenched personality cults to perceive any form of dissent or criticism as a direct threat to their authority and, by extension, to the nation itself. One glaring instance is in Eritrea, where President Isaias Afwerki has maintained an iron grip on power for decades, cultivating a cult-like reverence around himself. Under Afwerki's regime, dissent is not tolerated. Any form of opposition, whether from political activists, journalists, or ordinary citizens, is swiftly and ruthlessly suppressed. The media is tightly controlled, serving as a propaganda tool for the government rather than a platform for free expression. Political space is virtually non-existent, leaving little room for alternative voices to be heard.

The impact of this suppression on young people in Eritrea is particularly disheartening. They are denied the opportunity to engage in meaningful political discourse, express their opinions, or advocate for change. Their aspirations for a more democratic and inclusive society are stifled, and their potential for civic engagement is thwarted. Instead of being encouraged to participate actively in shaping their country's future, they are forced into silence and submission.

Cultural and National Identity Manipulation:

Among the myriad concerns is the manipulation of cultural and national identities, a tactic often employed by leaders entrenched in personality cults. This manipulation profoundly impacts the people, shaping their perceptions and influencing their sense of belonging and agency.

In many African countries, including Cameroon, leaders like Paul Biya have cultivated personality cults that extend far beyond politics. Biya's prolonged rule has been marked by the deliberate construction of his image as not just a political leader but as a symbol of Cameroon's cultural and national identity. The Spotlight (2023) notes that football has been utilized to reinforce the constant presence of President Paul Biya. This tactic struck a chord with many due to Cameroon's fervent passion for the game, as he adopted the nickname 'Lion Man', reminiscent of the national team, the Indomitable Lions, and in honor of Cameroon's unprecedented feat in reaching the World Cup Quarterfinals in 1990.

Economic Consequences:

The pervasive personality cult surrounding President Teodoro Obiang Nguema in Equatorial Guinea has facilitated economic mismanagement and widespread corruption, leaving the country's economy at the behest of the president and his son, the vice president. As a result, the poor rural population bears the brunt of these consequences. Inequitable distribution of resources and limited economic opportunities perpetuate poverty in rural areas. The mismanagement of funds escalates these issues, further marginalizing vulnerable communities. The cost of living is comparatively high, with prices slightly surpassing those in the United States (Travel tabs, 2023). Basic needs such as healthcare, education, and accommodation become luxuries, while food prices and education remain expensive.

It's a grim reality, one that weighs heavily on those of us who have fled such environments, seeking safety and opportunity elsewhere. However, it also underscores the urgent need for accountability, transparency, and good governance to break free from this cycle of economic exploitation and ensure a brighter future for all Africans, especially the most vulnerable among us.

Succession Challenges:

Succession challenges often attend the phenomenon of personality cults and pose difficulties in ensuring a smooth transition of power. A sense of indispensability is created around leaders, making them reluctant to groom successors or relinquish power. In the case of Togo, the Gnassingbé family's personality cult, particularly under Gnassingbé Eyadéma, entrenched a dynastic rule that made succession beyond the family circle virtually inconceivable. Despite his advanced age and health concerns, Paul Biya has shown little willingness to groom a successor and generated concerns over the country's political stability and democratic future.

In each of these cases, personality cults have contributed to dynastic rule, stifled political pluralism, and undermined democratic principles. The reluctance of leaders to groom successors or relinquish power has perpetuated autocratic governance, hindered institutional development, and fostered a culture where loyalty to the leader supersedes democratic norms. These examples underscore the significant obstacles that personality cults pose to democratic governance and political stability across Africa.

Ultimately, when leaders consolidate power through personality cults, they often undermine democratic institutions and stifle dissent, creating a volatile political environment. Their adverse effects on governance, democracy, and stability in our continent can catalyze UCGs, with ordinary citizens bearing the brunt of political unrest, economic instability, and human rights abuses. This concentration of power and erosion of democratic principles can lead to frustration among opposition groups, civil society organizations, and ordinary citizens who seek greater political participation and accountability. Consequently, these groups may resort to unconstitutional means, such as coups or violent uprisings, to challenge the entrenched leadership and demand political change. Additionally, the entrenchment of dynastic rule further exacerbates grievances, as it reinforces a system of inherited power that marginalizes alternative voices and perpetuates socio-economic disparities.

References

1. Abanyie, S.; Boateng, A.; Ampofo, S. (2016)
   Investigating the potability of water from dug wells:
   A case study of the Bolgatanga Township, Ghana.

African Journal of Environmental Science and Technology.

2. Adeyemi, S. (2017) Africa doesn't need charity, it needs good leadership. World Economic Forum.

3. Amnesty International. (2023) Sierra Leone: Still no justice for victims of August 2022 violent protests more than one year on.

4. Ampofo, A. A., & Boateng, S. K. (2016). The role of traditional leaders in local governance in Ghana: A study of the Akuapem Traditional Area. Journal of African Studies and Development.

5. Bah, C., Anderson, M., Feldman, M. (2021) Sierra Leone: President illegally suspends audit officials amidst controversy over presidential travel expenses and other financial irregularities. Africanist Press.

6. Byman, A.; Hardy, M.; Collinson, D.; Keith Grint, Brad Jackson; Mary Uhl-Bien (2011) The Sage Handbook of Leadership. SAGE Publications Ltd.

7. Cole, G. F. (1982). Sierra Leone's Post-Colonial Government: The Politics of Disillusionment. African Affairs.

8. Cole, T. (2014). The Krio of Sierra Leone: An Interpretive History. C. Hurst & Co. Publishers.

9. De Witte, L. (2003) The Assassination of Lumumba. Verso Books.

10. Dion, E.; Sany, J. (2021) After Two Coups, Mali Needs Regional Support to Bolster Democracy. United States Institute for Peace.

11. Eze, M.O. (2010). Cult of Personalities and Politics of Domination. In: The Politics of History in Contemporary Africa. Palgrave Macmillan, New York.

12. French, H. (1997) Anatomy of an Autocracy: Mobutu's 32-Year Reign. The New York Times.

13. Friedman, S. (2019) Power in Action: Democracy, Citizenship and Social Justice. Wits University Press.

14. Herbst, J. (2000). States and Power in Africa: Comparative Lessons in Authority and Control. Princeton University Press.

15. Karikari, E. (2013) African Postcolonial Leadership: The Contribution of African Student Leaders in the United States. Minnesota State University, Mankato.

16. Libya: A War on Africa? - Foreign Policy in Focus.

17. Makeka, M. (2016) Why it's time for a new generation of African leaders. World Economic Forum.

18. Mamdani, M. (1996) Citizen and Subject: Contemporary Africa and the Legacy of Late Colonialism. Princeton University Press.

19. Mamdani, M. (2001). When Victims Become Killers: Colonialism, Nativism, and the Genocide in Rwanda. Princeton University Press.

20. Mbigi, L. and Maree, J. (1995). Ubuntu: The Spirit of African Transformation Management. Knowledge Resources.

21. Miriri, D. (2022) Explainer: The legal procedure for contesting Kenyan election results. Reuters.

22. Moyo, D. (2009) Dead Aid: Why Aid Is Not Working and How There Is a Better Way for Africa. Farrar, Straus and Giroux.

23. NATO and Libya: Five Years On - NATO.

24. Ogunleye, T. K. (2013). The relevance of traditional rulers in contemporary governance in Nigeria: A

case study of Akure in Ondo State, Nigeria. Journal of Sustainable Development in Africa.

25. Prison Massacre, Sierra Leone Government Destroys Incriminating Evidence. Sierraloaded (2022).

26. Richards, P. (1996). Fighting for the Rain Forest: War, Youth, and Resources in Sierra Leone. James Currey Publishers.

27. Russia's Mercenaries, The Wagner Group, And the War in Mali - Radio Free Europe/Radio Liberty (RFE/RL).

28. Sarah, C. (2017) When Corruption Is the Operating System: The Case of South Africa. Carnegie Endowment for International Peace.

29. Sesay, Amin. (2020) Long Awaited COI White Paper... Sierra Leone Government Endorses Recommendations of COI. The Calabash Newspaper.

30. Source: International Crisis Group - The Wagner Group: Russia's Shadowy Private Military Company.

31. Source: RFE/RL - Russia's Mercenaries, The Wagner Group, And the War in Mali.

32. Source: The New York Times - Russian Mercenaries' Role in Libya Grows with Heavy Losses.

33. Spotlight. (2023) The Persistence of Cults of Personality in African Governance. Africa Center for Strategic Studies.

34. Stockwell, J. (1978). In Search of Enemies: A CIA Story. George J. McLeod Limited.

35. Sudan Crisis Explained. (2024) USA for UNHCR.

36. The Bee Hive. (2024) Leadership In Your Home and Beyond.

37. The Intervention in Libya Was Such a Tragic Mistake - The Atlantic.

38. The Wagner Group: Russia's Shadowy Private Military Company - International Crisis Group.

39. Travel Tabs. (2023) Cost of living and prices in Equatorial Guinea, prices of food, rent, shopping, etc. Updated Jul 2023.

40. Yates, D. (2024) Dynastic rule in Equatorial Guinea. African Journal of Political Science and International Relations.

EIGHT

LEADERSHIP AND SOCIAL DYNAMICS

Examination of Societal Factors Influencing Leadership

Social factors influencing leadership in Africa are diverse and shaped by the continent's rich cultural, historical, and socio-economic contexts. Here are some key social factors and instances specific to Africa:

Cultural Diversity

Africa's rich cultural diversity contributes to varied leadership expectations and norms across different regions and ethnic groups. Cultural values such as respect for elders, communal decision-making, and consensus-building often influence leadership styles and approaches. In addition to Ghana's Akan culture, other examples include the Ubuntu philosophy in Southern Africa, which emphasizes interconnectedness and collective responsibility, influencing leadership styles that prioritize community welfare over individual interests.

Traditional Leadership Structures

Traditional leadership structures, such as tribal chiefs, kings, and paramount rulers, have historical significance and continue to wield influence in many African societies. These traditional leaders often serve as custodians of culture, mediating disputes and providing guidance to their communities. In Nigeria, traditional rulers known as Obas, Emirs, and Obis hold significant sway in their respective regions. Their authority, derived from centuries-old traditions, shapes local governance and community development initiatives, influencing contemporary leadership dynamics. The Ashanti king (Asantehene) in Ghana holds a revered traditional leadership role that influences societal values and expectations.

Gender Roles and Expectations

Traditional gender roles and expectations can pose challenges for women aspiring to leadership positions, as they may face cultural barriers and stereotypes that undermine their authority and legitimacy as leaders. Cultural stereotypes may associate leadership traits such as assertiveness and decisiveness with masculinity while stereotyping women as nurturing and less suited for leadership. These stereotypes can influence societal attitudes, making it challenging for women to be perceived as capable leaders. While Ellen Johnson Sirleaf's presidency in Liberia represented a groundbreaking achievement for women's leadership in Africa, her tenure also highlighted the persistence of gender biases and societal expectations. Sirleaf's leadership challenged traditional gender roles, demonstrating that women can effectively lead nations and contribute to socio-economic development.

Rwanda has one of the highest percentages of women in

parliament globally, with over 60% representation. Gender-sensitive policies and efforts to challenge traditional gender roles have contributed to increased opportunities for women in leadership positions. While progress has been made in some African countries, challenges persist, and the impact of gender roles on leadership opportunities remains a complex and multifaceted issue. It requires ongoing efforts to challenge stereotypes, promote equal educational opportunities, address workplace discrimination, and create supportive policies to facilitate women's participation and advancement in leadership roles.

Youth Engagement and its Effect on Leadership Dynamics

Young people in Africa have been actively involved in political activism and mobilization, advocating for social justice, human rights, and political reform. Youth activism has the potential to influence political agendas, challenge existing power structures, and drive demands for more inclusive and accountable governance. Here's an explanation of youth engagement and instances illustrating its impact on leadership in Africa.

First, Africa has one of the youngest populations globally, with a significant portion being under the age of 30. The aspirations, frustrations, and demands of young people exert considerable influence on leadership dynamics, particularly in the context of youth unemployment, social inequality, and political disenfranchisement. Leaders are increasingly compelled to engage with youth issues and prioritize policies that address the needs and aspirations of young people, recognizing their potential as agents of change and drivers of socio-economic development. The #EndSARS protests in Nigeria in 2020, led by young activists, highlighted the role of the youth in demanding accountability, advocating for police reform and an end to brutality.

Second, the increasing access to digital platforms and social media has empowered youth to connect, share information, and mobilize for various causes. Digital connectivity enables rapid dissemination of ideas, facilitates coordination of movements, and amplifies the youth voice in shaping public opinion and policy discussions. Improved access to education empowers young people to engage in intellectual and social discourse, enhancing their ability to participate in political processes and challenge existing norms. It was evident in movements like #FeesMustFall in South Africa (2015-2017). Also led predominantly by youth, this movement demanded free, accessible, and quality education in South Africa. These instances underscored the influence of educated youth in shaping policy discussions, prompting concessions from leadership and initiating broader societal dialogues on pertinent issues. As young people continue to play an active role in various spheres, their impact on leadership in Africa is likely to grow, challenging traditional norms and contributing to more inclusive and responsive governance.

Colonial Legacy

The legacy of colonialism has left an indelible mark on African societies, influencing political structures, governance systems, and leadership norms. Colonial powers often imposed hierarchical governance models that marginalized certain ethnic groups or favored specific elites, perpetuating social inequalities and power imbalances. Post-colonial leaders have grappled with the legacy of colonialism, navigating between traditional cultural values and modern governance principles as they seek to assert their authority and legitimacy. Countries like Zimbabwe and South Africa have grappled with the legacies of colonialism, impacting political and social structures.

Religious Values and Influences

Religious values wield significant influence on leadership across Africa, guiding societal expectations and moral conduct. Leaders are often expected to align with dominant religious principles, whether it be Islam, Christianity, or indigenous beliefs. The expectation shapes political discourse and decision-making, as leaders are scrutinized based on their adherence to religious ethics. Religious leaders also play a vital role in influencing public opinion and engaging with political leaders on social justice issues. Interfaith dynamics and challenges of religious extremism further complicate the relationship between religion and leadership. Effective leaders navigate these complexities by promoting interfaith dialogue, fostering tolerance, and upholding principles of religious freedom. The role of Islam in Senegal's political landscape, where leaders are often expected to align with Islamic principles.

Adaptation and Evolution

Despite the influence of cultural dynamics on leadership in Africa, it's essential to recognize that leadership practices are not static and can evolve over time. Leaders often navigate between traditional cultural values and contemporary demands, adapting their leadership styles to meet the challenges of a changing world. In contemporary Africa, leaders like Rwanda's President Paul Kagame have embraced a blend of traditional values and modern governance principles to drive national development. Kagame's leadership style incorporates elements of consensus-building and accountability while prioritizing innovation and technological advancement.

Rural-Urban Dynamics

Rural-urban dynamics shape leadership priorities in Africa, with leaders facing distinct challenges and expectations in each context. In rural areas, agricultural issues and basic infrastructure are priorities, while urban leaders focus on infrastructure, housing, and job creation. Effective leadership requires a balanced approach that addresses the diverse needs of both rural and urban populations, promoting inclusive and sustainable development across the country. Examples from countries like Ethiopia, Nigeria, and Rwanda demonstrate strategies to bridge rural-urban divides and promote equitable growth.

Educational Disparities

Educational disparities significantly impact leadership expectations and problem-solving approaches in Africa. Disparities between urban and rural areas shape perceptions of leaders' intellectual capabilities, with higher expectations for formal education in urban centers. Leaders with better education are equipped to analyze complex issues and implement effective solutions. Initiatives to address disparities, such as community-based schools and free education policies, demonstrate the role of leadership in promoting equitable access to quality education.

Effective leadership entails prioritizing equitable access to quality education for all citizens. Leaders must invest in educational infrastructure, teacher training, curriculum development, and student support services to narrow educational disparities and promote inclusive development. Moreover, leaders should prioritize policies that address the root causes of educational inequities, such as poverty, gender discrimination, and geographic isolation. However, disparities in educational access between urban and rural areas influence leadership perceptions in many African countries.

Media and Information Access

Media and information access are pivotal in shaping public perceptions and influencing leadership in Africa. Traditional and social media platforms serve as conduits for information dissemination and public discourse, impacting how citizens view their leaders. Social media, in particular, empowers citizens to mobilize collective action and hold leaders accountable, as seen in movements like #FeesMustFall in South Africa. However, challenges such as misinformation and fake news persist, requiring leaders to promote media literacy and combat disinformation.

Transitional Justice and Reconciliation

Transitional justice and reconciliation processes are vital for post-conflict societies in Africa, significantly influencing leadership priorities and national healing. Examples such as the Truth and Reconciliation Commission (TRC) in South Africa, led by Nelson Mandela, and the similar commission in Liberia and Sierra Leone illustrate the importance of these mechanisms in uncovering past injustices, promoting accountability, and fostering reconciliation. Efforts to address past human rights abuses and promote reconciliation in Liberia were hindered by political instability, resource constraints, and societal divisions. The establishment of the TRC was delayed and faced resistance, underscoring the challenges in confronting the legacy of civil wars. Despite these obstacles, civil society organizations, religious leaders, and grassroots initiatives persist in advocating for truth, justice, and reconciliation, showcasing Liberia's resilience in peacebuilding efforts.

Leadership effectiveness in our continent often involves a nuanced understanding of these social dynamics to build trust and promote sustainable development. Therefore, there is the need for leaders to navigate diverse cultural contexts and respond to the evolving expectations of their populations.

Leadership and the Problem of the Home and the Community

The Bee Hive, a Christian online platform, posits that if leadership is influenced, then every one of us is called to leadership. In this sense, God has called and equipped parents to influence their homes. This call aligns with both the divine and natural order, where leadership is meant to begin from the home before it cascades outward. Many of our leaders since independence are enchanted by the prospect of leading in external realms. Such an ambition can indeed be considered sacred. However, if we endeavor to lead in these external domains before establishing leadership within ourselves and our families, we have disrupted the divine order of leadership's intended purpose. The result of this disruption of divine design has habitually manifested in palpable spectacles of economic hardship, internecine conflict, and poverty. That is why, in this third decade of the 21st century, the image of a child trekking through both rural and urban landscapes with a bucket of water balanced precariously on their head remains all too common.

In rural areas, where infrastructure may be scarce, the burden is particularly heavy. Children rise with the dawn, their small frames bearing the weight of the day's first chore. In urban settings, where one might expect modern conveniences to prevail, the reality is not so different. Amidst towering skyscrapers and bustling streets, there are communities forgotten by progress. Here, too, children embark on their daily pilgrimage for water, navigating crowded alleys and busy intersections with practiced ease yet burdened by a task that should belong to the past. This scene is a poignant reminder of the enduring disparities that persist in our world despite the march of time and progress. It speaks to the fundamental challenges of the home, and this child that is deprived of access and equity is a stark reminder of the failure of present leadership and the blight of the future leader he embodies.

The home, as the foundational unit of society, has a profound impact on leadership in any country. The cultural, social, and familial dynamics within homes shape individuals' values, attitudes, and behaviors, which, in turn, influence their approach to leadership. We have identified several ways in which the home impacts leadership in our continent.

To start with, it is the primary environment for imparting leadership ideals. Individuals learn cultural values, traditions, and norms. Leaders often draw on cultural values learned at home, influencing their leadership style and decision-making. For example, respect for elders, communal responsibility, and the importance of consensus-building may be deeply ingrained in leaders' approaches.

Secondly, the home provides a critical space for education and the transmission of knowledge, and family members serve as role models. Educational values instilled at home have far-reaching effects in shaping leaders' attitudes toward continuous learning and innovation. Positive role modeling within the family may inspire leadership qualities such as empathy, integrity, and a commitment to service.

Thirdly, leaders may carry with them the gender expectations learned at home, affecting the representation and leadership opportunities for women in various sectors. Traditional gender roles are often reinforced at home, impacting perceptions of leadership roles for men and women.

Fourth, the home environment contributes significantly to the development of a work ethic, discipline, and perseverance. Leaders who were raised in homes that emphasized hard work and discipline may exhibit strong work ethics and resilience in their leadership roles.

Fifth, communication patterns within the home shape individuals' communication styles, including how they express themselves and listen to others. People who grew up in environments that encouraged open communication and dialogue may exhibit strong communication skills in their leadership roles, fostering collaboration and understanding.

Sixth, homes that encourage entrepreneurship and innovation contribute to the development of an entrepreneurial spirit, and children raised in such environments may exhibit a willingness to take risks, embrace innovation, and drive economic development.

Furthermore, the home often instills a sense of community and social responsibility, emphasizing the importance of giving back to society. This may equip one to prioritize community development and social impact in their leadership roles. It also places the value of philanthropy and community engagement to inspire a sense of giving back. Leaders with a philanthropic mindset may actively engage in community development initiatives, contributing to social welfare.

Finally, a person's first brush with conflict resolution occurs in the home. Those who were exposed to healthy conflict resolution models at home are in good stead to exhibit such skills in their leadership roles, contributing to organizational harmony and national cohesion.

Understanding the impact of the home on leadership in Africa highlights the interconnectedness of personal and professional development. Leaders who are attuned to these influences can leverage their upbringing to shape positive leadership qualities, contribute to community development, and foster inclusive and culturally sensitive leadership approaches.

The foregoing notwithstanding, our leadership deficit could be attributed to a varied assortment of factors stemming from the home's failure to provide the above instructions and to serve as the first institution of learning. The vicious cycle of lack, lawlessness, and abuse since independence has ensured that the home impacts leadership, albeit in a less complimentary way. I consider myself fortunate to have been brought up by two parents who were educators. Their influence instilled in me a valuable blend of discipline, contentment, and critical thinking that have guided me through the trials of youth. Yet, I recognize that my experience is far from the norm.

In my community, many young men find themselves navigating broken homes or households where parental presence is overshadowed by the relentless pursuit of livelihood. For these children, the concept of a nurturing upbringing often remains elusive. Instead, their formative years are marked by a stark absence of guidance and structure. School becomes optional, and the boundaries of acceptable behavior blur within the confines of home. In such environments, lying and profanity are normalized, shaping the everyday reality for countless African youths. This is the life of the everyday African. The one who would later vote and be voted for. The future President of the Republic.

However, aside from poor parental oversight, a number of other factors have inhibited the effectiveness of the home as the first bastion of leadership. Extended family units, while offering numerous benefits, can sometimes hinder leadership development in the home. The constraints on resources due to the needs of many family members can restrict access to educational and developmental opportunities vital for nurturing leadership skills.

One major socioeconomic change affecting African homes is migration for better livelihood or employment opportunities. As individuals and sometimes whole families move from rural to urban areas, or even abroad, in search of better economic prospects, the traditional family structure becomes fragmented. Such migration often results in the separation of family members, not just physically but also emotionally and culturally. Children may grow up without the close guidance of parents. This can lead to a weakening of familial ties and a dilution of cultural continuity, as the rich tapestry of oral histories, moral lessons, and leadership examples that would typically be imparted by parents are lost.

Moreover, the rise in technology and digital communication, while beneficial in many ways, can also serve as a distraction and a substitute for face-to-face interactions and communal activities that are essential for developing leadership skills. Young people might spend more time engaging with global cultures through screens than participating in their local communities.

Also, rapid urbanization, globalization, and exposure to Western norms challenge the primacy of traditional family values. Younger generations may prioritize individualism and materialism over communal responsibility and respect for elders, leading to a disconnect between traditional values and contemporary leadership practices.

More importantly, the formal education system in many African countries often prioritizes Western curricula and neglects indigenous knowledge systems. As a result, there is limited emphasis on teaching national values and traditions in schools, undermining the transmission of these values to future leaders.

These experiences are but a reflection of the systemic challenges that plague many communities across the continent. They underscore a fundamental challenge in the African home as the first institution of leadership and mirror the inadequacies of the seat of power. Accordingly, it is only natural that both institutions share commonalities in their behavioral expressions —the first culminating in the latter.

Leadership and a Conscientious Citizenry

Kemoh and Lamin frequently visit the Atire Base, a popular tea shop in Freetown's busy east end, where local youths often gather to discuss topics from politics to football, often engaging in heated debates. One such debate erupted over the president's numerous trips abroad, including a controversial honeymoon during the COVID-19 pandemic. Kemoh, a supporter of the president's party, the SLPP, defended these travels, dismissing opposition criticisms as mere fuss. Despite widespread media criticism over the president's travels, Kemoh and other SLPP supporters appeared unfazed, viewing it as their party's time to exert influence. Meanwhile, Lamin, an opposition party supporter who holds a degree in Social Sciences and is unemployed, is critical of the government and hopeful for his party's return to power to improve his job prospects.

The story of Kemoh and his debates at the Atire Base captures a broader issue affecting leadership in Africa—the lack of objectivity in the citizenry and its impact on fostering effective leadership. This narrative highlights how personal biases, party loyalty, and a disconnect from civic responsibilities can perpetuate bad leadership and undermine democratic principles.

The bustling tea shop, where politics interlaces with daily life, reflects a microcosm of national discourse. Discussions like the one between Lamin and Kemoh often devolve into partisan arguments rather than objective analyses of leadership performance. Kemoh's position illustrates how partisan loyalty can overshadow critical evaluation of leaders' actions. This blind loyalty is a crucial factor; it means that even when leaders perform poorly or make questionable decisions, they are still defended by their party's supporters. This scenario shows a lack of objectivity where personal benefit from political affiliations trumps the common good.

Lamin's situation sheds light on another critical aspect—the expectation of personal gain from political affiliations. Despite his education, Lamin remains unemployed and sees his future job prospects as tied to his party's access to power. This dependency on political patronage for personal advancement is common and detrimental. It leads to a cycle where the primary concern for many of our compatriots is not the competence or integrity of the leaders but rather what those leaders can provide to them personally. This mindset reduces the incentive for political leaders to perform well in office since their support base may remain loyal as long as patronage is maintained.

Moreover, the narrative touches on a national concern, highlighted by the media, about the president's behavior and the perceived lack of accountability. Yet, this critical issue becomes just another point of contention drowned out by partisan noise rather than a catalyst for collective action demanding better leadership. The result is a diminished commitment to democratic values and reduced accountability, where leaders are not held to standards that would typically promote good governance.

The situation is further heightened by dishonest leadership. In a sense, Kemoh and Lamin can be excused for allowing their personal sentiments to trump the patriotic imperative. President Ahmed Tejan Kabbah's decision to campaign for Julius Maada Bio in Sierra Leone's 2012 elections, despite previously accusing him of significant corruption, highlights a troubling inconsistency in leadership that can demoralize citizens and weaken their trust in the political system. This flip-flop not only causes confusion and distrust among voters but also normalizes corruption, undermines democratic values, and discourages civic participation. It illustrates the broader impact of dishonest leadership, reinforcing cynicism and creating barriers to new, ethical leadership.

The absence of a conscientious citizenry can also lead to increased corruption. Leaders, sensing limited oversight and weak public outcry, may engage in corrupt practices with impunity, knowing that their actions will likely go unchallenged by a populace that is more interested in what benefits they can derive from their affiliations rather than the broader impact on the nation's welfare. In Nigeria, corruption has been a longstanding issue, with numerous government officials accused of embezzling vast sums. Public sector corruption, especially, has flourished in environments where there is little public scrutiny and where citizens are more focused on ethnic or regional loyalties than on holding leaders accountable.

Another effect of the lack of an active citizenry is that leaders may disregard democratic norms, limit political pluralism, and undermine institutions. Instances of leaders extending their terms, manipulating electoral processes, or restricting political opposition have occurred aplenty with the collusion of a huge bulk of the citizenry. President Paul Biya's long tenure has been marked by allegations of electoral fraud and constitutional manipulations to extend his presidency. These actions, coupled with a relatively subdued public response, have weakened political institutions and limited effective governance.

Addressing these challenges requires widespread civic engagement, which is largely missing in our continent. Such lack can lead to apathy, diminishing the effectiveness of democratic practices and community development efforts. Voter apathy and low turnout in elections, in several instances, are indicative of a less engaged citizenry, weakening the democratic process.

In essence, when citizens lack objectivity, when they are not actively engaged in upholding ethical standards and are primarily driven by personal or partisan interests, it can create an environment where leaders are more prone to prioritize personal interests over the common good. This case points out a critical gap in the collective consciousness. It often creates a degree of disenchantment that provides a strong motivation for UCGs. Civic education, broader political engagement, and a strong public demand for accountability and transparency are essential to break this cycle and foster leaders who can truly advance the public good.

"The glue that holds all of Africa's opportunities together is good leadership" Fred Swanika, Founder and CEO of African Leadership Group.

References

1. Adeyemi, S. (2017). Africa doesn't need charity, it needs good leadership. World Economic Forum.

2. Amnesty International. (2023). Sierra Leone: Still no justice for victims of August 2022 violent protests more than one year on.

3. Ampofo, A. A., & Boateng, S. K. (2016). The role of traditional leaders in local governance in Ghana: A study of the Akuapem Traditional Area. Journal of African Studies and Development.

4. Bah, C., Anderson, M., Feldman, M. (2021). Sierra Leone: President illegally suspends audit officials amidst controversy over presidential travel expenses and other financial irregularities. Africanist Press.

5. Byman, A.; Hardy, M.; Collinson, D.; Keith Grint, Brad Jackson; Mary Uhl-Bien. (2011). The Sage Handbook of Leadership. SAGE Publications Ltd.

6. Cheruiyot, D. K. (2016). Media, Democracy, and Development in Africa. Palgrave Macmillan.

7. Cooper, F. (2002). Africa since 1940: The Past of the Present. Cambridge University Press.

8. De Witte, L. (2003). The Assassination of Lumumba. Verso Books.

9. Deutsch, J. (2006). The Malevolent Leaders: Popular Discontent in America. Yale University Press.

10. Fassin, D. (2013). Enforcing Order: An Ethnography of Urban Policing. Polity.

11. French, H. (1997). Anatomy of an Autocracy: Mobutu's 32-Year Reign. The New York Times.

12. Geschiere, P. (2009). Witchcraft, Intimacy, and Trust: Africa in Comparison. University of Chicago Press.

13. Hofstede, G. (2001). Culture's Consequences: Comparing Values, Behaviors, Institutions, and Organizations Across Nations. Sage.

14. Jenkins, P. (2002). The Next Christendom: The Coming of Global Christianity. Oxford University Press.

15. Kaggia, S. (2010). My Dilemma is a River: An Urban African Poet's Prayer for Rain. Africa World Press.

16. Lambert, T. (2015). Religion in Africa: Its Plurality and Plurality of Meanings. EJ Brill.

17. Mamdani, M. (1996). Citizen and Subject: Contemporary Africa and the Legacy of Late Colonialism. Princeton University Press.

18. Mamdani, M. (2005). Politics and Class Formation in Uganda. Monthly Review Press.

19. Mazrui, A. A. (1997). The Africans: A Triple Heritage. Little, Brown and Company.

20. Mbiti, J. S. (1991). African Religions and Philosophy. Heinemann.

21. Mbigi, L. and Maree, J. (1995). Ubuntu: The Spirit of African Transformation Management. Knowledge Resources.

22. Mustapha, A. R. (2009). Sects & Social Disorder: Muslim Identities & Conflict in Northern Nigeria. James Currey Publishers.

23. Moyo, D. (2009). Dead Aid: Why Aid Is Not Working and How There Is a Better Way for Africa. Farrar, Straus and Giroux.

24. Nwankwo, A. (2013). Youth, HIV/AIDS, and Social Transformation in Africa. Lexington Books.

25. Olorunnisola, A. A. (2004). Globalization and Mass Communication in Africa. Lexington Books.

26. Rodney, W. (2018). How Europe Underdeveloped Africa. Verso.

27. Shaw, R. (2009). Memories of the Slave Trade: Ritual and the Historical Imagination in Sierra Leone. University of Chicago Press.

28. Sirleaf, E. J. (2009). This Child Will Be Great: Memoir of a Remarkable Life by Africa's First Woman President. HarperCollins.

29. The Bee Hive. (2024). Leadership In Your Home and Beyond.

30. Wuthnow, R. (1999). After Heaven: Spirituality in America Since the 1950s. University of California Press.

31. Yates, D. (2024). Dynastic rule in Equatorial Guinea. African Journal of Political Science and International Relations.

NINE

POPULAR MISCONCEPTIONS AND PARALLELS

What Africans don't Get about Democracy

THE CONCEPT OF WESTERN DEMOCRACY HAS GENERATED one too many theorizing, not least about its operationalization on African soil. Several misconceptions exist about African democracy, often fueled by stereotypes, limited understanding of diverse political contexts, and historical narratives. Africans' disillusionment with democratic institutions and processes is commonplace, but it also mirrors assumptions that may or may not reflect the practical import of the concept. Since independence, democracy carried its own corollaries to political governance. It has taken on different forms, echoing the diversity of democratic nations around the world, for there are so many different models of democratic government that it is sometimes easier to understand the idea in terms of what it definitely is not. In answer to the elusive nature of the concept, Kofi Anan noted that "there are as many different forms of democracy as there are democratic nations in the world." The aim of this chapter is to delve into the mindset of Africans and uncover their aspirations regarding democracy, seeking to grasp why disillusionment with its implementation persists.

Colonial Legacy

The wake of independence signaled a new political construct but an extension of the old economic order. What France Fanon emoted as 'artillery shelling and scorched earth policy' fizzled out and left in its wake a formalized system of economic dependence. This is one area where Africans got their hopes dashed. Throughout this period, Africans were imbued with the belief that the primary concern of Western nations revolves around the transfer of power between political factions, neglecting the reality that their core focus lies in economic policies.

In as much as many scholars believe that one of the most significant legacies of colonialism in Africa is the displacement of the traditional acquisition of political authority through familial ties, substituting it with a mandate derived from the people, Africans, too, were not immune to the idea that democracy's exclusive domain is power transitions. However, the impact of colonial economic structures on post-independence African economies belie that binary assumption.

Newly independent nations grappled with limited economic autonomy because colonial powers often established economic systems that prioritized the extraction of resources, for instance, and the exploitation of labor for the benefit of the colonizers. France maintained economic control over many states through a system known as "Françafrique." This system involved close political and economic ties between French and African elites, often at the expense of the local population.

French companies continued to dominate key sectors of the economy, such as mining, agriculture, and energy, extracting natural resources and exploiting cheap labor. Additionally, France exerted influence over the monetary policies of its former colonies through the CFA franc, a currency that is fixed to the value of the French currency, which limited the countries' economic sovereignty. British multinational corporations maintained a significant presence in former colonies while labor exploitation, including low wages, poor working conditions, and limited workers' rights, persisted.

Africans held lofty expectations for self-governance, sovereignty, and the ability to shape their own destinies free from colonial rule. Harking back to Chapter 1, the nationalists had scarcely foreseen the difficulties inherent in assuming control of a governance structure that Africans were not inherently accustomed to. This structure was discordant with their economic circumstances and, most importantly, relied heavily on the support of the very people from whom they sought to gain freedom. Decades on the lot of the African was still tethered to daily sustenance, with wars and insecurity escalating under the full glare of a polity called democracy.

Against this bleak reality, there existed a power elite whose focus on personal enrichment took precedence over the well-being of the populace, fostering a widespread sense of disillusionment and a feeling of disappointment in the colonial legacy.

That Capitalism is an Inherent Outcome of Democracy

Perhaps the biggest misconception Africans had about democracy was to insert it in the picture frame of capitalism lock, stock, and barrel. Consequently, after gaining independence, there was a rush to embrace full-fledged capitalism, overlooking the existing mixed economy framework prevalent on the continent. A fine blend of capitalism and socialism was in operation during independence.

At the outset, collective interest was a fundamental aspect of the traditional African economy. Economic activities were often community-oriented instead of individualistic. Decisions regarding resource allocation, trade, and production were made with the collective benefit of the community in mind rather than solely focusing on individual profit or gain. That collectivism was what the independent African state embodied. The state played a significant role in the economy, with public ownership and control of key industries, infrastructure, and natural resources. This role placed the welfare of citizens at the heart of state policy and, at the same time, imputed to the state primary responsibility over the citizenry.

However, the form of capitalism imposed by colonial powers has not consistently catered to the African reality. It continues to be heavily influenced and guided by external powers (Kenneth Amaeshi, 2015). Multinational corporations often prioritize their own prosperity over that of the communities in which they function. This tendency is particularly characteristic of many Western multinational firms, as they originate from a culture that prioritizes individual pursuits over collective welfare.

In the early years of independence, although the state played a prominent role in the economy, there was space for private enterprise and entrepreneurship to thrive. Private businesses coexisted with state-owned enterprises, fostering economic diversification and driving innovation. Ghana, under the leadership of Kwame Nkrumah, implemented socialist-leaning economic policies, including the establishment of state-owned enterprises in key sectors such as agriculture, manufacturing, and mining. However, private enterprises also operated alongside these state entities, particularly in trade, retail, and small-scale industries.

Governments implemented social welfare programs to address poverty, inequality, and basic needs such as healthcare, education, and housing. These programs aimed to improve living standards and promote social equity, reflecting socialist ideals of economic justice and redistribution. Many African countries prioritized education as a fundamental aspect of development and implemented programs to expand access to schooling. For instance, countries like Ghana, Tanzania, and Kenya established free or subsidized primary education programs to ensure that all children had the opportunity to receive basic education regardless of their socio-economic background.

Nations pursued import substitution industrialization (ISI) as a strategy for economic development. This involved promoting domestic industries to produce goods that were previously imported, reducing dependence on foreign imports, and fostering industrial growth and self-sufficiency. Agriculture remained a vital sector of the economy, with efforts to modernize and increase productivity through state-led initiatives such as land reform, agricultural cooperatives, and rural development programs. However, the legacy of colonial land tenure systems and unequal access to resources persisted as challenges.

A significant shift occurred in Africa's economic policy during the 1980s and 1990s, marked by the introduction of structural adjustment programs (SAPs) enforced by international financial institutions like the International Monetary Fund (IMF) and the World Bank. Economies were pressured to privatize state-owned enterprises across various sectors, including telecommunications, energy, and transportation. For example, in Nigeria, state-owned enterprises like Nigerian Airways and Nigerian Telecommunications were privatized, allowing for increased private sector involvement in these industries. In Zambia, for instance, trade liberalization measures led to the influx of imported goods, particularly agricultural products, which negatively impacted local farmers and industries. Nations were also required to deregulate their economies by removing price controls and reducing government intervention in markets. In Ghana, the deregulation of the cocoa industry led to the liberalization of cocoa prices, allowing for greater market competition but also exposing small-scale farmers to price volatility and exploitation by large multinational corporations.

These programs had far-reaching impacts on African economies, resulting in austerity measures, etc. which often escalated poverty and inequality. The underlying ideology was rooted in the principles of free-market capitalism, aiming to promote economic growth through market-oriented reforms. Moreover, the enduring legacy of colonialism and ongoing neoliberal economic dynamics continue to shape trade patterns, investment flows, and development strategies across African nations. In contemporary times, nations are mandated to create National Commissions for Privatization, with the primary aim of divesting the last vestiges of state-owned enterprises, most of which were in moribund states due to willful neglect.

Entities in the telecoms, electricity, sea ports, air transport, and water sectors in most countries, including Kenya, Nigeria, Sierra Leone, South Africa, Zambia, etc., ended up in private hands based on the urging of the Bretton Woods. Yet service delivery still remains a challenge. What is clear is that African governments failed to countenance certain realities in the continent when ingesting neoliberal prescriptions hook, line, and sinker. Firstly, Africa inherited deeply entrenched economic structures established by colonial powers, characterized by resource extraction, unequal trade relationships, and limited industrial development. This legacy hindered the transition to a market-based economy and perpetuated dependency on primary commodity exports.

Secondly, countries lacked robust legal and regulatory frameworks to support capitalist activities, including property rights protection, contract enforcement, and investor confidence. Weak institutions bred corruption, bureaucratic inefficiency, and political instability, undermining the business environment.

Thirdly, inadequate infrastructure, including transportation networks, energy supply, and telecommunications, constrained economic productivity and hindered private sector growth. Without reliable infrastructure, businesses faced logistical challenges, higher operating costs, and reduced competitiveness.

Fourth, the lack of skilled labor and technical expertise hampered efforts to diversify economies and promote entrepreneurship. Insufficient investment in education, healthcare, and skills development resulted in a poorly educated and unhealthy workforce, limiting productivity and innovation.

Fifth, widespread poverty, income inequality, and social exclusion persisted in many African countries, exacerbating social tensions and undermining social cohesion. The concentration of wealth and resources in the hands of a few elites limited the potential benefits of capitalism from trickling down to the broader population.

There are numerous additional factors contributing to the ineffectiveness of this economic model in improving the lives of Africans. Rather than critically assessing its implementation, our leaders are subjected to further adherence, often without a clear understanding or with self-serving motives.

Plenty more reasons abound for the ineffectiveness of this economic model to transform the lives of Africans. Rather than critically assessing its operationalization, our leaders get more dosage of it, often without a clear understanding or with self-serving motives. Worthy of note is that European nations' transition to capitalism was gradual and complex, and different regions experienced it at different rates and in different ways. Moreover, capitalism coexisted with other economic systems during this period, such as mercantilism and early forms of industrial capitalism, before becoming the predominant economic paradigm in the modern era.

Under the leadership of Julius Nyerere, Tanzania adopted a policy of African socialism, known as Ujamaa, which emphasized communal ownership and collective farming. While the government nationalized key industries such as banking, transportation, and mining, private enterprises, including small-scale farms and businesses, continued to operate within the economy.

That Neocolonialism is Responsible for Africa's Misfortune

To what extent do Africans bear the blame for the deplorable state of their democracies is under-addressed throughout academic scholarship and political discourse. The assumption that neocolonialism is solely responsible for Africa's misfortunes is flawed and overly simplistic. While neocolonialism, which refers to continued economic, political, and cultural influence exerted by former colonial powers or other foreign entities, has undoubtedly played a role in shaping Africa's trajectory, it is just one factor among many. Africa faces a multitude of challenges, including governance issues, corruption, internal conflicts, economic disparities, and environmental degradation, which cannot be solely attributed to neocolonialism. Many African countries have struggled with governance issues such as corruption, lack of transparency, and authoritarianism, which hinder development and progress. Leaders like Mobutu Sese Seko in the Democratic Republic of Congo and Robert Mugabe in Zimbabwe were notorious for their corrupt and authoritarian regimes, which significantly contributed to their countries' economic decline.

Numerous internal conflicts have plagued African countries, leading to instability, displacement of populations, and loss of lives. The civil wars in Liberia, Sierra Leone, and South Sudan, which caused immense suffering and hindered development efforts, could more be attributed to internal schisms than any external influence.

Additionally, Africa is home to some of the world's poorest countries and faces significant economic disparities both within and between nations. While neocolonial economic policies may have contributed to some of these disparities, factors such as ineffective economic management, overreliance on natural resources, weak institutions, and lack of investment in infrastructure and human capital also play a significant role. Environmental issues are no less debilitating to Africa's growth. Deforestation, desertification, and climate change pose significant challenges to development. These issues exacerbate poverty, food insecurity, and displacement of populations, impacting millions of people across the continent.

Most importantly, Africa's position within the global economic system, characterized by unequal trade relations, debt burdens, and dependence on foreign aid, also contributes to its challenges. While neocolonial economic policies may have perpetuated some of these dynamics, broader global economic forces and policies also play a significant role.

That Democracy Means Immediate Growth

Africans, from independence to date, expect that simply adopting democratic practices would rapidly solve economic and development challenges. However, the reality is much more nuanced. Democracy is a complex process that interacts with various factors influencing development. Based on its checkered past, it requires time, institutional capacity, and inclusive policies to contribute to sustainable development. Similarly, there is a palpable misconception that the holding of democratic elections automatically leads to economic prosperity. While democracy can indeed contribute to economic development, its impact depends on several factors. Effective governance, sound economic policies, and favorable global economic conditions are essential for realizing the economic benefits of democracy. Without these conditions in place, the mere presence of democratic institutions may not guarantee economic prosperity.

Modern democratic systems in the West began to take shape during the Enlightenment period in the 17th and 18th centuries. Fundamentally, the core democratic tenets of popular sovereignty, political equality, and individual rights were established for centuries, whereas the modern African state has only had decades to undergo its transition. However, international financial institutions impose directives on African countries, aiming to leash them in a way that would not realistically apply to countries in the global north during their formative periods. Political entrepreneurs who replaced the visionary independence leaders were complicit about this arrangement.

The Industrial Revolution, which began in the late 18th century, played a crucial role in the economic development of Western countries. Industrialization led to significant advancements in technology, infrastructure, and productivity, laying the foundation for modern economies.

While Western countries are generally considered fully democratic and developed today, they continue to face challenges such as inequality, political polarization, and globalization. These challenges underscore the ongoing nature of democratic governance and the need for constant vigilance and adaptation to evolving circumstances.

A Black Continent and One-size-fits-all Solution

Africa consists of 54 countries, each with its own unique political systems, governance structures, and experiences with democracy. One common misconception is the assumption of homogeneity of views among Africans regarding democracy. In reality, Africa is characterized by linguistic, cultural, and political diversity, leading to significant variations in perspectives on democracy among different regions, ethnic groups, and individuals. Countries like Nigeria and South Africa have diverse economies with significant contributions from multiple sectors, while countries like Chad and Niger rely heavily on agriculture and natural resource extraction. This economic diversity influences development strategies and policies across the continent.

The role of traditional leaders in governance differs between countries like Botswana, where traditional leaders play a significant role in local administration, and countries like Tanzania, where centralized government structures are more dominant.

Another misconception is the assumption of a single, universally accepted interpretation of human rights across all African societies. In reality, human rights can be interpreted differently based on cultural, historical, and religious contexts within African societies. This diversity leads to varied perspectives on issues such as freedom of expression and gender equality among different communities and regions across the continent.

However, despite the varied interpretations of human rights across different cultural contexts, it is crucial for governments to adhere to the principles outlined in the Universal Declaration of Human Rights (UDHR). These principles serve as a global standard for protecting fundamental human rights and ensuring dignity for all individuals. Our governments have often failed to apply these universal standards, maintain respect for cultural diversity, and uphold basic human rights. Such neglect has led to the erosion of freedoms and equality, perpetuating injustice and hindering development. It is the responsibility of governments to navigate these complexities, ensuring that human rights are protected and promoted for every citizen, regardless of cultural differences.

That Regular Elections Guarantee Good Governance

Regular elections are often perceived as a hallmark of good governance and democratic progress. In Africa, the assumption that holding regular elections automatically ensures good governance is false. While elections are a crucial component of democracy, their effectiveness depends on broader factors such as the rule of law, respect for human rights, and the strength of democratic institutions.

In many cases, countries may hold regular elections but still struggle with issues such as corruption, political repression, and lack of accountability. Without robust institutions to safeguard democratic principles, elections can be manipulated or undermined, leading to flawed outcomes and perpetuating governance challenges. In Zimbabwe, elections have been held regularly, but they have often been marred by allegations of voter intimidation, electoral fraud, and violence. The 2018 elections, while relatively peaceful, still faced accusations of irregularities and a lack of transparency, undermining public trust in the electoral process and the legitimacy of elected officials. For example, in some African countries, elections have been marred by irregularities, voter intimidation, and lack of transparency, undermining public trust in the electoral process and the legitimacy of elected officials.

Moreover, the mere act of holding elections does not address deeper structural issues within society, such as inequality, poverty, and social exclusion. In some cases, electoral processes may exacerbate existing divisions or inequalities within society, leading to social unrest or political instability. Therefore, the assumption that regular elections alone can guarantee good governance overlooks the need for comprehensive reforms and institutional strengthening to uphold democratic values and ensure effective governance.

Ultimately, good governance requires more than just periodic elections; it necessitates the establishment of strong democratic institutions, adherence to the rule of law, protection of human rights, and meaningful citizen participation in decision-making processes. Without addressing these fundamental aspects, the mere act of holding regular elections may not lead to genuine democratic progress or improved governance outcomes.

That the West will Invariably Defend Democracy

Historical evidence demonstrates that Western intervention in African affairs has often been motivated by strategic interests rather than a genuine commitment to democracy. Instances of Western support for authoritarian regimes or interference in democratic processes for geopolitical gain under-mine the notion that the West prioritizes democracy in Africa.

Moreover, relying on external actors to safeguard democracy undermines African agency and sovereignty. Sustainable democratic development requires homegrown solutions that are rooted in the aspirations and needs of African citizens. Outsourcing the responsibility for democracy to external actors perpetuates a dependency mindset and undermines efforts to build strong, independent democratic institutions.

Furthermore, Western interventions in African democracies have sometimes been counterproductive or even detrimental to democratic progress. Examples of Western-backed regime changes or interventions that have led to instability and conflict highlight the risks of external interference in African affairs. Additionally, conditional aid or support from Western donors may come with strings attached, leading to compromises on democratic principles or policies that serve Western interests rather than African priorities.

Ultimately, the responsibility for protecting and advancing democracy in Africa lies with African governments, institutions, and citizens themselves. While international support and cooperation can be valuable, true democratic development requires self-determination, accountability, and active participation from all stakeholders within Africa. By empowering African nations to lead their own democratic transitions and address governance challenges, the continent can chart a path towards sustainable democratic governance that reflects its unique needs and aspirations.

The defense of democracy in Africa is the exclusive mandate of Africans. The thinking that the West will intervene for the mere sabotage of democracy has proven untenable over the years. Following the June 2023 General Elections in Sierra Leone, the international community refrained from intervention until the opposition staged an unusual demonstration of civil disobedience. Despite complaints of electoral irregularities from credible international observers like the EU Election Observation Mission and the Carter Center, the Electoral Commission for Sierra Leone declared the incumbent president, Julius Maada Bio, the winner with 56.17 percent of the votes, surpassing the required 55 percent threshold for avoiding a run-off election.

The opposition rejected the results and opted not to seek judicial recourse due to a profound lack of trust in the judiciary. Instead, they urged their elected officials in parliament and local councils to boycott the government, marking a rare instance of protest in Africa that stopped short of mobilizing supporters to the streets but proved potent in challenging the government's authority.

This approach of civil disobedience bears a striking resemblance to Gandhi's philosophy, characterized by peaceful protests, boycotts, and noncooperation with oppressive authorities. African leaders and activists have often drawn upon Gandhi's principles of nonviolent resistance to advocate for democratic rights and freedoms. In Sierra Leone, the All People's Congress effectively employed tactics such as boycotts and sit-at-home protests to confront the government for its irregularities and excesses. This impasse prompted the government to seek a mediated dialogue facilitated by the Commonwealth, the African Union, and ECOWAS.

Gandhi's belief in the moral and spiritual strength of individuals to peacefully resist injustice and tyranny resonated in the nonviolent resistance witnessed in Sierra Leone. Led by Samura Kamara, the leader of the APC, this resistance spared the country massive bloodletting, as the Bio government had gained notoriety for its violent crackdown on protesters. Ultimately, the opposition's pressure compelled the government to agree to an independent and impartial investigation into the rigged elections, bypassing the need for a court judgment.

Definitely, without this action by the opposition, Sierra Leon would have joined the litany of democracies characterized by abuse of due processes with no remedial intervention by the West. It is hoped that the opposition in other countries would find smarter ways to defend their democracies.

That the West is Free from Corruption

The notion that the West is free from corruption is pervasive and is often reinforced by portrayals of Western societies in the media, educational systems, and political discourse, where corruption scandals in Western countries may receive less attention compared to those in African nations.

The West's role in promoting anti-corruption initiatives and providing development assistance to African countries may contribute to the perception that Western nations have effectively addressed corruption within their own borders. Development aid often comes with conditions related to governance reforms and anti-corruption measures, leading some Africans to believe that corruption is primarily a problem in their own countries rather than in the West. They may associate corruption with developing or authoritarian regimes, overlooking the reality that corruption exists in all societies, regardless of their level of economic development or political structure.

One prominent example is the United States, where corruption scandals have rocked both federal and state governments. For instance, the Watergate scandal in the 1970s exposed widespread corruption within the Nixon administration, leading to the resignation of President Richard Nixon. More recently, numerous cases of political corruption, like bribery have been uncovered at various levels of government including the presidency.

Similarly, corruption scandals have plagued European countries, including France, Italy, and Spain. In France, former President Jacques Chirac was convicted of corruption and embezzlement during his time as mayor of Paris. Italy has faced persistent issues with corruption within its political and business sectors, leading to the downfall of several government officials and business leaders. In Spain, the Gürtel case revealed a widespread network of corruption involving politicians, businessmen, and civil servants.

Worthy of note is the lobbying phenomenon that is normalized in the West. The Bio administration of Sierra Leone, for instance, hired a US-based lobbyist to launder their image following significant electoral irregularities in the 2023 elections. This lobbyist's task is to influence the US government, which has yet to congratulate Julius Maada Bio and his administration due to concerns raised by international election observers. The lobbyist's mission is to engage stakeholders in the US, including Congressmen, Senators, and the US Ambassador, to soften the US stance against the Sierra Leone Government. Much of it is not unconnected with financial inducement.

Moreover, corruption within Western financial institutions has also been exposed, particularly during the global financial crisis of 2008. Banks and financial services firms in the United States and Europe were implicated in unethical practices such as mortgage fraud, predatory lending, and market manipulation, contributing to the economic downturn and necessitating significant regulatory reforms.

That All Citizens Are Actively Engaged in Democratic
Processes and Civic Activities.

While democratic ideals promote the involvement of citizens in governance and decision-making, the reality is far more nuanced.

One significant challenge to widespread civic participation is voter apathy. Despite the existence of electoral processes, many citizens may feel disillusioned or disenchanted with the political system, leading to low voter turnout and limited engagement in electoral activities. Factors contributing to voter apathy may include perceptions of electoral fraud, lack of trust in political institutions, and dissatisfaction with political candidates or parties.

Limited access to information also hinders civic engagement in Africa. In many cases, marginalized communities, rural areas, and underserved populations may lack adequate access to reliable information about political processes, candidates, and policy issues. Without access to unbiased and comprehensive information, citizens may struggle to make informed decisions and actively participate in democratic processes.

Socio-economic disparities further exacerbate challenges to civic engagement. Inequities in wealth, education, and social status can create barriers to participation, with marginalized groups facing systemic obstacles to engaging in political activism or civic initiatives. Economic constraints, time limitations, and competing priorities may prevent individuals from fully participating in democratic processes, particularly those from disadvantaged backgrounds.

To address the misconception about civic participation, it is crucial to recognize and acknowledge the diverse factors that influence citizen engagement in Africa. Efforts to promote civic participation should focus on enhancing access to information, addressing socio-economic disparities, and fostering inclusive and participatory political environments. By empowering citizens with knowledge, resources, and opportunities for meaningful participation, African societies can strengthen their democratic institutions and ensure that all voices are heard in the political process.

Consistent with the foregoing, a thorough comprehension of democracy in Africa requires delving into the interwoven dynamics between political transformations and economic policies shaped by both historical legacies and present-day influences. These diverse experiences across the continent underscore the significance of appreciating each nation's distinct historical, cultural, and political backdrop in discussions on democracy. Oversimplifying the challenges and triumphs within the region by assuming a uniform trajectory for African democracies can overlook the nuanced realities that exist.

Parallels with Asia

My heart aches with the weight of Africa's turbulent journey. The coups, the corruption, the unfulfilled promises of democracy—these haunt my thoughts daily. My curiosity, restless and insatiable, turns towards the East, towards Asia, where nations that once mirrored our struggles now rise as beacons of economic prosperity and political stability. How did they manage to forge paths of progress, to cultivate growth where we still grapple with unrest? Their stories, both a contrast and a mirror to our own, beckon me to delve deeper, to uncover the lessons we might learn and the paths we might tread to transform our own fate.

Political Stability and Transitions

Asia has generally experienced more political stability and successful transitions to civilian rule compared to much of Africa. For instance, Indonesia's transition to democracy in 1998, following the fall of the authoritarian regime of Suharto, stands as a testament to Asia's political resilience (Peou, 2009). Similarly, South Korea's transition from military rule to a democratic government in the late 1980s highlights a successful shift towards civilian governance. After decades of authoritarian rule, South Korea held direct presidential elections in 1987, leading to the establishment of a stable and prosperous democracy (Kang, 2003). Another notable example is Taiwan, which transitioned from one-party rule under the Kuomintang to a multi-party democratic system in the 1990s. This peaceful transition has enabled Taiwan to become one of the most vibrant democracies in Asia, characterized by regular, free, and fair elections (Rigger, 2001).

In contrast, many African countries continue to struggle with political instability and repeated coups. Sudan, for example, has faced numerous internal conflicts since independence, including the 1st and 2nd civil wars and the war in Darfur. The conflict in 2021 marked the overthrow of the transitional government established after Omar al-Bashir's ousting in 2019 and the latest conflict in 2023 is between rival military groups. Similarly, Mali has experienced multiple coups, with the latest in 2021 undermining efforts for stable democratic governance. Zimbabwe's political landscape, marred by instability and contested elections, saw a military intervention in 2017, leading to the resignation of long-time leader Robert Mugabe. These contrasts highlight the varied paths and challenges that Africa and Asia face in their pursuit of political stability and democratic governance.

Economic Development and Governance

The economic strides of certain Asian countries starkly contrast with the struggles faced by many African nations. Singapore, South Korea, and Taiwan, once mired in poverty and conflict, have achieved rapid economic development and established stable governance (Stubbs, 2005). These success stories highlight the potential for transformation, a potential that Africa still strives to fully realize amidst its challenges.

Regional Cooperation and Organizations

Regional cooperation plays a pivotal role in political stability. Asia's Association of Southeast Asian Nations (ASEAN) focuses on economic cooperation and regional stability but has little need to be interventionist compared to the African Union (AU), which actively addresses coups and promotes democratic governance (He, 2016). The AU's direct interventions in Mali and Sudan demonstrate a commitment to maintaining order and democratic principles, but at the same time, it presupposes a high incidence of regional instability occasioned by frequent disruptions.

Foreign Intervention and Influence

Both Africa and Asia have experienced significant foreign interventions that have profoundly influenced their political landscapes. These interventions often complicate internal political environments, adding layers of external pressure to already volatile situations. However, while both continents have faced foreign interference to similar extents, Asia has largely moved past the era of frequent coups, with a few exceptions, whereas Africa continues to grapple with recurrent coups and political instability.

In Asia, the U.S.-backed coup in Iran in 1953 is a notable example of foreign intervention. The coup, orchestrated by the CIA and MI6, overthrew Prime Minister Mohammad Mossadegh and reinstated the Shah, leading to decades of autocratic rule and significant anti-Western sentiment (Kinzer, 2003). Despite this, many Asian countries have successfully transitioned to stable civilian rule. Indonesia's transition to democracy in 1998, following the fall of Suharto's authoritarian regime, and Mongolia's peaceful shift to democracy in the early 1990s are prime examples (Peou, 2009).

In recent years, Asia has generally seen fewer coups. Thailand's 2014 military coup is a notable exception, but even Thailand has maintained relative stability compared to the persistent instability seen in many African nations (Chambers & Waitoolkiat, 2016). This relative stability in Asia can be attributed to several factors, including stronger institutional frameworks, economic development, and successful integration of traditional governance structures with modern democratic principles.

Conversely, Africa continues to struggle with political instability and repeated coups. Sudan, for example, has faced numerous military coups since its independence, with the most recent one in 2021 overthrowing the transitional government established after the ousting of Omar al-Bashir in 2019 (Francis, 2005). Similarly, Mali has experienced multiple coups, undermining efforts to establish a stable democratic governance structure (Vines, 2021).

Foreign influences in Africa have also played a significant role in shaping political dynamics. France's involvement in the Central African Republic (CAR) and Russia's Wagner Group's activities in Libya and the Sahel are prominent examples.

These interventions, often driven by geopolitical interests, have frequently exacerbated local conflicts and undermined democratic processes (Marchal, 2015; McGregor, 2020).

In contrast, many Asian countries have managed to navigate foreign interventions while maintaining relative political stability. For instance, South Korea and Taiwan, despite experiencing significant foreign influence during the Cold War, have developed into stable democracies with strong economies (Koo, 2018). China's rise as a global power, while controversial, has been marked by a stable, albeit authoritarian, governance model that has avoided military coups (Shambaugh, 2020).

Civil Society and Activism

Civil society movements have been catalysts for change in both regions, though their impacts vary. The People Power Movement in the Philippines in 1986 exemplifies the power of civil activism in Asia (Thompson, 1995). In Africa, movements in Sudan and Tunisia have similarly driven significant political change (Gallopin, 2021). These instances underscore the vital role of grassroots activism in challenging entrenched power structures and advocating for democratic reforms.

Post-Cold War Dynamics

The post-Cold War era brought significant political shifts, with some Asian countries embracing democratic reforms more successfully than their African counterparts. Mongolia's transition to democracy in the early 1990s illustrates a successful democratic transition in Asia (Rossabi, 2005). In contrast, many of our countries in Africa continue to navigate the remnants of Cold War politics, which still influence their governance landscapes.

Military Involvement in Politics

Military coups have occurred in both Africa and Asia, but their frequency and outcomes differ. The 2014 coup in Thailand illustrates military involvement in politics, impacting the country's governance and political stability in the Asian context. In Africa, nations like Burkina Faso and Guinea have experienced frequent military coups, reflecting ongoing challenges in civil-military relations (Francis, 2005).

In reflecting upon these parallels, it becomes evident that Africa and Asia, despite their shared histories of colonialism and struggle, have diverged in their paths toward stability and prosperity. Asia's successes offer valuable lessons, yet the unique challenges faced by African nations require tailored approaches and solutions. As we strive to understand and emulate these successes, we must also recognize and address the distinctive contexts of our own continent, forging a path that acknowledges our history while aspiring towards a future of stability and growth.

References

1. Chachavalpongpun, P. (2014). Thailand: The Politics of Despair. Journal of Democracy.
2. Chambers, P., & Waitoolkiat, N. (2016). Khaki Capital: The Political Economy of the Military in Southeast Asia. NIAS Press.
3. Francis, D. J. (2005). Civil Militia: Africa's Intractable Security Menace? Ashgate Publishing.

4. Gallopin, J. B. (2021). Protest and Political Change in the Arab World. Routledge.

5. He, B. (2016). The Institutional Dynamics of China's Great Transformation. Cambridge University Press.

6. Kinzer, S. (2003). All the Shah's Men: An American Coup and the Roots of Middle East Terror. John Wiley & Sons.

7. Koo, B. (2018). The Political Economy of South Korea's Economic Growth. In South Korea's Rise: Economic Development, Power, and Foreign Relations. Cambridge University Press.

8. Marchal, R. (2015). Central African Republic: Back to War Again? The World Today.

9. Marchal, R. (2015). The Central African Republic: Back to War Again? In M. Boas & K. Dunn (Eds.), African Guerrillas: Raging Against the Machine. Lynne Rienner Publishers.

10. McGregor, A. (2020). Russia's Wagner Group in Libya: Real Influence or Illusion? Terrorism Monitor, 18(10).

11. Ndlovu-Gatsheni, S. J. (2009). Do 'Zimbabweans' Exist? Trajectories of Nationalism, National Identity Formation and Crisis in a Postcolonial State. Peter Lang.

12. Peou, S. (2009). International Democracy Assistance for Peacebuilding: Cambodia and Beyond. Palgrave Macmillan.

13. Rossabi, M. (2005). Modern Mongolia: From Khans to Commissars to Capitalists. University of California Press.

14. Shambaugh, D. (2020). China's Future. Polity.

15. Stubbs, R. (2005). Rethinking Asia's Economic Miracle: The Political Economy of War, Prosperity, and Crisis. Palgrave Macmillan.

16. Thompson, M. R. (1995). The Anti-Marcos Struggle: Personalistic Rule and Democratic Transition in the Philippines. Yale University Press.

17. Vines, A. (2021). The New Era of Coups in Africa: What is Happening? Chatham House.

TEN
IMPACT AND CONSEQUENCES

Negative impact

Despite the optimistic forecast of AU Agenda 2063, which envisioned Africa achieving peace and "silencing the guns by 2020," the continent has instead witnessed a resurgence of forceful takeovers, with no signs of abatement in the foreseeable future. This trend has punctuated the political calendars of numerous countries, casting a shadow over prospects for stability and development.

Coups d'état in Africa carry profound and varied impacts that reverberate across countries, societies, and governance structures. I am distraught by the unfolding events that mar the continent's progress. These consequences are multifaceted and intricate, affecting not only political stability but also economic development, human rights, and diplomatic relations.

Economic development, too, bears the brunt of these upheavals. The uncertainty wrought by coups deters investment, disrupts trade, and hampers economic growth. In countries like Zimbabwe, the military intervention of 2017, which led to the resignation of long-time leader Robert Mugabe, has not resulted in the anticipated economic revival. Instead, the economy remains in tatters, weighed down by political instability and poor governance. The dream of prosperity for many Africans is deferred, if not altogether shattered, by the economic stagnation that follows in the wake of coups.

Human rights violations often accompany these forceful takeovers. The immediate aftermath of a coup can see the suspension of civil liberties, crackdowns on dissent, and widespread abuses by the military. In places like Guinea, the military coup of 2021 saw brutal suppression of protests and dissenting voices, further entrenching a culture of fear and repression. The promise of democracy, which includes the protection of human rights, is betrayed as citizens find themselves at the mercy of authoritarian rule.

Diplomatic relations are another casualty of coups. Countries that experience frequent military takeovers find themselves isolated on the international stage their governments' legitimacy questioned. This diplomatic isolation can lead to sanctions and a reduction in foreign aid, compounding the economic and social challenges faced by the nation. The African Union, which aims to foster unity and development, finds its efforts undermined by the very instability it seeks to eradicate.

As an asylee, reflecting on these events from afar, I am gripped by a profound sense of disillusionment. The resurgence of coups d'état across Africa feels like a betrayal of the continent's potential. The path to progress seems perpetually obstructed by the specter of political instability and poor governance. These coups are not just political events; they are catastrophic disruptions that ripple through every facet of life, stifling the dreams and aspirations of countless Africans.

The dire consequences of poor governance and political

instability only exacerbate existing challenges and hinder progress. The echoes of these events resonate deeply within me, fueling a longing for a future where Africa can finally break free from the chains of its turbulent past and move towards a horizon of peace, prosperity, and true democratic governance.

The Ripple Effects of Political Instability

The reverberations of coups are deeply felt in the disruption of political stability. Our nations in the Sahel, like Mali and Burkina Faso, have experienced repeated coups, each instance shattering the fragile scaffolding of their fledgling democracies. The incessant political upheaval undermines the very foundations of governance, leading to a cycle of instability that is hard to break. The vision of a peaceful Africa seems to recede further into the horizon with each coup, dashing the hopes of millions for a stable future.

Imagine the life of Fatou, a small business owner in Bamako, Mali. She runs a modest textile shop, providing for her family and employing a few local artisans. Each coup disrupts her business operations, as curfews, roadblocks, and uncertainty drive away customers and suppliers. The once-bustling markets fall silent, and her sales plummet. The fragile supply chains break down, and the cost of materials skyrockets. Fatou's dreams of expanding her business and sending her children to school are shattered by the relentless waves of political turmoil. Her artisans, who rely on daily wages, find themselves on the brink of poverty.

Bad governance often serves as a significant catalyst for political instability in Africa. When governments fail to uphold the rule of law, respect human rights, and provide basic services to their citizens, it breeds discontent and erodes trust in institutions. This can lead to widespread protests, civil unrest, and even violent conflicts as people demand accountability and change. In the Democratic Republic of Congo (DRC), for example, decades of corruption, weak governance, and conflict fueled by competition over vast natural resources have plagued the nation. Under former President Joseph Kabila, the DRC experienced prolonged political instability and violence. Kabila's refusal to step down after his constitutionally mandated two terms led to widespread protests and a political crisis. The government's crackdown on dissent, including arbitrary arrests and violence against protesters, further destabilized the country.

The ripple effects of political instability extend beyond national borders, affecting regional stability and economic development. Countries experiencing political turmoil often struggle to attract investment, maintain essential services, and address pressing social and economic challenges, perpetuating a cycle of underdevelopment and instability. The political instability in Libya, for instance, has had far-reaching implications for the region. Following the overthrow of Muammar Gaddafi in 2011, Libya descended into chaos, with rival factions vying for power and control. The power vacuum and ongoing conflict in Libya have fueled arms trafficking, terrorism, and irregular migration, affecting neighboring countries such as Tunisia, Egypt, Chad, and Niger.

The instability in Libya has strained diplomatic relations between these countries and Libya, as well as among themselves. Neighboring countries have been forced to manage security threats emanating from Libya's instability, including terrorist activities and the proliferation of weapons. The conflict has also disrupted regional cooperation initiatives and efforts to address common challenges, such as migration and counterterrorism.

Consider also the story of a young university student,

Amina, in Sudan. She dreams of becoming a doctor to serve her community. However, the repeated coups and resulting instability disrupt her education. Universities shut down, her professors flee the country, and the future she has worked so hard for seems increasingly uncertain. The instability forces her family to prioritize survival over education, and Amina's dreams fade in the harsh light of political chaos.

These personal stories are reflective of a broader malaise affecting countless Africans. The constant state of flux not only stifles economic progress but also sows seeds of disillusionment and despair. Political instability tears at the fabric of society, leaving behind a trail of unfulfilled potential and broken dreams. Reflecting on these realities, the weight of disenchantment in me grows heavier. The hope for a stable and prosperous Africa remains a distant dream, overshadowed by the persistent shadow of political turmoil.

Erosion of Democratic Institutions

Political instability in Africa is like a relentless storm, eroding the democratic institutions meant to protect and uplift the lives of ordinary citizens. To address this instability, comprehensive strategies are needed that delve into the roots of coups and bad governance. These strategies must promote democratic governance, strengthen institutions, foster inclusive political processes, and tackle underlying socio-economic grievances.

Amadou is a small business owner in Kinshasa, Congo. He runs a modest electronics store, providing for his family and contributing to his community. Yet, the Democratic Republic of Congo (DRC) is plagued by weak institutions, endemic corruption, and political repression. President Joseph Kabila's refusal to step down after his term ended in 2016 triggered political instability and widespread protests, deepening the country's crisis. For Amadou, this instability is devastating. His customers stay away, fearing the violence in the streets. Suppliers hesitate to deliver goods, worried about the safety of their shipments. Banks, uncertain of the future, deny him the loans needed to sustain his business. Each day, Amadou watches his livelihood slip away, his dreams eclipsed by the turmoil engulfing his nation.

Similarly, the #EndSARS protests in Nigeria, sparked by institutional abuses committed by the police force, plunged the country into a period of turmoil. The movement, led by young Nigerians demanding an end to police brutality and corruption, highlighted the deep flaws within the nation's institutions. For educational institutions like universities, this turmoil is particularly disruptive. Picture a university in Lagos where lectures are frequently canceled, exams postponed, and research halted due to the chaos. Students and faculty find themselves in a state of limbo, their academic and professional pursuits constantly interrupted. A bright student with aspirations of studying abroad or securing a prestigious scholarship sees her plans derailed. The constant disruptions mean she cannot complete her studies on time, and her future remains uncertain.

In Burkina Faso, a military coup in 2014 overthrew the democratically elected government, ushering in a period of political turmoil and uncertainty. This coup disrupted the country's democratic transition and undermined the progress made towards establishing accountable governance structures. Despite subsequent efforts to restore democracy, including elections and transitional governments, Burkina Faso continues to grapple with political instability and insecurity. Consider a health clinic in Ouagadougou, the capital city. The coup and ongoing instability result in erratic funding for health services.

Essential supplies like vaccines and medicines are often delayed or completely unavailable. The clinic staff, though dedicated, are overworked and under-resourced. Patients, especially the most vulnerable—pregnant women, children, and the elderly—suffer the most. What was once a beacon of hope and health for the community now struggles to keep its doors open.

These scenarios illustrate how the erosion of democratic institutions due to coups and unconstitutional changes of government (UCGs) profoundly impacts the average African. The constant state of political flux disrupts daily life, stifles economic progress, and sows seeds of despair. The hope for a stable and prosperous Africa seems a distant dream, overshadowed by the persistent shadow of political turmoil. Amadou's electronics store, the disrupted university in Lagos, and the struggling health clinic in Ouagadougou are fragments of a larger, troubling mosaic—a tapestry of dreams deferred, potential unrealized, and lives caught in the relentless grip of instability.

Human Rights Violations

Coups and political instability in Africa often coincide with egregious human rights violations perpetrated by those seeking to consolidate power or suppress opposition. These violations have wide-ranging impacts on the affected populations and the broader society, exacerbating tensions and undermining the prospects for peace and stability.

The escalation of human rights abuses can take various forms. Following a coup, the new regime may resort to tactics such as the suppression of dissent, political persecution of opponents, and violence against civilians to maintain control and silence opposition voices. For example, in the aftermath of a coup, arbitrary arrests, extrajudicial killings, and forced disappearances may become commonplace as the new leadership seeks to assert its authority and eliminate perceived threats.

A stark example can be seen in the case of Sudan. Following the military coup in April 2019 that ousted President Omar al-Bashir, the transitional military council cracked down violently on peaceful protesters demanding civilian rule. Security forces used live ammunition, tear gas, and arbitrary arrests to suppress dissent, resulting in numerous casualties and widespread human rights abuses. However, the crackdown only served to galvanize opposition to the military regime, eventually leading to a power-sharing agreement between the military and civilian forces.

Similarly, in the Sahel, the military coup in August 2020 led to a surge in human rights violations, including arbitrary detentions, torture, and extrajudicial killings by security forces. The coup exacerbated existing ethnic tensions and fueled violence in the countries, leading to a humanitarian crisis and further destabilizing the fragile political situation.

These examples underscore the devastating impact of human rights violations in the wake of coups and political instability, highlighting the urgent need for accountability, justice, and respect for human rights in Africa's democratic transitions.

Economic Disruptions

The shadows of coups and political instability often cast long, dark clouds over the economic landscape. The disruptions manifest in various ways, dismantling existing economic structures and thwarting the prospects of development. The impact is profound, affecting every layer of society and stalling the march toward a brighter future.

The first major casualty of political unrest is investor confidence. Political turmoil creates uncertainty among investors, both domestic and foreign, leading to a reluctance to commit capital to long-term investments or business ventures. This uncertainty often results in capital flight, where investors withdraw their funds from the country and seek safer investment opportunities elsewhere. The sudden outflow of capital exacerbates existing economic challenges and impedes efforts to stimulate growth and development.

Imagine a nation in the aftermath of a coup. The streets are filled with tension, and the air is thick with uncertainty. Foreign investors, their hearts heavy with doubt, begin to divest. Projects that once promised jobs and prosperity are abandoned. Their skeletal remains are a stark reminder of what could have been. Economic activity contracts, and with it, the hope of new employment and increased government revenue fades. Domestic businesses, too, retreat into survival mode, scaling back operations and halting expansion plans. The gears of progress grind to a halt, and the once vibrant economy slows to a painful crawl.

Consider Zimbabwe, a nation once brimming with potential, now a poignant example of the havoc wrought by political instability. Under the rule of President Robert Mugabe, the country endured electoral violence, human rights abuses, and economic mismanagement. The uncertainty surrounding land reform policies and property rights scared away foreign investors, leading to a precipitous decline in foreign direct investment. Hyperinflation soared, the currency crumbled, and productivity plummeted. Poverty and unemployment became the norm, a harsh testament to the devastating economic disruptions born of political turmoil.

In the Democratic Republic of Congo (DRC), the story is eerily similar. Rich in mineral wealth, the country attracted the attention of foreign investors. Yet, ongoing political instability, corruption, and armed conflict have created an environment fraught with risk. Investment opportunities wither, and economic growth remains a distant hope. The DRC continues to grapple with poverty, low living standards, and the elusive goal of sustainable development.

These narratives, though tragic, are not tales of inevitability. They serve as a clarion call for stability and reform. For Africa to rise, it must shed the shackles of political instability and embrace a future where investment can flow freely and economic structures can be rebuilt. Only then can the continent's true potential be realized, ushering in an era of growth, prosperity, and hope.

International Isolation

Coups and political instability in African states not only have domestic repercussions but also often lead to international isolation, as the global community typically condemns such unconstitutional changes of government.

When a coup occurs, it often triggers swift condemnation from the international community, including regional organizations such as the African Union and international bodies like the United Nations. The condemnation stems from the violation of democratic principles and the rule of law, which are fundamental to international norms and standards. As a result, the affected country may face diplomatic isolation, with other nations and organizations suspending diplomatic relations or imposing sanctions in response to the coup.

The consequences of international isolation can be severe for the affected country. Diplomatic isolation hinders the country's ability to maintain diplomatic relations, access international markets, and engage in trade and investment. This can lead to a contraction in economic activity, reduced foreign direct investment, and a decline in government revenue. The suspension of aid and development assistance can exacerbate existing economic challenges and impede efforts to stimulate growth and development.

Moreover, international isolation can strain diplomatic ties with neighboring countries and undermine efforts to address regional challenges such as security threats and cross-border issues. The affected country may find it difficult to participate in regional cooperation initiatives and may be excluded from important decision-making processes that impact the region.

Refugee and Migration Flows

Coups and political instability in African states often have profound consequences on refugee and migration flows, worsening existing humanitarian challenges and contributing to regional instability. These upheavals prompt individuals and families to flee their homes, seeking safety and economic opportunities elsewhere, thus creating waves of displacement that ripple across borders and continents.

When political turmoil erupts, the immediate atmosphere of insecurity and uncertainty forces people to make difficult decisions. Families hastily gather their belongings, leaving behind homes, livelihoods, and sometimes loved ones. The internal displacement sees people moving to safer regions within the country while others cross borders into neighboring states or embark on perilous journeys to distant lands.

Consider the plight of a family from the Democratic Republic of Congo (DRC). Amidst escalating violence and instability, they flee their village under the cover of night. The father, Jean, carries his youngest child, while the mother, Amina, clutches the hands of their two older children. They trek through dense forests, avoiding conflict zones and relying on the kindness of strangers for food and shelter. Their destination: a refugee camp in Uganda, where they hope to find safety and the possibility of a new beginning.

Upon reaching the camp, they face the harsh realities of life as refugees. The camp is overcrowded, resources are scarce, and the future remains uncertain. Jean, a skilled carpenter, struggles to find work, while Amina worries about the children's education and health. The family's story is a reflection of countless others, each marked by loss, resilience, and the hope for a better tomorrow.

In Sudan and South Sudan, similar stories unfold. People flee from violence and persecution, crossing into neighboring countries like Kenya, Ethiopia, and Tanzania. These nations, already grappling with their own challenges, strain under the weight of providing for large refugee populations. Humanitarian organizations step in, offering shelter, food, water, and healthcare, but the resources are often stretched thin.

The influx of refugees and migrants creates social tensions in host communities. In Kenya, a local farmer named Kamau finds his small plot of land increasingly crowded by new arrivals. Competition for jobs intensifies, and resources like water and healthcare become even more limited. Kamau feels a mix of compassion and frustration, reflecting a broader sentiment that can lead to xenophobia, discrimination, and sometimes violence.

The mass movement of people also disrupts regional stability and security. Borders become porous, and managing the cross-border dynamics becomes a herculean task. Neighboring countries grapple with the diplomatic and logistical challenges of hosting large refugee populations while maintaining security and order. This strain on diplomatic relations hinders efforts to address broader regional issues such as security cooperation and economic integration.

In a reflective moment, one might ponder the broader

implications of these human migrations. The sight of refugees queuing for aid, children playing in the dust of overcrowded camps, and families huddling together against the cold nights evokes a profound sense of the human cost of political instability. Each person in these stories carries a tale of resilience, of a life uprooted and the unyielding hope for peace and stability.

Impaired Development Efforts

The impact of coups on development efforts is significant, as they disrupt ongoing development programs and projects. In the aftermath of a coup, there is often a diversion of resources away from essential services such as healthcare, education, and infrastructure development towards addressing immediate security concerns and consolidating power. This redirection of resources can stall or even reverse progress in key areas of development, leaving communities without access to vital services and infrastructure.

In Guinea Bissau, development projects funded by international donors have been suspended or delayed due to political instability. This has had serious implications for the delivery of basic services and the implementation of initiatives aimed at poverty reduction, healthcare, and education.

The consequences of impaired development efforts are far-reaching and can have lasting effects on economic growth and poverty reduction. When development projects are disrupted or delayed, it not only affects the immediate beneficiaries but also undermines the overall resilience and capacity of communities to withstand future shocks and challenges.

Moreover, the lack of progress in development efforts perpetuates cycles of poverty and inequality, further marginalizing vulnerable populations and hindering social and economic mobility. This, in turn, creates fertile ground for social unrest, discontent, and further political instability. The effect is a vicious cycle of underdevelopment and insecurity.

Military Influence in Politics

Coups and political instability in African states often lead to increased military influence in politics, with significant implications for governance and stability.

The impact of successful coups on military influence in politics is profound. When the military successfully seizes power, it often establishes itself as the dominant force in governance, leading to a militarized form of governance where armed personnel play a central role in decision-making processes. This can undermine civilian-led democratic institutions and erode the principles of democratic governance.

For example, in countries like Egypt and Sudan, military coups have resulted in the establishment of military-led governments that have sidelined civilian authorities and curtailed political freedoms. The military has played a dominant role in shaping government policies and controlling key institutions, leading to a concentration of power in the hands of the military elite.

The consequences of prolonged military influence in politics are detrimental to democratic consolidation and stability. When the military becomes entrenched in political affairs, it often perpetuates a cycle of instability by undermining efforts to establish civilian-led democratic institutions. This can lead to political repression, human rights abuses, and a lack of accountability, further fueling social unrest and political turmoil.

Moreover, military involvement in politics can hinder economic development and deter foreign investment, as investors may perceive military-dominated governments as unstable and unpredictable. This can exacerbate economic challenges and perpetuate cycles of poverty and underdevelopment in affected countries.

Social Cohesion Challenges

Coups and political instability in African states often lead to significant challenges in social cohesion, exacerbating divisions and tensions within society.

The impact of coups on social cohesion is profound. The sudden overthrow of a government and the subsequent power vacuum can create uncertainty and anxiety among the population, leading to heightened social divisions along political, ethnic, or regional lines. In some cases, coups may be perceived as benefiting one group over others, further exacerbating existing social tensions.

In Sudan, coups have led to increased ethnic and political polarization, with different groups vying for power and influence in the aftermath of political upheaval. This has resulted in social unrest, intercommunal violence, and challenges in fostering national unity and reconciliation.

The consequences of social cohesion challenges are far-reaching and can contribute to further political instability. When society is deeply divided along ethnic or political lines, efforts to establish inclusive governance structures and promote national reconciliation are hindered. This can perpetuate cycles of instability and conflict, making it difficult to achieve lasting peace and stability.

Moreover, social cohesion challenges can undermine efforts at economic development and social progress, as resources and energy are diverted towards managing internal divisions and addressing social unrest. This can impede efforts to reduce poverty, promote social justice, and improve living standards for all citizens.

Foreign Policy Realignment

Coups and political instability in African states often lead to significant shifts in foreign policy alignment, impacting diplomatic relations and international cooperation.

When a government is overthrown through a coup, the incoming leadership may seek to redefine the country's foreign policy objectives and alliances. This could involve reevaluating existing partnerships and seeking new alliances with other nations that align more closely with the interests of the new regime.

In the aftermath of coups in countries like Egypt and Zimbabwe, there were notable shifts in foreign policy alignment, with the new governments pursuing different diplomatic strategies and alliances compared to their predecessors. These changes can have far-reaching consequences for international relations and cooperation in areas such as trade, security, and development assistance.

The consequences of foreign policy realignment can impact various aspects of a country's engagement with the international community. Changes in diplomatic relations may affect trade agreements, development assistance, and regional alliances, potentially disrupting established networks of cooperation and collaboration.

Shifts in foreign policy alignment can also influence regional dynamics and power balances. A country's decision to align itself with certain regional blocs or alliances may have implications for regional stability and security, affecting neighboring countries and broader regional cooperation efforts.

Diminished Confidence in Democracy

The occurrence of coups or political instability in African states often leads to a significant decline in public confidence in democratic governance, with far-reaching consequences for the stability and resilience of democratic systems.

Repeated instances of coups can have a profound impact on public perceptions of democracy. When citizens witness frequent disruptions to democratic processes and the overthrow of elected governments, it fosters skepticism about the effectiveness and stability of democratic systems. This erosion of confidence stems from the perception that democratic institutions are unable to prevent or withstand political upheaval, undermining faith in the democratic process as a means of governance.

Picture a young woman named Fatima living in Mali, where coups have become a recurrent nightmare. Growing up, she believed in the promise of democracy, inspired by the hope that her vote could shape the future of her country. However, witnessing the government overthrown multiple times, her faith in democracy begins to wane. She sees elected leaders deposed, often replaced by military figures who promise stability but deliver uncertainty and fear. Fatima's initial optimism fades into disillusionment as she begins to view democracy not as a beacon of hope but as a fragile construct easily shattered by those in power.

In Guinea, similar stories unfold. A young farmer, Moussa, recalls the days when he proudly cast his vote, believing in the power of the people's voice. But repeated coups have left him jaded. He sees the cycle of elections, brief periods of hope, followed by the abrupt seizure of power. Each coup deepens his distrust in the democratic system, making him question whether his participation in the electoral process matters at all.

The promise of democracy feels increasingly hollow, overshadowed by the harsh reality of political instability.

The consequences of diminished confidence in democracy are significant and multifaceted. When citizens like Fatima and Moussa lose faith in democratic governance, they may disengage from political participation, leading to political apathy and reduced civic engagement. This disengagement further weakens democratic institutions and processes, as active citizen participation is essential for holding governments accountable and ensuring democratic resilience.

Moreover, diminished confidence in democracy poses challenges in building a resilient democratic culture. Trust and legitimacy are foundational elements of democratic governance. When these are eroded, fostering a culture of democratic values, norms, and practices within society becomes increasingly difficult. The cycle of distrust perpetuates itself, creating a society where cynicism towards governance is pervasive.

Reflecting on these scenarios, one can see the broader implications for the future of democracy in Africa. The constant threat of coups creates an environment where the principles of democracy are continuously undermined. Citizens become weary of the instability, and their disillusionment with democratic processes grows. Rebuilding trust in democracy requires not only restoring democratic governance but also promoting transparency, accountability, and genuine engagement between the state and its citizens.

In conclusion, coups and political instability in Africa can have a detrimental effect on public confidence in democracy, leading to skepticism about the effectiveness and stability of democratic systems. Addressing this challenge necessitates efforts to strengthen democratic institutions, promote transparency and accountability, and rebuild trust between citizens and the state. International support and diplomatic initiatives can play a crucial role in facilitating peaceful transitions and preventing the recurrence of coups, thereby fostering a more stable and democratic future for the continent.

Positive Impacts

While coups are generally viewed as detrimental to democratic governance, there have been instances in Africa where they have led to positive changes or addressed issues of bad governance, albeit rarely. Some potential positive impacts of coups in Africa as a means to address bad governance include:

Removal of Corrupt or Ineffective Leaders

In some cases, coups have resulted in the removal of leaders who were perceived as corrupt, authoritarian, or ineffective in addressing the needs of their citizens. By overthrowing such leaders, coups can create opportunities for new leadership and governance structures to emerge. The coup in Burkina Faso in 2014 led to the ousting of President Blaise Compaoré, who had been in power for 27 years and faced widespread allegations of corruption and authoritarianism. The coup paved the way for a transitional government and eventually free and fair elections, ushering in a new era of democratic governance in the country, or perhaps not.

Correction of Electoral Fraud

In cases where electoral fraud or manipulation is suspected, coups may occur as a response to perceived electoral injustices. While coups themselves are undemocratic, they can sometimes prompt electoral reforms and the restoration of democratic processes. The military intervention in Zimbabwe in 2017, which resulted in the ousting of President Robert Mugabe, was prompted by concerns over electoral fraud and the manipulation of democratic processes. While the coup itself was not democratic, it led to the resignation of Mugabe and paved the way for subsequent elections.

Sierra Leone finds itself in a precarious position, potentially on the brink of usurpation. The country's recent political climate has been marked by allegations of electoral fraud and manipulation, undermining public trust in the democratic process. As history shows, such conditions can create a fertile ground for coups, especially when the populace feels disenfranchised and the integrity of elections is in question. The November 26 attempted coup may just be the start of a series of such attempts if electoral justice is not provided for the people of that country.

Reforms and Accountability Measures

In rare cases, coups have been followed by efforts to implement governance reforms and hold leaders accountable for their actions. This can include measures to combat corruption, improve transparency, and strengthen democratic institutions. Following the coup in The Gambia in 1994, the new government led by Yahya Jammeh initially promised to address corruption and implement governance reforms. While Jammeh's regime ultimately became known for its human rights abuses and authoritarianism, the coup initially raised hopes for positive change in the country.

It's important to note that while coups may sometimes result in short-term improvements or changes in governance, they often come at a significant cost to democratic norms, stability, and human rights.

Regional and Global Ramifications

Dismayed by the regional and global ramifications of coups, I reflect on the ripple effects that these political upheavals have on my homeland and beyond. The fabric of regional stability unravels with each coup, casting shadows of unrest and tension. Neighboring countries, once bastions of relative peace, find themselves drawn into the vortex of conflict. The coup in Mali in 2012 exemplifies this, where regional instability in the Sahel prompted neighboring nations to intervene, striving to restore balance in a region teetering on the brink.

Refugee flows surge like torrents through porous borders, carrying with them the stories of families torn apart by violence and uncertainty. South Sudan's civil war in 2013 unleashed a humanitarian crisis, forcing hundreds of thousands to seek refuge in Uganda, Ethiopia, and Kenya. These migrations strain the resources and patience of host countries, echoing the cries of displaced souls across the land.

Diplomatic relations fray under the strain of coups, as nations grapple with governance issues that test their alliances. The military coup in Zimbabwe in 2017 is a stark reminder of how political upheaval can sour regional ties, with the Southern African Development Community (SADC) urging a peaceful return to civilian rule amidst growing discord.

International interventions become inevitable as regional bodies like the African Union and ECOWAS step in to mediate and restore democratic governance. The 2020 intervention in Mali by ECOWAS, imposing sanctions and demanding a civilian-led government, underscores the global community's commitment to stability, even as the specter of further unrest looms large.

The economic impacts of these usurpations are devastating even at a regional level, disrupting trade and investment and stifling development efforts. Burundi's political crisis in 2015 led to sanctions and a decline in foreign investment, reverberating through the economies of the East African Community (EAC) and deepening the region's economic woes.

Global security concerns mount as political instability provides fertile ground for armed conflict and terrorism. Somalia's descent into chaos post-1991 birthed Al-Shabaab, a terrorist group whose influence extends beyond the region, threatening international peace and security. Humanitarian consequences compound the misery, with displacement, food insecurity, and human rights abuses becoming grim realities. The Democratic Republic of Congo (DRC) illustrates this tragedy, where political crises have led to widespread suffering, calling for urgent international humanitarian assistance.

These reflections remind me of the interconnectedness of our world, where the turmoil in one nation reverberates globally. Addressing these challenges holistically is paramount, requiring concerted efforts to foster democratic governance, peace, and security. Only then can Africa hope to build resilient and stable political systems that nurture peace, prosperity, and development, allowing its people to dream of brighter futures once more.

References

1. African Union. (2014). African Union's Response to Unconstitutional Changes of Government.
2. Aisen, A., & Veiga, F. J. (2013). How Does Political Instability Affect Economic Growth? European Journal of Political Economy.

3. Autesserre, S. (2010). The Trouble with the Congo: Local Violence and the Failure of International Peacebuilding. Cambridge University Press.

4. Cilliers, J. (2017) What drives instability in Africa and what can be done about it. The Conversation.

5. Collier, P., & Hoeffler, A. (2004). Greed and Grievance in Civil War. Oxford Economic Papers.

6. Diamond, L. (2008). The Spirit of Democracy: The Struggle to Build Free Societies Throughout the World. Henry Holt and Company.

7. Gyimah-Boadi, E. (2015). Africa's Waning Democratic Commitment. Journal of Democracy.

8. Hammar, A., McGregor, J., & Landau, L. B. (Eds.). (2010). Displacing Zimbabwe: Crisis and Transition. Journal of Southern African Studies.

9. Human Rights Watch. (2021). World Report 2021: Democratic Republic of Congo.

10. International Crisis Group. (2011). Somalia: The Transitional Government on Life Support.

11. International Organization for Migration (IOM). (2020). World Migration Report 2020.

12. Norris, P. (2011). Democratic Deficit: Critical Citizens Revisited. Cambridge University Press.

13. Posner, D. N., & Young, D. J. (2007). The Institutionalization of Political Power in Africa. Journal of Democracy.

14. United Nations. (2019). UN Policy on Unconstitutional Changes of Government.

15. United Nations Conference on Trade and Development (UNCTAD). (2020). World Investment Report 2020.

16. United Nations High Commissioner for Refugees (UNHCR). (2021). Global Trends: Forced Displacement in 2020. Available at: UNHCR.

17. United Nations Office for the Coordination of Humanitarian Affairs (OCHA). (2020). Humanitarian Needs Overview: Democratic Republic of the Congo. Available at: OCHA.

18. United Nations Security Council. (2020). Report on the Situation in Somalia.

19. World Bank. (2021). Political Stability and Absence of Violence/Terrorism: Overview. Available at: World Bank.

ELEVEN

THE ROLE OF THE AU AND REGIONAL ECONOMIC COOPERATION (RECS)

THE LATEST SURGE OF COUPS HAS PLACED THE RELEVANCE of the African Union and regional bodies on the duck of public opinion once again. These bodies are hard-pressed, responding to coups in their preponderance and frequency. No sooner have they meted sanctions, suspension, and ultimatum on one onslaught than they convened for another, putting a strain on their resolve and a hindrance on their collectivism and effectiveness. Since 2019, the flurry of attempts to usurp power in West Africa and the Sahel almost equals the number of moves made by incumbents to subvert democracy. Both military and non-military claims to power are making the list, the effect being invariably the same—liberal democracy is on stranglehold.

The AU comprises all 54 nations on the continent, with a mandate to foster unity and solidarity among Africans. It is supposed to delineate binding positions on governance and democracy with the aim of addressing issues of critical importance to Africa. Indeed, it has taken significant steps to instill democratic norms and deter unconstitutional changes of government (UCGs), or maybe not.

The myriad of challenges notwithstanding, the AU has developed policies which aim to put an end to power seizures, namely the Lome Declaration in 2000 and the African Charter on Democracy, Elections, and Governance. Regional Groupings have done likewise and, in few instances, have backed rhetoric with action. ECOWAS adopted a Protocol on Democracy and Good Governance (2001) while their counterparts in the East, Southern, and Central Africa developed similar instruments, all aimed at addressing unconstitutionality in its motley forms.

The role of these bodies, including the AU, evolved significantly from a teflon approach to domestic affairs to a more hands-on interest in nations' democratic trail. In Liberia and Sierra Leone, ECOWAS, through their military wing, ECOMOG intervened. In Sierra Leone, they toppled the junta regime and reversed the 1997 coup. In 2000, the newly christened AU (from OAU) carried its resolve against unconstitutionality further through policies and protocols, signaling a collective commitment to democratic governance.

With increased regional cooperation attested in efforts by SADC and ECOWAS, response became even more coordinated by the 2010s. The AU's Peace and Security Council and the establishment of the Panel of the Wise (PoW) underscored the commitment to mediation and conflict prevention. Mali and Burkina Faso spurred a unified response through collaborative efforts and rapid condemnation. The 2021 usurpations in Guinea also warranted swift condemnation, sanctions, and efforts towards the restoration of constitutional order.

Through its February (2022) Pledges, the AU examined the connections between human rights violations and the occurrences of insurgencies and coups in Africa and convened a summit to address five coups and growing insurrections in Cameroon, Mozambique, Somalia, Central African Republic, and the Sahel.

During its 16th extraordinary summit held in Malabo, Equatorial Guinea, the AU aimed to address the challenges posed by terrorism and UCGs. The Chairperson of the AU Commission, Moussa Faki Mahamat, commented on how security threats and usurpations are impeding Africa's progress toward its aspirations of becoming a peaceful and prosperous continent. By this point, the leadership of the AU had come to realize the urgent necessity for more assertive responses or stronger deterrent measures.

The heads of state gave their endorsement to the recommendations made by the Peace and Security Council (PSC) on strengthening the fight against terrorism and UCGs. This reflects a commitment at the continental level to the two threats and their resulting menace. However, the ISS/PSC report 2022 noted that this resolve does not indicate a substantial policy shift from the AU's typical response to these challenges. Despite the strong persuasion the theme carried-- 'robust response, deepening democracy and collective security', it was seen as a mere statement of solidarity to previous AU positions.

The report acknowledged 'significant financial and human resource restrictions' as a fetter to the Commission's operationalization. Conversely, it is crucial to know that in the large scheme of things, the continent's downward spiral on governance and democracy could be traced beyond logistical issues to more fundamental matters relating to the configuration of the AU instrument.

Perhaps the AU's biggest handicap is its lack of qualification for membership other than geography. Although the AU Charter emphasizes principles such as respect for sovereignty, democracy, and human rights among its member states, there are no specific criteria related to governance, democracy, or human rights for AU membership. In the GGA publication titled Coups in West Africa – a Critical Analysis of AU and ECOWAS responses (2022), Lileti Maluleke and Monique Bennett point out that unlike the EU (which has membership criteria based on certain democratic credentials—other than mere location in Europe) the AU action on unconstitutionality is not collective and unified.

The absence of specific governance criteria for AU membership means that countries with varying levels of democratic practices and respect for constitutional order can be part of the organization. Oftentimes, the organization gets to be chaired by a head of state who is on a default presidential term and whose human rights and governance credentials are deplorable. What leverage could Robert Mugabe, Omar Al-Bashir, Teodoro Obiang Nguema, and a host of others wield over any military junta? This inconsistency in governance standards undermines the AU's collective ability to promote and enforce democratic principles uniformly. While they adopt preventive diplomacy and administrative methods to forestall coups, little has been done to prevent peers from committing constitutional manipulations or actions that constitute democratic backsliding.

Burundi and South Sudan faced significant political turmoil and violence, including allegations of electoral irregularities, political repression, and armed conflict. The late President Pierre Nkurunziza of Burundi sought a controversial third term, leading to widespread protests and violence, and got away with it before he succumbed to cardiac arrest at the end of that term. Human Rights Watch disclosed on March 1, 2022, that South Sudan had incarcerated two government critics, Abraham Chol Akech and Kuel Aguer Kuel, in 2021. They remained in detention for a while without any indication of impending trials or other legal proceedings. Despite these challenges, the membership of these countries was never brought into question, nor were there considerations about sanctions.

One prevalent critique of regional policies aimed at preventing coups centers on irregular enforcement. Although regional organizations like ECOWAS and SADC have established protocols and frameworks, the application of measures such as sanctions and diplomatic isolation often lacks uniformity. Certain leaders accused of unconstitutional behavior may evade substantial repercussions, fostering perceptions of biased enforcement and eroding trust in regional interventions.

At the risk of overstating the need for democratic criteria for membership of the AU, the lack of it gives heads of state a palpable sense of entitlement and keeps the bar of representative democracy forever low. Autocratic regimes exploit the lack of membership criteria to gain legitimacy through mere AU participation. At the Sixty-third Ordinary Session of ECOWAS held in Guinea-Bissau, Sierra Leone's Julius Maada Bio, after purloining the most controversial election victory in his country's democratic history, was in attendance to reassert his legitimacy. Despite disapproval of the election results by the country's election watchdog, National Elections Watch (NEW), and credible international observers like the European Union Elections Observation Mission (EU EOM) and the Carter Center, the president was receiving a tap on the back by his peers at ECOWAS and even the UN. The UN Secretary General, through his Special Representative for West Africa and the Sahel, congratulated Bio for the *'successful'* conduct of the multi-tier elections, with no consideration towards concerns raised by credible institutions. Additionally, there is a general hesitancy to take strong measures, such as suspending membership or imposing sanctions, against member states found responsible for perpetuating unconstitutionality. This definitely undermines the organization's commitment to democratic governance and hinders its effectiveness in discouraging UCGs. It only serves to embolden coup leaders and undermine the AU's commitment to democratic principles.

Maluleke and Bennett (2022) argue that the African Union's dilemma reflects its involvement in two overlapping scenarios—addressing immediate security concerns while also advancing normative goals such as democracy and good governance. The opposing response to the situations in Chad and Mali emphasizes the vagaries of realpolitik, which the continental body is forced to deal with. Its decision not to slam sanctions on Chad or suspend it from the AU runs contrary to its principles on UCGs. Howbeit, justified for security considerations, the Chad decision casts a slur on the effectiveness of AU responses.

Furthermore, critiques arise concerning the restricted capability of the AU and regional organizations to enforce decisions and interventions adequately. When confronted with formidable military regimes like Chad, which has a strong sway over neighboring countries, enforcing compliance with the AU mandate poses a tall order. The absence of a robust enforcement mechanism, therefore, diminishes the effectiveness of sanctions and diplomatic measures, enabling illegitimate regimes to govern with impunity. Rectifying these criticisms necessitates continuous endeavors to bolster regional mechanisms, improve coordination, and guarantee prompt and consistent enforcement of measures to prevent and address coups.

Another criticism pertains to the delay in responding to coup incidents. The prolonged duration it takes for the AU and regional organizations to intervene in crises provides coup leaders with the opportunity to solidify their power and quell opposition before meaningful action is initiated. Delay is not only attested in the time it takes such bodies to make a position, it is also seen in the allowance of time given to military juntas to return their countries to democratic rule. Sometimes, a second coup erupts before an initial deadline expires. Mali and Burkina Faso are vivid illustrations.

In Guinea, the Transition Charter drafted by the junta is open-ended. Speculations abound whether the National Transition Council (CNT) will last for 24 or 36 months or even longer. ECOWAS expressed significant apprehension regarding the prolonged duration of the transition period. If 36 months, the lifespan of the (CNT) will almost equal a typical presidential term, not reckoning the pre-Charter period. Such delayed responses contribute to the entrenchment of illegitimate regimes, making it attractive to stage a putsch and challenging to restore democratic governance.

A huge damper to AU and regional bodies' credibility is the lack of proper accountability mechanisms concerning human rights abuses by heads of state. The perpetrators face inadequate consequences for their actions. This lack of accountability can have far-reaching implications, contributing to a culture of impunity within countries. When individuals responsible for such violations evade justice, it fosters a cycle of coups and political instability. Without effective accountability measures in place, there is little deterrent against future abuses of power, perpetuating a damaging cycle that undermines the rule of law and democratic institutions.

Dovetailing with the foregoing is inadequate preventive diplomacy efforts. The AU and regional bodies still face challenges in proactively preventing conflicts and political crises that could lead to coups. They have gained notoriety for rubber-stamping controversial elections and turning a blind eye to controversial constitutional amendments that spark uprisings. Maluleke and Bennett (2022) noted that in certain times, they are perceived as prioritizing power over justice. This approach is, at best, reactionary rather than proactive in addressing the root causes of political instability.

There is a seeming disconnect between the regional bodies and the AU in their legal framework. Instruments delineating the mandate of regional bodies hardly capitulate to the continental body. At the operational front, the disparity of positions is no less visible. During periods of political instability in Zimbabwe, the Southern African Development Community (SADC) took a more lenient approach compared to the AU. While the AU has been critical of Zimbabwe's electoral processes and human rights violations, SADC was more inclined towards non-interference and quiet diplomacy, leading to differences in their responses and priorities. Hence, there is a sense in which these bodies sometimes find it hard to defer to the AU in dealing with their member states.

A special look at the roles of these bodies in fostering good governance and promoting peace in their respective regions would lend further insight into democratic backsliding in Africa.

East African Community (EAC)

The East African Community (EAC) promotes economic, political, and social integration among its member states in East Africa. It traces its origins back to the 1960s when the first attempt at regional integration, known as the East African Community (1967-1977), was established. This initial community collapsed due to political differences among its founding members—Kenya, Tanzania, and Uganda.

In November 1999, the EAC was revived with the signing of the Treaty for the Establishment of the East African Community, which aimed to enhance cooperation and integration among its member states. The treaty was signed by the presidents of Kenya, Tanzania, and Uganda in Arusha. Since then, the EAC has expanded its membership to include Burundi and Rwanda, which joined in 2007.

The thrust of its establishment is to promote economic development, regional integration, trade, investment, cooperation in infrastructure, health, education, agriculture, and peace and security in the region. Operating through institutions like the Summit of EAC Heads of State, the Council of Ministers, the East African Legislative Assembly (EALA), and the East African Court of Justice (EACJ), the EAC implements policies and programs to achieve its objectives. Article 124 of The Treaty for the Establishment of the East African Community acknowledges the importance of peace and security, and despite challenges such as economic disparities, trade barriers, and political differences, the EAC has achieved some degree of regional integration, and is on course with establishment of a common market and customs union. It is working towards a monetary union and political federation, all with the goal of creating a politically stable, economically prosperous, and socially cohesive East Africa. In 2006, the EAC also embraced a Regional Strategy for Peace and Security.

Additionally, member states have signed a Memorandum of Understanding on Cooperation in Defence. Other important documents include the Protocol on an Early Warning and Response Mechanism and a Regional Framework for Conflict Prevention, Management, and Resolution. However, like many such instruments with other Regional Economic Cooperations (RECs) the operationalization is mostly a matter of rhetoric.

It is crucial to note that because of the varying levels of democratic governance among member states and their conflicting aspirations for dominance, there is no primary organization for security collaboration. The landscape is largely marred by governance deficits, including limitations on political freedoms, human rights abuses, and flawed electoral processes.

Conflicts and security threats, such as border disputes, ethnic tensions, and terrorism, pose significant challenges to regional stability. The EAC's ability to effectively address these security concerns is often constrained by limited resources, institutional capacity, and coordination among member states. Moreover, divergent national interests and political dynamics sometimes impede collective action on security issues, undermining the EAC's efforts to foster peace and stability in the sub-region.

A more potent attempt at combatting peace and security threats is found in the establishment, in 1996, of the Inter-Governmental Authority on Development (IGAD), with a more bloated circle of members. Djibouti, Eritrea, Ethiopia, Sudan, South Sudan, and Somalia were added to the existing members of the EAC.

It delineates various comprehensive approaches for implementation aimed at fostering a stable and secure environment within the region.

Yet the rate of democratic backsliding in the region remains appalling. Political instability is rife, not least regarding contested elections, government crackdowns on dissent, and power struggles. There are severe disputes over territorial boundaries, such as the conflict between Ethiopia and Sudan over the Al-Fashaga region. The region has been a target for terrorist groups such as Al-Shabaab, which operates primarily in Somalia but has also carried out attacks in neighboring countries like Kenya. Additionally, there are insurgent groups active in various parts of the region, such as in the Cabo Delgado province of Mozambique. Competition over natural resources, including land, water, and minerals, is a common driver of conflict. For instance, disputes over grazing land and water sources have led to violence between pastoralist communities in Kenya and Ethiopia.

According to the IGAD Peace and Security Strategy, most significant conflicts in the region stem from issues related to deficiencies in democratic governance, poverty, and inadequate development, as well as a political atmosphere characterized by intolerance and disregard for the rule of law. However, this position is more a lamentation of the problem than a resolve for action. Invariably, RECs' position on issues could not readily translate to action. Constraints facing these bodies are wide ranging.

Firstly, initiatives promoted by RECs and not member states, in so far as they relate to democratic governance, are hardly binding on heads of states, the majority of which are authoritarian in body and spirit. Neither EAC nor IGAD have the wherewithal to enforce compliance. The East African Standby Force (EASF) is fraught with logistical and operational challenges. Elowson and Albuquerque (2016) noted a key concern arising from the unclear process for authorizing EASF deployments. Despite the AU's control over decision-making concerning the African Standby Force, troop-contributing countries ultimately decide on deployments. Additionally, uncertainties persist regarding troop pledges from all ten EASF member states, leaving doubts about their commitment to honor these pledges during actual peace operations. For instance, no regional peacekeeping mission was deployed to South Sudan during the 2013 crisis, despite the EASF being on standby. There was hesitancy among member states to deploy the force due to political considerations and disagreements.

Secondly, the EASF faces logistical and operational challenges, including inadequate equipment, training, and infrastructure. For instance, during the EASF's deployment to support the African Union Mission in Somalia (AMISOM), logistical constraints hampered its effectiveness, leading to delays and limitations in its operations.

In essence, the East African Community has made limited progress in peace and security efforts, with political leaders often preferring to handle conflicts themselves rather than involving the EAC. Internal divisions among member states, based on economic integration, differing leadership styles, and regime types further hinder the organization's effectiveness. These divisions have made it challenging for the EAC to act decisively on peace and security issues, as evidenced by its inability to intervene effectively in political crises in member states.

Economic Community of West African States (ECOWAS)

ECOWAS has a similar configuration like the EAC. Established in 1975, it aims to foster economic integration and cooperation among West African states. Its institutions include the ECOWAS Commission, Parliament, and Court of Justice. ECOWAS operates in areas such as trade, infrastructure, peace, and security, with initiatives like the ECOWAS Trade Liberalization Scheme (ETLS), the West African Monetary Zone (WAMZ), and the ECOWAS Protocol on Free Movement of Persons, Residence, and Establishment. The EOWAS Monitoring Group (ECOMOG) constitutes its military wing. ECOMOG has built a reputation of deploying boots on the ground and reversing UCGs, boosting the interventionist efforts of ECOWAS and making it stand out among other RECs.

ECOMOG's intervention in Liberia during the first phase of the Liberian civil war (1989-1997) was one of its most notable operations. Troops were deployed to enforce a ceasefire agreement and oversee the disarmament process. The intervention helped end the civil war and paved the way for the election of Charles Taylor as president. In Sierra Leone, forces were deployed to support the government against rebel forces, particularly the Revolutionary United Front (RUF). During the ECOWAS Chairmanship of General Sani Abacha (himself a military ruler of Nigeria), ECOMOG played a significant role in the Armed Forces Revolutionary Council (AFRC) coup in Sierra Leone in 1997.

Following the overthrow of President Ahmad Tejan Kabbah by the AFRC, ECOMOG intervened to restore constitutional. Their forces, primarily composed of troops from Nigeria and other ECOWAS member states, engaged in military operations to counter the AFRC's control and enforce the return of the legitimate government. The intervention ultimately led to the defeat of the AFRC and the restoration of President Ahmad Tejan Kabbah to power. ECOMOG's intervention contributed to stabilizing the situation and facilitating peace negotiations.

In essence, ECOWAS has played a significant role in regional development and conflict resolution, epitomizing its commitment to promoting peace and stability in West Africa.

Ironically, one of the more potent RECs is now home to the largest continuous stretch of UCGs in the world, a sure indictment of its influence and usefulness. The Protocol on Democracy and Good Governance, endorsed in 2001, incorporates a framework to address unconstitutional changes of government. The protocol outlines guidelines for democratic governance within ECOWAS member states, encompassing aspects such as electoral processes, the independence of the judiciary, and the neutrality of security forces. However, despite all ECOWAS members being signatories to the protocol, some do not comply with these requirements, while the rest are merely complicit in their violations. Of course, instances of non-compliance vary, and they range from issues related to electoral processes and judicial independence to the conduct of security forces.

One can argue that the biggest culprit to democratic backsliding and ultimately to UCGs in West Africa is ECOWAS' failure to address blatant actions by heads of member states to amend constitutions and extend their term limits. Alpha Condé of Guinea and Alassane Ouattara of Côte d'Ivoire, manipulated constitutions to extend their time in power. Both instances were treated by the regional body with a feeble call for dialogue, justifying the critique that AU sanctions are only meant to target UCGs. Indeed, Condé did not survive his manipulations much long. The head of his Presidential guard deposed him in a coup and became head of state. Colonel Mamadi Dumbuya and his military cohort established the National Council for Reunification and Development to run the state, but not long before the ECOWAS cabal slammed their sanctions. These actions only raise concerns about democratic governance and adherence to constitutional norms in the region.

Apparently, the only test for constitutionality is the holding of elections. Presidential term limits, where in place, have been frequently circumvented through so-called constitutional coups. Heads of state have deftly manipulated social cleavages and played up fears of malevolent foreign interference to deflect popular pressure away from their illiberal rule. President Faure Gnassingbé of Togo declared victory in the 2020 presidential elections amid extensive protests. In Guinea, President Alpha Condé had pushed forward with a constitutional referendum aimed at prolonging the presidential term to six years, a move that could enable him to argue that the extant five-year term did not count. Meanwhile, in Benin, opposition parties opted to boycott the 2019 parliamentary elections, citing accusations of electoral fraud and the implementation of stringent security measures, which subsequently led to diminished voter participation.

Unlike unconstitutional actions perpetrated by heads of states, ECOWAS has promptly denounced coups and imposed sanctions on those responsible, demonstrating a steadfast dedication to anti-coup principles enshrined in the Protocol on Democracy and Good Governance. That notwithstanding, obstacles to the efficacy of sanctions reflect constraints of coercive diplomacy (Pape, 1997). The effectiveness of sanctions or coercion has been irregular due to diverse political contexts and unequal adherence to democratic values among member states. Moreover, like other RECs, ECOWAS faces challenges in converting condemnations into swift action of penalties and restoration.

Economic Community of Central African States (ECCAS)

ECCAS operates across multiple fronts in Central Africa, focusing on peace, security, democracy, regional integration, humanitarian assistance, and capacity building. Through mechanisms like the Central African Multinational Force (FOMAC), ECCAS addresses conflicts, supports democratic governance, and promotes economic cooperation. It facilitates dialogue, mediates disputes, and monitors elections while providing humanitarian aid and developmental support. Despite facing challenges, ECCAS plays a crucial role in fostering stability, development, and cooperation in the region.

A notable feature of the ECCAS configuration is its establishment of the Early Warning Mechanism of Central Africa (MARAC) to monitor and analyze potential threats to peace and security in the region. Tasked with gathering and analyzing data to avert conflicts, it comprises a central unit located at the ECCAS headquarters and decentralized units within member states tasked with collecting and analyzing information. While there may not be specific publicized instances attributed directly to MARAC, its work is often integrated into broader regional peace and security efforts. It includes issuing early warnings on electoral violence, conducting risk assessments on cross-border conflicts, providing mediation support for inter-communal disputes, offering capacity-building for early warning systems, and coordinating humanitarian assistance. These actions demonstrate MARAC's potential role in promoting peace, stability, and security in Central Africa through various means, including early warning, mediation, capacity building, and coordination efforts.

Central Africa may still rank among the most volatile regions in the continent, but the concept behind an early warning structure represents a proactive initiative for deterrence of UCGs. Implementation of its protocols is often a tall order based on a variety of considerations.

While MARAC plays a crucial role in conflict prevention efforts in Central Africa, its impact may be influenced by broader regional dynamics and the challenges inherent in addressing complex and multifaceted security threats.

Southern African Development Cooperation (SADC)

Like other RECs, SADC was the culmination of efforts to improve on existing structures for better performance. Established on August 17, 1992, it emerged from the Southern African Development Coordination Conference (SADCC) with a broader mandate encompassing economic, political, and social integration. Its operationalization involves a multi-faceted approach, with key institutions and mechanisms driving its agenda. At the apex is the SADC Summit, where Heads of State and Government convene annually to provide policy direction. The SADC Council of Ministers oversees implementation, while the Secretariat in Gaborone serves as the administrative arm. The SADC Tribunal, although suspended since 2010, serves as the judicial entity, and sectoral committees focus on specific areas of cooperation. The Regional Indicative Strategic Development Plan (RISDP) guides development efforts, while economic integration initiatives like the SADC Free Trade Area and protocols on trade and industrialization advance regional economic goals. Overall, SADC's operationalization reflects a concerted effort towards sustainable development, peace, and security in Southern Africa through regional cooperation and integration.

True to the intent and purpose of its formation, SADC's earliest priorities were hardly governance and security related. They were more focused on boosting economic ties between partner states. Objectives such as enhancing the rail and road systems connecting member states and aiming to lessen reliance on South African ports and transportation routes for imports and exports were high on their scale of preference. (Britannica, 2024). This was prior to the emergence of black rule in South Africa and its membership in 1994.

Southern Africa has experienced sporadic instances of political instability and challenges to democratic governance, although UCGs in the form of traditional military coups have been relatively rare compared to other regions. Zimbabwe experienced a coup in 2017 in the midst of political and economic tensions. Lesotho had an attempted coup, while Madagascar faced the coup in 2009. There are ongoing calls for democratic reforms in Eswatini. These cases highlight the region's struggles with political turmoil and contested elections, although UCGs have not been as prevalent as in some neighboring regions.

Through various means, including diplomatic engagement, peacekeeping missions, observer missions, sanctions, and capacity building, SADC has made interventions in conflicts in the region. In Lesotho, the biggest recipient of SDC interventions, the regional body deployed peacekeeping forces in 1998 and 2017 to address political tensions and violence. Additionally, SADC has frequently deployed observer missions to monitor elections in member states in an attempt to promote transparency and credibility in electoral processes. In Zimbabwe, SADC engaged in diplomatic efforts to mediate the political crisis following the 2017 de facto coup, facilitating negotiations for a peaceful transition of power. SADC's interventions aim to promote peace, stability, and democratic governance in the region, demonstrating its commitment to addressing conflicts and political challenges in Southern Africa. But, achieving democratic stability leaves much to be desired.

Arab Maghreb Union (AMU)

During the Treaty approval of the AMU in Marrakesh in 1989, member States consented to the coordination, harmonization, and rationalization of their policies and strategies to attain sustainable development across all sectors of human activities. Alongside the Treaty, the Marrakesh Summit endorsed the Solemn Declaration concerning the establishment of AMU and its agenda of work. Among its myriad objectives, it aspires to contribute to the "preservation of peace based on justice and equity."

The Arab Maghreb Union (AMU) has made strides since its establishment, though challenges have impeded its progress.

Notable instances include facilitating dialogue among member states on political, economic, and cultural fronts, resulting in initiatives like the Free Trade Agreement and the Arab Maghreb Union Investment Bank aimed at bolstering intra-regional trade. Infrastructure projects, such as the Trans-Maghreb Highway and the Trans-Maghreb Railway, have been initiated to enhance connectivity and integration, though progress has been hampered by political tensions, such as the Western Sahara conflict, hindering regional cooperation. Efforts to counter terrorism, illustrated by joint military exercises like "African Lion," demonstrate AMU's commitment to security collaboration. Despite these achievements, ongoing political discord, exemplified by the Morocco-Algeria rivalry, and economic disparities have stifled deeper integration and cooperation among member states, undermining the union's potential.

Indeed, AMU faces multiple threats to peace and stability. The Western Sahara conflict between Morocco and the Polisario Front has strained relations with Algeria, impacting regional stability. Such political disagreements and rivalries hinder cooperation and integration efforts. Security threats from terrorism, extremism, and transnational criminal networks, exemplified by groups like Al-Qaeda in the Islamic Maghreb (AQIM), contribute to instability. Economic disparities and trade barriers within the region further impede progress toward stability and prosperity.

The Arab Spring had a profound impact on AMU, disrupting political stability, exacerbating security challenges, and impeding progress toward regional integration and cooperation. The uprisings in member states such as Tunisia, Libya, and Egypt led to regime changes, internal instability, and shifts in foreign policy priorities, diverting attention and resources away from regional cooperation efforts. Increased security risks along borders, economic downturns, and delays in regional cooperation initiatives further hindered the AMU's functioning. The aftermath of the Arab Spring continues to influence the dynamics of the AMU, highlighting the complex interplay between domestic and regional factors in shaping Maghreb politics and cooperation. Without effective collaboration and resolution of underlying tensions, peace and stability in the Arab Maghreb Union will remain elusive.

Community of Sahel- Saharan States (CEN-SAD)

CEN-SAD's main goal is to establish a comprehensive economic union and remove any barriers hindering the unity of its member states, with the aim of fostering economic, cultural, political, and social integration. The updated treaty underscores two additional areas of collaboration: regional security and sustainable development. It has made notable strides since its inception, focusing on fostering regional cooperation, infrastructure development, humanitarian assistance, cultural exchange, and security cooperation among its member states. Through dialogue and collaboration, CEN-SAD has provided a platform for addressing common challenges and opportunities in the Sahel-Saharan region. Infrastructure projects, particularly in transportation and energy sectors, have aimed to enhance connectivity and facilitate trade and commerce among member states.

It has made significant strides in enhancing regional security through various initiatives. Joint military exercises and training programs have been conducted among member states to improve their capacity to combat security threats, exemplified by the joint military exercises held in Chad in 2019. Information sharing mechanisms have been established to facilitate early warning and response to security challenges, demonstrated by the creation of the CEN-SAD Regional Security Observatory. Counterterrorism strategies and action plans have been developed to address the threat of terrorism in the region, including measures to disrupt terrorist networks and strengthen border security, as seen in the joint efforts to combat Boko Haram and other extremist groups in the Sahel. Additionally, capacity-building programs have been implemented to enhance the capabilities of member states' security forces, exemplified by the training programs conducted by Algeria to enhance counterterrorism tactics.

CEN-SAD faces significant challenges in promoting regional security in the Sahel-Saharan region. Political instability, limited resources, transnational threats, border insecurity, and ethnic conflicts hinder efforts to address security challenges effectively. For instance, political instability in Libya creates a conducive environment for terrorist groups, while resource constraints in Niger affect border patrols, allowing illicit activities to thrive. Transnational threats like terrorism transcend borders, requiring coordinated responses. Weak border controls exacerbate security challenges, facilitating the movement of criminals and armed groups. Ethnic conflicts further destabilize member states, hindering efforts for peace and stability. Addressing these challenges necessitates concerted efforts to enhance political stability, strengthen security institutions, improve border management, and promote socioeconomic development. Without effective cooperation, the security situation in the region is likely to remain fragile.

Relationship with AU

The Regional Economic communities and the African Union share a vision rooted in the ideals of regional economic integration and continental unity. Established under the Abuja Treaty of 1991 and the 1980 Lagos Plan of Action, RECs were conceived as the building blocks for the broader African Economic Community (AEC). Their primary aim is to promote regional economic integration among member states within their respective regions and contribute to the overarching goal of an integrated and prosperous Africa.

However, the interplay between RECs and the AU is often fraught with challenges, particularly in the context of preventing unconstitutional changes of government (UCGs) and political instability. This delicate dance between regional and continental priorities shapes their effectiveness and coherence in addressing Africa's multifaceted crises.

Differing Priorities: RECs often prioritize regional concerns and interests over broader continental objectives. This divergence can lead to differing approaches in addressing political instability. For instance, the Southern African Development Community (SADC) and the Economic Community of West African States (ECOWAS) have distinct regional focuses, sometimes at the expense of the AU's broader mandates. This can create a fragmented landscape where regional stability is pursued in isolation, potentially undermining cohesive continental strategies.

Coordination Challenges: Limited coordination and communication between RECs and the AU can result in disjointed efforts to address political crises. The political turmoil in Burundi in 2015 exemplifies this challenge. Both the AU and the East African Community (EAC) attempted to mediate the crisis separately, leading to overlapping initiatives and a lack of coherence in their responses. The result was a fragmented approach that diluted the overall impact of mediation efforts.

Overlapping Mandates: The overlapping mandates of RECs and the AU in conflict prevention and resolution can lead to competition and duplication of efforts. In the case of the Democratic Republic of Congo (DRC), both the AU and the International Conference on the Great Lakes Region (ICGLR) were involved in mediation efforts. The overlap created coordination challenges and mixed messages to stakeholders, complicating the resolution process.

Resource Constraints: Resource limitations within RECs can hinder their ability to effectively address political instability and prevent UCGs. The constraint often strains relations with the AU, which may expect more robust action from regional bodies. The limited capacity to enforce decisions undermines the effectiveness of sanctions and diplomatic isolation, weakening collective influence and allowing coup leaders to exploit divisions.

Insufficient Accountability Mechanisms: The lack of robust accountability mechanisms for human rights abuses and unconstitutional changes of government contributes to a culture of impunity. This deficiency is evident in many AU member states, where perpetrators often face inadequate consequences for their actions. The resulting impunity fosters a cycle of coups and political instability, undermining efforts to build resilient democratic systems.

Inadequate Engagement with Civil Society: Engagement with civil society organizations and grassroots movements is often insufficient, limiting the inclusion of diverse perspectives and grassroots solutions in response strategies. Ignoring civil society can result in missed opportunities for bottom-up solutions and a comprehensive understanding of political dynamics. Effective engagement with civil society is crucial for developing holistic and sustainable responses to political crises.

Political Mediation Challenges: Political mediation efforts by RECs and the AU often face challenges such as a lack of trust between conflicting parties and difficulties in finding common ground for dialogue. These challenges hinder the success of mediation initiatives, perpetuating political crises and instability. Addressing these issues requires building trust, fostering dialogue, and creating inclusive mediation frameworks that consider the interests of all stakeholders.

Addressing Root Causes: Responses to coups and political instability often focus on immediate consequences rather than addressing the root causes of instability, such as governance, inequality, and socio-economic challenges. Failure to address these underlying issues leads to recurring crises and coups. A proactive approach to conflict prevention that tackles the root causes is essential for sustainable peace and stability in Africa.

Peace and Mediation Efforts in Sierra Leone: After the June 2023 elections in Sierra Leone, the African Union (AU), ECOWAS, and the Commonwealth played crucial roles in mediating between the government and the main opposition, which had boycotted parliament and local government over alleged electoral fraud. Their coordinated efforts facilitated a dialogue aimed at addressing the opposition's grievances and restoring political stability.

While these interventions highlight the potential for effective collaboration in promoting electoral justice and democratic governance, ongoing challenges in other regions underscore the need for consistent and cohesive approaches across Africa. Sierra Leone's experience demonstrates the importance of regional and continental coordination in achieving political reconciliation and stability.

References

1. African Union. (2007). African Charter on Democracy, Elections, and Governance.
2. African Union. (2021). Communiqué of the Peace and Security Council on the Situation in Guinea.
3. African Union. (2021). Report of the Chairperson of the African Union Commission on the Situation in Mali.
4. African Union. (2022). AU Panel of the Wise: Efforts in Conflict Mediation and Prevention.
5. African Union. (2022). Report on the February Summit: Addressing Insurgencies and Coups in Africa.
6. African Union. (2022). Sixteenth Extraordinary Summit of the African Union in Malabo, Equatorial Guinea.
7. African Union Commission (AUC). (2000). The Lome Declaration on the Framework for an OAU Response to Unconstitutional Changes of Government.
8. Britannica. (2024). Southern African Development Community (SADC).
9. Britannica. (2024). Southern African Development Community: African organization. Britannica.
10. Council on Foreign Relations (CFR). (2021). The Role of Regional Organizations in Addressing African Coups.
11. Economic Community of Central African States (ECCAS). (2006). ECCAS Early Warning Mechanism (MARAC).

12. Economic Community of West African States (ECOWAS). (2001). Protocol on Democracy and Good Governance.

13. ECOWAS. (1999). ECOWAS Protocol Relating to the Mechanism for Conflict Prevention, Management, Resolution, Peacekeeping, and Security.

14. ECOWAS. (2020). ECOWAS Communiqué on the Situation in Mali.

15. East African Community (EAC). (1999). Treaty for the Establishment of the East African Community.

16. Elowson, C., & Albuquerque, A. (2016). Challenges to Peace and Security in Eastern Africa: The role of IGAD, EAC and EASF. Studies in African Security.

17. Elowson, C., & Albuquerque, A. (2016). Challenges to the African Standby Force: The Case of the East African Standby Force. Swedish Defence Research Agency (FOI).

18. Freedom House. (2022). Nations in Transit: Decline in Democratic Governance in Africa.

19. Human Rights Watch. (2022). South Sudan: Free Detained Critics, End Repression.

20. Institute for Security Studies (ISS). (2021). The Efficacy of Sanctions in Addressing Unconstitutional Changes of Government in Africa.

21. Institute for Security Studies (ISS). (2022). The Peace and Security Council Report: Africa's Responses to Coups and Unconstitutional Changes of Government.

22. Inter-Governmental Authority on Development (IGAD). (2016). IGAD Peace and Security Strategy.

23. International Crisis Group. (2011). Somalia: The Transitional Government on Life Support.

24. International Crisis Group. (2022). Burkina Faso: Preventing a New Cycle of Instability.

25. Maluleke, L., & Bennett, M. (2022). Coups in West Africa – A Critical Analysis of AU and ECOWAS Responses. Good Governance Africa (GGA).

26. Pape, R. (1997). Why Economic Sanctions Do Not Work. MIT Press Direct.

27. Southern African Development Community (SADC). (2006). SADC Regional Indicative Strategic Development Plan (RISDP).

28. United Nations. (2021). UN Secretary-General's Report on Peace and Security in Africa.

29. United Nations High Commissioner for Refugees (UNHCR). (2021). Global Trends: Forced Displacement in 2020.

30. United Nations Office for the Coordination of Humanitarian Affairs (OCHA). (2020). Humanitarian Needs Overview: Democratic Republic of the Congo.

31. World Bank. (2021). Political Stability and Absence of Violence/Terrorism: Overview.

POTENTIAL HOTSPOTS

THE DYNAMICS OF MILITARY INVOLVEMENT IN AFRICAN politics remain a critical concern for democratic governance. Perverted processes are being regularized to fit into the democratic construct, albeit with enough room for concern. Other elements of anxiety are primordially present but addressed in muted tones. Together, these constitute hotspots that need a sustainable fix.

Constitutions

Constitutional instruments are sometimes the biggest sources of controversy and recipe for usurpations. Constitutions drafted by civilian administrations may exhibit either oversight of the proclivities of the military or embody potential loopholes for exploitation by those with actual might. The constitution of Egypt historically granted extensive powers to the military, including jurisdiction over civilians in certain cases. This scenario is common, where military leaders have metamorphosed into civilian presidents. In Egypt, under Hosni Mubarak, a former air force commander, the military exerted significant influence over political decision-making and undermined democratic governance. They enjoyed significant privileges under the constitution.

Constitutions have not always clearly delineated the role of the military in governance, leading to ambiguity and potential for military intervention in power politics. Despite the multitude of experiences by states for instance, constitutions hardly expressly forbid the intervention of people in uniform in governance. Ironically, military junta have invariably cited protecting the constitution as justification for their putsch. An express provision otherwise would bar them from finding constitutional justification for their unconstitutionality. Nigeria would have addressed military tendencies far better and probably altered a protracted history of military nuisance. In essence, a military leader would be hard-pressed to look for justification elsewhere if the grand nom to which all elements of the state pivot clearly bars them from seizing power by any means.

Additionally, these constitutions may inadvertently create loopholes that can be exploited by military leaders seeking to assert control. For instance, provisions related to national security or emergency powers may grant broad authority to the military, potentially undermining civilian authority and democratic principles. In Zimbabwe, for example, the military played a significant role in the ousting of long-time ruler Robert Mugabe in 2017, leading to concerns about the military's influence over the country's political transition.

Civilian Rule by all Means

Military leaders, in a bid to gain legitimacy, have fashioned a way to transition to civilian leadership positions through democratic processes. While this may appear to signal a move towards civilian rule, it sure is a red flag for continued influence of the military in governance. In Egypt, former military general Abdel Fattah el-Sisi assumed the presidency in 2014 after leading a military coup against the elected government. Despite becoming a civilian President through elections, el-Sisi's presidency has been marked by authoritarian practices and a crackdown on political dissent, raising questions about the military's commitment to democratic norms.

Thus, civilianization has been a recurring theme in the continent's political landscape. The trend often arises from military coups or periods of authoritarian rule, where military leaders assume power and subsequently seek to legitimize their authority through elections or constitutional means. While some military leaders turned civilian presidents have overseen successful transitions to democracy, others have perpetuated authoritarian practices and undermined democratic institutions. Robert Mugabe, a former guerrilla leader who led Zimbabwe to independence in 1980, civilianized and later perpetrated widespread human rights abuses, electoral fraud, and economic mismanagement, leading to the country's economic collapse and international isolation.

Hence, it wouldn't be unexpected if over half of the recent surge of military leaders in Africa chose to participate as civilian candidates in forthcoming elections. The transition to civilian roles often entices military takeovers and poses a danger area that both the AU and regional bodies need to tackle. Guinea's Transition Charter explicitly prohibits individuals from the current CNT from running in the next democratic elections. Therefore, a comprehensive reassessment of the military's role in governance structures necessitates the inclusion of anti-civilianization clauses within AU and REC protocols.

Elections Howbeit

The interpretation of democracy by both the AU and regional organizations has been narrowed down primarily to conducting elections, often overlooking broader issues like term limits and respect for democratic institutions (Akum et al, 2020). Coups may be symptomatic of deeper issues, such as leaders' refusal to peacefully step down, citing security concerns, whether genuine or fabricated. These challenges contribute to political instability and hinder democratic transitions, creating fertile ground for coups to occur. The ECOWAS Protocol on Democracy and Good Governance, which provides that "every accession to power must be made through free, fair and transparent elections," is only paying ink-service to an increasingly volatile situation. All leaders need to do is prove that they were elected through the ballot box, and then they are deemed legitimate. Leonie Mills (2022) describes this as a 'narrow framing of democracy.' It occasions an erosion of electoral integrity, weakens the foundation of democracy, and constitutes a recipe for disorder. This situation ties in with third term bids, another common obstacle to democratic transitions. Leaders, sometimes citing either genuine or fabricated security concerns, refuse to peacefully relinquish power. They blatantly amend constitutions to perpetuate themselves to third terms, to the muted glare of regional organizations. An arrangement characterized by serious application of protocols would have suspensions and sanctions visited on these actions, for they are no less unconstitutional as usurpations. Some leaders perpetrate multiple amendments to cement their perpetual stay in power.

Yoweri Museveni, who has been in power since 1986, has amended Uganda's constitution multiple times to extend his stay in office. In 2005, the presidential term limit was repealed to avoid further recourse to the constitution every now and again. This allowed Museveni to run for a third term in 2006 and subsequent terms thereafter. Paul Kagame and the late Pierre Nkurunziza, in 2015, executed controversial amendments to their countries' constitutions to eke out third-term endorsements. Despite massive condemnations from human rights groups and opposition politicians as well as riots, in the case of Burundi, they secured their bid.

Population Boom

The African population is projected to grow significantly by 2050, necessitating the creation of millions of decent jobs annually to accommodate this growth. However, limited access to education and skills gaps impede the continent's ability to capitalize on its demographic dividend and harness the potential of its youthful workforce.

A considerable portion of the global workforce is projected to reside in Africa by 2030. Going by current growth rate, the continent will experience a demographic dividend that drives the continent's progress. Nonetheless, it is clear that without strategic investments in policy and education, tapping into this dividend and leveraging the benefits of accommodating a significant portion of the world's workforce could present considerable challenges. (World Economic Forum 2016). Many face restricted access to university education, while those who complete school struggle for gainful placement.

In perspective, Africa's current tertiary enrollment rate

averages a mere 7%. Contrasting this, the United States exhibits a tertiary enrollment rate exceeding 72%, while China's stands at around 30%. This discrepancy suggests that even if Africa were to construct 200 new universities equivalent to Harvard's size annually for the next 15 years, it would still face challenges in closing its existing skills gap with India and would only marginally impact the prospects of its youth population. High youth unemployment rates were a significant factor in the Tunisian revolution of 2010-2011. Frustrated by limited economic opportunities and political repression, many young Tunisians took to the streets in protests that eventually led to the overthrow of President Zine El Abidine Ben Ali.

Moreover, Competition over scarce resources, such as land, water, and food, could escalate into conflicts, particularly in regions where resources are already scarce or unevenly distributed. These conflicts can further exacerbate instability and hinder economic development. South Sudan and the Delta Region of Nigeria will pale in the face of the next possible eruptions. The new media will have handed the people's consciousness about every facet of their rights in their palms. Just a tap on the palm will afford them the knowledge of every mineral and attendant royalties that are due to them.

Migration

Africans opt for perilous journeys to seek economic opportunities abroad rather than facing unemployment and economic challenges at home. Sometimes, they move to other countries in the continent, where they either settle or transit en route to some destination in Europe. This trend of migration is a trouble spot in foreign policy circles. Nations' migration policies and their treatment of migrants have become a critical subject in their democratic scorecard and a determiner of their perceived level of political stability. The tell-tale dynamics of migration in Africa speak volumes about the democratic landscape in the continent.

In North Africa, leaders with diminished democratic credibility have suddenly contrived a means to deflect attention from their style of governance by adopting stringent migration policies to appease European nations. In March 2024, the European Union unveiled a 7.4 billion-euro ($8 billion) aid package for Egypt due to the latter's stance on migration to European territories. The agreement, signed in Cairo by President Abdel Fattah el-Sissi and European Commission President Ursula von der Leyen, sparked criticism from human rights organizations due to Egypt's track record on human rights. The assistance package comprises both grants and loans to be disbursed over the course of the next three years.

This comes in addition to Egypt, the most populous Arab nation, being declared a strategic partner. El-Sissi tightening or even closing of the Egyptian frontier to migrants using the country as a transit point to Europe earned him the goodwill of nations on the other side of the Mediterranean. Countries in Europe plagued by the migrant crisis are inclined to ignore the erosion of democratic principles from any nation that helps them stem the rising tide of migrants. The deal also comes at a time of increasing concerns about the potential for Israel's anticipated ground offensive in Rafah, Gaza's southernmost town, to trigger a mass movement of people into Egypt's Sinai Peninsula. The ongoing Israel-Hamas conflict, now in its sixth month, has led to over a million individuals seeking refuge in Rafah. (Associated Press, 2024).

Amid this geopolitical maneuvering, consider the plight of Ibrahim, a young man from Sudan. Fleeing violence and economic despair, he journeys north, hoping to cross into Europe from Egypt. However, with the Egyptian frontier closed, Ibrahim finds himself stranded in a border town. The promised land of safety and opportunity remains out of reach as he confronts the harsh reality of being stuck in a country tightening its grip on migrants.

Ibrahim's story reflects broader regional trends. In Tunisia, President Kais Saied has leveraged his crackdown on migrants to secure a 1-billion-euro loan package from the European Union, influenced by Italian Prime Minister Giorgia Meloni. This financial support came despite Tunisia's stifling of dissent and human rights abuses. Meloni did not only influence the EU to provide this package, she also pressured the IMF to make good on an initial promise of nearly $2bn in help. (Aljazeera.com, 2023). Migrants like Ibrahim, aiming to reach Europe through Tunisia, now face increased obstacles and hostility.

Mohamed Ould Ghazouani, a former military junta in Mauritania, is another addition to the list of dictators getting the carrot from Europe. Reports of arbitrary arrests and detentions of political opponents and activists characterize his administration. Additionally, issues such as discrimination against certain ethnic groups, particularly Haratines and Afro-Mauritanians, and the persistence of slavery and caste-based discrimination in the country have been highlighted by international human rights observers. That notwithstanding, the EU unveiled a 210-million-euro aid package aimed at assisting Mauritania in combating human smugglers and preventing migrant boats from departing, amidst a significant increase in the number of individuals attempting the perilous journey across the Atlantic from West Africa to Europe. (Associated Press, 2024).

These leaders are receiving a tap on the back for so much as playing by the rules of Western powers despite oppressing their own people. Their poor democratic credentials only bear an inverse proportionality to their level of appreciation from the so-called proponents of democracy. The EU rhetoric of promoting democracy and human rights runs out of kilter with their action in the continent, a fact that should dawn on Africans. It is surely not a matter to curse and wail but a phenomenon to brood over, for it is a geopolitical reality that nations prioritize their interests beyond principles and that morality and ethics in politics are but patents of the major powers. You manifest ethics when they deem it so. This degree of incentivization of African autocrats only serves to embolden other backsliders in the continent and poses a problem for AU and regional efforts to consolidate democracy and good governance.

An equally volatile situation is the degree of xenophobia displayed in some countries in the continent. In South Africa, xenophobic violence targeting migrants from other African countries, especially Nigeria, has erupted periodically, leading to loss of life and displacement. Not only that, in countries facing economic challenges, competition for resources and jobs can exacerbate tensions between migrants and host communities. In Zimbabwe, for instance, economic hardship led to tensions between Zimbabwean citizens and migrants from neighboring countries, particularly in the informal sector. Such competition for scarce resources can fuel resentment and instability. It surely poses a challenge over building continental consensus to safeguard fundamental principles of human rights and democracy.

Migration can also strain relations between neighboring countries, leading to diplomatic tensions and even conflict. The movement of refugees and migrants across borders has strained relations between countries in the Great Lakes region, such as Burundi, Rwanda, and Tanzania. Disputes over refugee flows and border security have occasionally escalated into diplomatic standoffs and border skirmishes.

The treatment of migrants in detention centers and refugee camps often raises human rights concerns. In Libya, migrants attempting to reach Europe are often subjected to arbitrary detention, extortion, and abuse by traffickers and authorities. Such violations not only contravene international human rights standards but also contribute to instability and insecurity in the region.

Thus, it is evident that with the rate of backsliding in democracy and human rights, the call of James Aggrey, an educator who believed that Africans should receive a college education abroad and return to effect change, will continue to remain a challenge. Tackling these challenges necessitates confronting deep-seated grievances that have been overlooked and often exacerbated by ineffective and sometimes oppressive governance prevalent across the African continent.

France

Recently, French President Emmanuel Macron has made overtures that appear to revisit the relationship between his country and its former colonies in the continent. His moves reflect a desire to rebrand his country's longstanding image as an exploiter of francophone Africa. He has increased support to the continent, maintained French troops in the Sahel to combat jihadist militants, reinforced ECOWAS in its democratic efforts, and initiated the repatriation of cultural artifacts taken during colonial conflicts (CNN.com, 2021). The aim is to expand engagement beyond traditional modes of cooperation. At the same time, the rising influence of other powers like China means Africa has elsewhere to look for strategic partnerships. This occasions the need for our continent to be approached more differently. Yet it does not seem to quell the growing level of disenchantment against France, especially among young Africans.

Among colonial powers, France maintains a more profound degree of influence over its former colonies, particularly in areas like politics, economics, and military affairs. Controversies surrounding its involvement in various facets of life in its former colonies have long held sway. In shaping their political landscape, France frequently involves itself (if not meddles) in their domestic affairs to protect its interests or support friendly governments. Economically, many of these countries remain closely linked to France through trade agreements, currency arrangements, and investment ties. Additionally, France maintains a military presence in several African countries, providing security assistance and training to local forces while also using its military presence to protect its strategic interests in the region.

One of the more contentious issues about French foreign policy with Africa is the currency arrangement between France and its former colonies. These countries have the CFA franc as a common currency. There are two separate versions of it—one used in West African countries (XOF) and another used in Central African countries (XAF). These currencies are pegged to the French Franc, now the euro, with a fixed exchange rate maintained by the French Treasury. Additionally, the former colonies are required to deposit a portion of their foreign exchange reserves into the French Treasury as a guarantee. The currencies get monetary stability for these countries but also limits their control over their monetary policy and sometimes constrains their economic sovereignty.

Politically, the French government has endorsed flawed elections and controversial third-term bids to preserve diplomatic relations with autocratic leaders, as seen in Chad in 2006. In the

Republic of Congo, President Denis Sassou Nguesso changed the constitution in 2015 to remove term limits, allowing him to run for a third consecutive term. Another instance is in Burkina Faso, where President Blaise Compaoré attempted to amend the constitution in 2014 to extend his 27-year rule, sparking mass protests and ultimately leading to his resignation. Guinea's Alpha Condé successfully changed the constitution in 2020 to allow him to run for a third-term despite widespread protests and accusations of undermining democratic principles. In Ivory Coast, President Alassane Ouattara similarly sought a third term in 2020, citing a controversial interpretation of the constitution's term limit provisions. In all of these attempts, France has not been able to rid itself of accusations of complicity or tacit support to the leaders due to historical ties, but above all, economic interests.

Before these latest instances of complicity, France's failure to support civil society movements in the north and Gulf states and the eventual eruption of the Arab Spring in 2010 attracted massive vilification. To salvage the ruin, Macron is actively seeking avenues to establish fresh collaborations with non-state entities in Africa.

Macron's recent approach to African diplomacy reflects a departure from traditional alliances with authoritarian regimes, particularly in Central African countries like Cameroon, Gabon, and the Republic of the Congo, which have increasingly turned to China (Cohen, 2022). France now aims to use its influence to support the aspirations of African citizens and prepare for impending leadership transitions as several long-serving presidents in the region approach old age. However, its failure to tackle unconstitutionality in the 2020s, as well as its meddling in their security and military affairs is irksome in the eyes of the citizens Macron intends to appease.

In November 2021, an investigative report by Disclose, based on leaked military intelligence documents and whistleblower revelations, exposed France's approval of a covert intelligence program aiding the Egyptian government. Despite being portrayed as counterterrorism cooperation, the program primarily facilitated extrajudicial killings of border crossers between Libya and Egypt. Officers involved admitted the program did little to address terrorism.

Additionally, France's withdrawal from Mali, ending Operation Barkhane in the country, is prominent among the panoply of reasons for the vilification of the former colonial power in the continent. In a bid to counter jihadist insurgency and prevent the toppling of the Malian government, Mali requested military support from France. The French military entered Mali in early 2013 and, without delay, reclaimed control of the northern region. France and its allies bolstered the capabilities of the Malian military and deployed advanced air and ground technologies. The mission was conducted in collaboration with five nations, all of which are former French colonies situated across the Sahel region—Burkina Faso, Chad, Mali, Mauritania, and Niger. In addition to Mali, it established two more permanent bases in Chad and Niger.

The contentious pullout from Mali, coupled with other counterinsurgency challenges, left the country prone to numerous civilian and military casualties, with over 2.5 million people displaced (Harvard International Review (HIR) 2023). Armed factions persist in launching severe assaults against the militaries combatting them and, increasingly, against civilians in the Sahel. Malians harbor a considerable degree of resentment about France for abandoning them during a period of heightened insecurity. While most French citizens consider Françafrique, France's historical sphere of economic, political, and military influence in its former colonies, as a relic of the past, many Malians still grapple with the adverse effects of this system (HIR, 2023).

The sad trend, though, is that France, for all its complicated stature in the continent, is in no hurry to back down on its operations. This presents a quandary when compared with the role of other colonial powers like Britain. The latter has, to a large extent, been measured in dealing with former territories and has maintained more fidelity with democratic principles.

The Bretton Woods

The Bretton Woods institutions, comprising the International Monetary Fund (IMF) and the World Bank, pose significant challenges to Africa's governance and economic progress. Their influence, intended to promote stability and growth, often constrains the continent's ability to develop autonomously. Loans and assistance from these institutions come with stringent conditions, such as austerity measures and structural adjustments, which are often unsuitable for the socio-economic contexts of African nations. This inflexible, one-size-fits-all approach can stifle unique development paths necessary for sustainable growth.

Memories from Nairobi, Kenya, of the 1990s highlight the negative impact of Structural Adjustment Programs (SAPs). These programs led to the closure of thriving industries and a reduction in public services, resulting in widespread job losses and social unrest. The legacy of SAPs is a cautionary tale of external economic intervention gone wrong.

In many other countries, the burden of debt from grand infrastructure projects financed by international loans is heavy. The government's focus on debt repayment, as dictated by the IMF and World Bank, has led to cuts in social spending, leaving schools and hospitals under-resourced and development dreams unfulfilled. This debt crisis has turned the aspirations of a generation into a struggle for survival.

Privatization of essential services, such as water, electricity, and healthcare, often results in higher costs and reduced access for the poor. Intended to improve efficiency, privatization has instead increased hardships for many, making improved services a privilege for the few.

In a typical local market in Africa, the challenges of trade liberalization loom. While intended to open markets and attract foreign investment, these policies often expose domestic industries to overwhelming competition from developed countries, undermining local producers and sustainable industry development.

In Addis Ababa, Ethiopia, the limitations of representation within the Bretton Woods institutions are evident. African leaders' voices are often muted in decision-making processes, and policies frequently do not reflect the continent's priorities. This disconnect hinders the effective addressing of Africa's unique economic challenges.

Reliance on external financial institutions fosters a dependency that stifles innovation. Bound by lenders' conditions, African countries struggle to develop and implement indigenous solutions to their economic challenges, perpetuating cycles of poverty and limiting autonomous progress.

These contemporary scenarios across Africa illustrate the profound and often detrimental impact of the Bretton Woods institutions on governance and economic development. The conditionalities, structural adjustments, and debt crises imposed by these institutions have left deep imprints on the continent's socio-economic landscape. As Africa moves forward, it must prioritize its unique needs and aspirations, fostering development from within and seeking alternatives that align with its diverse realities. Despite the challenges, the spirit of resilience and innovation in Africa holds the promise of a brighter future.

References

1. Akum, F. N., Chinyere, A. O., & Mbaku, J. M. (2020). African Leaders' Refusal to Step Down and Its Impact on Democratic Governance. Brookings Institution.

2. Akum, F.; Djilo, F. & Handy, P. (2020). What causes Africa's coups? That is the question. Institute for Security Studies (ISS).

3. Al Jazeera. (2023). Tunisia secures €1bn EU loan despite human rights concerns.

4. Aljazeera.com (2023). Why is the EU offering Tunisia a financial assistance package? Aljazeera.

5. Associated Press. (2024). EU offers €210 million aid to Mauritania for anti-smuggling efforts.

6. Associated Press. (2024). EU unveils €7.4 billion aid package for Egypt to curb migration.

7. Cohen, C. (2022). Will France's Africa Policy Hold Up? Carnegie Endowment for International Peace.

8. Cohen, J. (2022). Macron's Pivot to Africa: France's New Diplomatic Strategy. Foreign Policy.

9. CNN. (2021). Macron's New Africa Strategy: Rebranding France's Colonial Legacy.

10. CNN.com (2021). France returns 26 looted artifacts and artworks to Benin.

11. Disclose. (2021). Leaked Documents Reveal France's Covert Intelligence Program in Egypt.

12. ECOWAS. (2001). Protocol on Democracy and Good Governance.

13. Freedom House. (2022). Nations in Transit: Decline in Democratic Governance in Africa.

14. Harvard International Review (HIR). (2023). The Legacy of Françafrique in Mali and France's Withdrawal.

15. International Crisis Group. (2011). Somalia: The Transitional Government on Life Support.

16. International Crisis Group. (2022). Burkina Faso: Preventing a New Cycle of Instability.

17. King, I. (2023). How France Failed Mali: The End of Operation Barkhane. Harvard International Review.

18. Magdy, S. (2024). The European Union announces an $8 billion aid package for Egypt as concerns mount over migration. Associated Press.

19. Mills, L. (2022). Narrow Framing of Democracy in Africa. Democracy in Africa Blog.

20. Mills, L. (2022). The Effectiveness of ECOWAS in Mitigating Coups in West Africa. ipinst.org.

21. Pape, R. (1997). Why Economic Sanctions Do Not Work. MIT Press Direct.

22. Stahler, S. (2022). New Erosion: Democratic Backsliding in South Sudan. Democratic Erosion Consortium (DEC).

23. Swaniker, F. (2016). Great leaders aren't born – they're made. And Africa is showing us how. World Economic Forum.

24. United Nations High Commissioner for Refugees (UNHCR). (2021). Global Trends: Forced Displacement in 2020.

25. United Nations Office for the Coordination of Humanitarian Affairs (OCHA). (2020).

Humanitarian Needs Overview: Democratic Republic of the Congo.

26. Vantage with Palki Sharma (03/18/2024). YouTube.

27. World Bank. (2021). Political Stability and Absence of Violence/Terrorism: Overview.

28. World Economic Forum. (2016). The Future of Jobs and Skills in Africa.

THIRTEEN

EMERGING TRENDS

Africa, often overlooked in global narratives, is undergoing a profound transformation that challenges conventional perceptions. Amidst this shift, emerging trends in African politics are shaping the continent's future trajectory. The narrative of "Africa Rising" encompasses thriving economies, a burgeoning educated workforce, and vibrant expressions of entrepreneurial and cultural creativity. However, this narrative is not a sudden emergence but rather a gradual evolution, debunking the notion of Africa as a stagnant or ignored continent.

Two divergent futures loom on the horizon, each contingent upon the choices made by Africa's youth, who are increasingly empowered with technocratic skills. In one scenario, these young individuals embrace leadership as a vehicle for altruistic service, guided by ethical wisdom and a sense of collective responsibility. Conversely, in an alternative scenario, they may utilize their agency to perpetuate inequality, reinforcing entrenched post-colonial governance practices through sophisticated and resilient means.

As we delve into the emerging trends in African politics, it becomes evident that the continent's trajectory hinges on the choices made by its burgeoning youth population. The direction they choose will not only shape the future of Africa but also resonate globally, influencing perceptions and narratives about the continent's role in the 21st century. Several emerging trends are shaping African politics, reflecting evolving dynamics within the continent. Here are some notable trends:

Youth Mobilization and Leadership: African youth are increasingly asserting their political influence through activism, protests, and participation in electoral processes. For example, the #EndSARS protests in Nigeria in 2020, led predominantly by young people, demanded an end to police brutality and systemic corruption, highlighting youth dissatisfaction with the status quo.

Digital Transformation: The proliferation of digital technologies and social media platforms is revolutionizing political communication, activism, and mobilization in Africa. Social media platforms like Twitter, Facebook, and WhatsApp are being used to mobilize and organize political movements, disseminate information, monitor elections in real time, and hold governments accountable. Digital activism and online advocacy have become powerful tools for civic engagement and political change. The emergence of deep fake technology has only further escalated the phenomenon.

Regional Integration: African countries are deepening regional cooperation and integration to address common challenges and harness collective resources. Examples include the African Continental Free Trade Area (AfCFTA), which aims to boost intra-African trade and economic growth by creating a single market for goods and services.

Women's Political Participation: There is a growing push for gender equality and women's empowerment in African politics, with an increasing number of women holding leadership positions and participating in decision-making processes. For instance, Ethiopia appointed Sahle-Work Zewde as its first female president in 2018, marking a significant milestone for women's representation in African politics.

Environmental Sustainability: African countries are increasingly prioritizing environmental sustainability and climate resilience in their political agendas. For example, countries like Kenya and Rwanda have implemented ambitious green energy initiatives and conservation programs to mitigate climate change and protect natural resources.

Democratic Backsliding: Despite progress in democratization, some African countries are experiencing democratic backsliding, characterized by erosion of democratic norms, suppression of political dissent, and manipulation of electoral processes. Examples include the political crisis in Zimbabwe, where contested elections and human rights abuses have undermined democratic governance.

Security Challenges: Africa continues to grapple with security challenges, including terrorism, insurgency, and intercommunal violence. Instances include the ongoing conflict in the Sahel region, where jihadist groups like Boko Haram and Al-Qaeda operate, posing significant security threats to the region's stability.

Urbanization and Migration: Rapid urbanization and internal migration are reshaping the demographic and political landscapes of African countries. Urban areas are becoming hubs of economic activity, social change, and political contestation. Migration within and between countries is fueling demographic shifts, cultural exchange, and political tensions, influencing electoral dynamics and policy priorities.

Environmental Sustainability: Climate change and environmental degradation are emerging as significant political issues in Africa. Countries are grappling with the impacts of climate change, including extreme weather events, food insecurity, and displacement. There is growing awareness of the need for sustainable development practices, renewable energy solutions, and conservation efforts to mitigate environmental risks and promote resilience.

Using LGBTQ Legislation to Divert Attention

In the west end of Freetown, my childhood friend Abdul Karim lived a life shadowed by prejudice and discrimination due to his sexual orientation. From childhood, he was never attracted to girls, but to appear regular to his us and society, he maintained a girlfriend named Martha while also forming a close relationship with a boyfriend, Kelvin Boyle. On July 15, 2021, Abdul Karim's hidden life was dramatically exposed, forcing him into exile.

On that fateful day, Martha visited Abdul Karim's residence unexpectedly and, without knocking, stumbled upon him and Kelvin in an intimate moment. Overwhelmed by shock, Martha screamed and ran out to seek help from the neighbors. The community quickly responded to her distress call and rushed to Abdul Karim's house. There, they found Abdul Karim and Kelvin in a compromising position. Fueled by anger and prejudice, the mob descended upon them, subjecting the couple to physical abuse.

As the mob's rage intensified, Abdul Karim managed to break free and fled, leaving Kelvin at the mercy of the angry crowd. In Sierra Leone, same-sex relationships are considered taboo, especially in certain communities and public opinion often turns violent before the police can intervene. In the aftermath of the incident, my friend found himself living in constant fear and discomfort. His friends in the neighborhood, once close allies, distanced themselves from him out of shame and embarrassment. To make matters worse, the police began searching for him, forcing him to go into hiding.

Traumatized and unsafe, Abdul Karim eloped through neighboring Guinea to France, where he is currently seeking asylum. Reflecting on this, it is evident that if the energy used to chase people with different social or sexual orientations were directed towards holding corrupt politicians accountable, Africa would be better off. Our politicians exploit societal prejudices to divert attention from their governance failures.

Poor leadership does not only disenfranchise geographically distinct communities but also targets socially different groupings as scapegoats for societal malaise. African leaders often use legislation against LGBTQ individuals to deflect attention from their governance failures or excesses. By focusing public attention on issues related to sexual orientation and gender identity, these leaders rally support from conservative segments of society, distract from pressing socio-economic challenges, and consolidate power.

In 2014, Uganda's President Yoweri Museveni signed into law the Anti-Homosexuality Act, imposing harsh penalties, including life imprisonment, for homosexual acts. Critics argued that Museveni, facing internal dissent and corruption allegations, used the legislation to divert attention from these issues and appeal to conservative elements within Ugandan society. Further scrutiny came with the 2009 Ugandan efforts to institute the death penalty for homosexuality. Museveni claimed that "European homosexuals are recruiting in Africa," diverting attention from governance issues by inflaming cultural and religious sentiments. In March 2023, the Ugandan Parliament passed the Anti-Homosexuality Act, which criminalizes consensual same-sex conduct with penalties up to life imprisonment, imposes 10-year prison terms for attempted homosexual acts, and prescribes the death penalty for "aggravated homosexuality."

Similarly, Nigeria's Same-Sex Marriage Prohibition Act of 2014 criminalized same-sex marriage and public displays of affection between same-sex couples. President Goodluck Jonathan signed the bill amidst criticism of his administration's handling of security challenges, such as the Boko Haram insurgency. The timing of the legislation suggested it was intended to divert attention from these pressing security concerns.

Zimbabwean leaders, including former President Robert Mugabe and his successor Emmerson Mnangagwa, have also used anti-LGBTQ rhetoric to bolster their political standing. Amidst economic challenges and allegations of electoral fraud, these leaders have employed inflammatory language against LGBTQ individuals to appeal to conservative sentiments and deflect criticism.

In general, African leaders are utilizing legislation targeting LGBTQ individuals as a means of diverting attention from governance shortcomings. By exploiting societal divisions and appealing to conservative values, these leaders maintain their grip on power and evade accountability for socio-economic and political challenges.

The Tendency to be Swayed by Economic Growth Despite Political Instability

As an asylee living far from Africa, I am deeply touched by the negative trend of economic growth entwined with political instability, which often motivates unconstitutional changes of government (UCGs). The prioritization of economic growth over addressing political instability presents significant risks for emerging Africa. While economic development is crucial, neglecting underlying political issues can lead to unsustainable growth, exacerbate social tensions, and undermine investor confidence.

Sustainable development concerns arise when short-term economic gains overshadow the need for long-term stability. Without addressing political instability, economic growth becomes fragile and prone to recurrent crises, hindering sustainable progress. The Democratic Republic of Congo (DRC), despite ongoing political instability and conflict, exemplifies this. Its abundant natural resources, including minerals and timber, have attracted significant foreign investment. However, the extraction of these resources has fueled conflict and corruption, aggravating political tensions and hindering efforts to establish lasting peace and democratic governance.

Moreover, ignoring social and political fragility intensifies existing issues. Economic growth alone cannot address grievances or foster social cohesion, potentially widening inequalities and deepening societal divisions. Investor confidence is also at stake, as political uncertainty can deter foreign investment despite positive economic indicators. Policy paralysis further compounds the problem, with governments struggling to implement effective strategies or enact necessary reforms in unstable environments.

Persistent political instability can tarnish a country's regional and global reputation, impacting diplomatic relations, trade partnerships, and international cooperation efforts. Negative perceptions deter tourists and undermine the country's image on the global stage. Thus, while economic growth is vital, it must be accompanied by efforts to address political instability and promote good governance to ensure the long-term prosperity of emerging Africa.

South Sudan, since its independence in 2011, has descended into a protracted civil war fueled by political power struggles, ethnic rivalries, and competition over natural resources. Despite the conflict, the country's oil reserves have remained a focal point for economic growth. However, the revenues from oil have fueled corruption and armed conflict, undermining efforts to achieve political stability and sustainable development.

These emerging trends underscore the complex and dynamic nature of African politics. They highlight both opportunities for positive change and persistent challenges that require innovative and inclusive solutions. It is a call to action for leaders and policymakers to recognize that sustainable development cannot be achieved without addressing the underlying political instabilities that plague the continent. The path to a prosperous Africa lies in a harmonious balance between economic growth and political stability, ensuring that progress is inclusive, enduring, and reflective of the continent's diverse realities.

Suppressing the Individual but not the Will

In many African countries, a trend has emerged where lesser known leaders have been created by oppressors in the stead of main opposition figures who might be in jail or are barred from competing for power. African leaders have a history of suppressing political opposition by imprisoning prominent figures or activists who pose a threat to their rule. These leaders often employ tactics such as arbitrary arrests, trumped-up charges, and prolonged detention to silence dissent and maintain their grip on power. However, this strategy has sometimes backfired, as it can inadvertently elevate lesser-known individuals within the opposition ranks.

They may unintentionally create martyrs or amplify the voices of lesser-known activists who step in to fill the void. Over time, these emerging leaders may gain credibility and support among disillusioned citizens who are discontent with the current regime's repression. As the opposition movement coalesces around new faces and voices, it may become more resilient and determined in its quest for political change. The latest instances could be found in Senegal, but before that, in July 2016, Jammeh detained Ousainou Darboe, the leader of Gambia's main opposition party, along with other UDP party officials. With no viable means to challenge Jammeh's rule. The formation of the "Coalition for Change 2016" was led by the relatively unknown Adama Barrow, a former Argos security guard and estate agent who took over Darboe's party when the latter was in jail. This sparked hope among many Gambians for a potential upset in the election, breaking Jammeh's streak of four consecutive electoral victories.

In Senegal, the charismatic opposition leader, Osman Sonko, was incarcerated and barred from contesting the March 2024 elections. In his stead, Bassirou Diomaye Faye, aged 44, who held a senior position within the Pastef party led by Sonko, contested and won the elections. Faye achieved victory a mere 10 days following his release from prison.

Diaspora Agency and the 'Mammy Cuss' Revolution

A compelling new trend has emerged in our body politic. Citizens living in the diaspora have taken on the mantle of opposition, challenging governments and confronting bad leadership from afar. These individuals, who reside in the safe havens of Europe and America, have become both the voice and the conscience of their homelands. From the bustling streets of London to the stately avenues of Washington, African diasporans are rallying. They are no longer just spectators but active participants, using their resources to support democratic causes back home. They organize demonstrations at United Nations offices, their chants for justice echoing through the corridors of international power. Financial contributions flow from them, funding movements and sustaining the fight for democracy. These actions exemplify a modern-day revolution where distance does not diminish resolve but strengthens it.

Back home, traditional avenues for dissent are stifled under the weight of repressive regimes. Free speech is a fragile dream, easily shattered by oppressive forces. In this void, a unique and potent form of protest has taken root—maternal invectives. Known as "Mammy Cuss" in the Krio language of Sierra Leone, these deeply personal insults target the sanctity of one's parents.

In African culture, where respect for elders, parents and ancestors is sacrosanct, invoking such curses is a powerful act of defiance. On social media, these invectives have become the rallying cry for the disillusioned. Commentators in the diaspora, or those hidden within the shadows of their own countries, hurl these curses with revolutionary fervor. The words cut deep, a stark departure from the usual accusations of corruption and dishonesty, signaling a profound desperation.

While the use of maternal invectives can be seen as a troubling development, it underscores the depth of discontent and the extremes to which people are driven. Traditional descriptors like "corrupt" and "dishonest" have lost their potency, giving way to this more visceral form of expression. It reveals how suppression of free speech can backfire, pushing citizens to find more radical and disruptive means to voice their grievances.

Moreover, the widespread adoption of these invectives highlights the desperation of a populace that feels voiceless and oppressed. It is a raw, unfiltered cry for justice and change, a testament to the power of words when all other avenues are closed. This phenomenon also reflects the strategic use of language as a tool for social and political leverage, illustrating how cultural nuances shape the contours of protest and resistance.

References

1. African Union. (2020). African Continental Free Trade Area (AfCFTA) Agreement.
2. Akum, F. N., Chinyere, A. O., & Mbaku, J. M. (2020). African Leaders' Refusal to Step Down and Its Impact on Democratic Governance. Brookings Institution.
3. Aisen, A., & Veiga, F. J. (2013). How Does Political Instability Affect Economic Growth?. European Journal of Political Economy.
4. Al Jazeera. (2023). Tunisia secures €1bn EU loan despite human rights concerns.
5. Asiedu, E. (2002). On the Determinants of Foreign Direct Investment to Developing Countries: Is Africa Different? World Development.
6. Associated Press. (2024). EU offers €210 million aid to Mauritania for anti-smuggling efforts.
7. Associated Press. (2024). EU unveils €7.4 billion aid package for Egypt to curb migration.
8. Autesserre, S. (2010). The Trouble with the Congo: Local Violence and the Failure of International Peacebuilding. Cambridge University Press.
9. Busse, M., & Hefeker, C. (2007). Political Risk, Institutions and Foreign Direct Investment. European Journal of Political Economy.

10. Cohen, J. (2022). Macron's Pivot to Africa: France's New Diplomatic Strategy. Foreign Policy.

11. Crocker, C. (2019). African Governance: Challenges and Their Implications. Hoover Institution.

12. Freedom House. (2022). Nations in Transit: Decline in Democratic Governance in Africa.

13. Human Rights Watch. (2024). Uganda: Court Upholds Anti-Homosexuality Act. Human Rights Watch.

14. International Monetary Fund (IMF). (2019). Regional Economic Outlook: Sub-Saharan Africa.

15. Johnson, D. H. (2016). South Sudan: A New History for a New Nation. Ohio University Press.

16. Mills, L. (2022). Narrow Framing of Democracy in Africa. Democracy in Africa Blog.

17. Ross, M. L. (2004). How Do Natural Resources Influence Civil War? Evidence from Thirteen Cases. International Organization.

18. Swaniker, F. (2016). Great leaders aren't born – they're made. And Africa is showing us how. World Economic Forum.

19. United Nations Conference on Trade and Development (UNCTAD). (2020). World Investment Report 2020.

20. World Bank. (2021). Political Stability and Absence of Violence/Terrorism: Overview.

FOURTEEN

STRATEGIES FOR PROGRESS AND STABILITY

"To say African democracies are dying is to accept that they were alive." Suleiman and Onapajo (2022).

To achieve stability and progress throughout Africa, it is crucial to tackle the complex history and diverse aspects of coups on the continent. Often perceived as a quick fix for poor governance, coups rarely offer a lasting solution. Instead, they underscore the necessity for reevaluating the neoliberal democratic project in Africa. Addressing the issue of coups demands a proactive stance; regional and continental organizations must revise their evaluation criteria and adopt active strategies rather than simply responding to crises as they occur.

Imagine a scenario where an African nation renegotiates its trade and aid agreements with a major world power to include clauses that prioritize human rights and the interests of the country. This strategic shift leads to more transparent dealings and reduces the ability of external parties to exert undue influence on domestic politics, contributing to a more stable political environment.

This hard reset is what our continent needs in all spheres of development, and it is not far-fetched. President John Magufuli of Tanzania, during his presidency from 2015 until his death in 2021, was known for his nationalistic approach to foreign investments, particularly evident in his dealings with the Bagamoyo port project. This project, initiated before his term and backed by Chinese and Omani investors, was intended to significantly boost Tanzania's shipping capabilities. However, Magufuli halted the project, criticizing the terms agreed upon by his predecessors as unfavorable and exploitative, citing issues like excessive control by foreign investors, substantial tax exemptions, and clauses restricting the development of other ports.

His decision to stop the project was part of a broader economic policy focused on protecting national interests and renegotiating unfair agreements. At the same time, it is an illustrative case of strong leadership and the will to take responsibility for our dealings with outsiders. While some criticized Magufuli's approach as draconian, many others in the continent praised him for protecting Tanzanian interests and sovereignty. My aim is not to celebrate dictatorship by any means but to underscore the need for our leaders to adopt a Magufuli-like posture in negotiating development programs in all facets of society. The level of seriousness and the degree of nationalism is imperative.

Adopting this approach is vital to our progress and stability, but before that, it requires a comprehensive strategy encompassing governance reform, judicial integrity, financial accountability, strong human rights standards, and inclusive political processes. Below is a narrative organization of various strategic elements aimed at averting coups and fostering political stability and prosperity across the continent.

Redefining Relationships with External Powers

Efforts to stabilize the political landscape require addressing the agency and complicity of external actors like France, China, and Russia which are viewed as factors in the deterioration of democracy in the continent. A strategic reevaluation of relationships with these countries, which often prioritize strategic gains over democratic values, is essential. By insisting that they include respect for human rights and democratic principles in their agreements, our nations can protect their sovereignty and prevent foreign interests from fostering corrupt or undemocratic practices. This might involve renegotiating trade deals or aid agreements to include more stringent requirements for transparency and adherence to democratic norms. The complicity of China must stop. As a whole, vigilance is required regarding the objectives of major powers in our continent. Eastern powers, for instance, prioritize establishing connections with governments over forming relationships with the people. They base their relationship on the most powerful rogue who assumes power. That does not demonstrate affection for a people.

- *Handling the Double-Edged Sword of Exclusivity Clauses*

The handling of exclusivity clauses in business agreements between African governments and foreign companies is a thread that must be carefully woven. These clauses, which often grant foreign entities exclusive rights over vast resources and significant sectors, have historically been double-edged swords. On one hand, they can attract much-needed investment, but on the other, they can stifle competition, local enterprise, and sustainable development. A more nuanced and equitable negotiation of these clauses is pivotal to realizing a vision of a prosperous and self-reliant Africa.

Exclusivity clauses have often been a staple in agreements involving natural resource extraction, telecommunications, and infrastructure development. While they can ensure steady revenue and foreign investment, the pitfalls are manifold.

For example, in the mining sector, exclusivity clauses have often led to situations where foreign companies extract vast amounts of minerals with little benefit to the local economy. The Democratic Republic of Congo (DRC), rich in cobalt and other minerals, has seen several such agreements. In many cases, these contracts have favored foreign corporations, leading to wealth extraction without corresponding improvements in local infrastructure or economic diversification (Ross, 2022).

Similarly, in the telecommunications sector, exclusivity agreements have sometimes hindered the development of competitive markets. In countries like Mozambique, early exclusivity clauses granted to certain foreign telecom companies stifled competition and delayed the expansion of affordable and accessible telecom services to rural areas (African Development Bank, 2021). To align exclusivity clauses with the vision of a new Africa, several strategies must be employed. These strategies involve rethinking how such clauses are negotiated and implemented, ensuring that they serve the broader goals of national development and economic empowerment.

i) Emphasizing Fair Terms and Conditions

Negotiating fairer terms in exclusivity clauses is critical. This involves ensuring that these clauses include provisions for local content, technology transfer, and infrastructure development. For instance, Ghana's approach to its oil sector has included clauses that mandate foreign companies to invest in local infrastructure and support local businesses (Andersson, 2022).

ii) Periodic Review and Flexibility

Incorporating clauses that allow for periodic review and adjustment of terms can help address changing economic and social conditions. It ensures that agreements remain beneficial over time and can adapt to new realities. Nigeria's renegotiation of its oil contracts in the 2000s to increase government take is a pertinent example (International Monetary Fund, 2022).

iii) Strengthening Local Enterprises

Encouraging joint ventures between foreign companies and local businesses can enhance the capacity of domestic enterprises. This approach not only fosters technology transfer but also builds local expertise and ensures that a greater share of profits remains within the country. Rwanda's partnership models in the tourism sector, which involve local communities in joint ventures, have proven successful (United Nations Development Programme, 2022).

iv) Transparency and Accountability

Ensuring transparency in the negotiation and implementation of exclusivity clauses is paramount. Public disclosure of contracts and the involvement of civil society in monitoring these agreements can prevent corruption and ensure that the terms are in the public interest.

Enhanced Accountability and Legal Frameworks

One of the foundational strategies to deter future coups is enhancing the accountability of leaders who overstay their mandated terms. Prohibiting such leaders from holding positions within regional or continental bodies can act as a significant deterrent. Recognizing the risks posed by such actions, the African Union (AU) may implement a new policy: any leader who extends their term beyond what is constitutionally mandated is ineligible to hold any position within AU bodies. This policy should be part of a broader initiative to enhance the accountability of political leaders across the continent.

The adoption of United Nations Security Council Resolution 2719 (UNSCR 2719) on December 21, 2023, has opened a new phase for peacekeeping missions in Africa. This resolution establishes a mechanism allowing AU-led peace operations to receive UN funding through assessed contributions. It could enhance the effectiveness and sustainability of peace operations while boosting African leadership in their administration. The resolution was prompted, in part, by a reduction in UN peacekeeping efforts and a transition towards missions led by Africans (Allen and Mazurova, 2024). The AU can leverage this platform to impose regulations that deter abuse of constitutional term limits and other undemocratic expressions of power.

- *Waiver of consent from host governments:* Often, without consent from the host government, peacekeepers are unable to make enforcements, and the mission's objectives would be compromised. However, despite being the norm for external peace operations, the consent of a host government may be overruled in the case of a military intervention, where the leadership has lost legitimacy. It is crucial that the peacekeeping framework of Resolution 2719 expressly provide such waiver, as consent is invariably withheld by rogue governments.

An example of regional bodies attempting to enforce democratic principles without the consent of the host government is ECOWAS, which has a history of intervening in member states to uphold democratic transitions. For instance, the regional body played a significant role in the 2017 Gambian presidential crisis, where it deployed troops after diplomatic efforts failed to enforce election results when the incumbent Yahya Jammeh refused to cede power to the democratically elected Adama Barrow. This intervention showcased how regional organizations could actively prevent leaders from defying democratic norms and extend their rule.

Early Warning Systems

Combatting coups requires a proactive approach instead of a reactionary one. In a polity where instability can quickly escalate into violence or coups, the importance of robust early warning systems and strategic deployment of regional military forces cannot be overstated. These tools serve as critical mechanisms for preempting crises and ensuring continuous stability across the continent. Establishing robust early warning systems to detect signs of political unrest early can prevent the escalation into coups.

The scenario involving the African Union's Continental Early Warning System (CEWS) underscores a critical challenge often faced across the continent, that is, the gap between the establishment of regulatory frameworks and their actual implementation. While the continent boasts numerous well-drafted legal and democratic frameworks intended to guide operations and enforce standards, the practical application and enforcement of these regulations frequently fall short.

a) Theoretical Framework vs. Practical Implementation:

Regulatory Frameworks in Theory: The CEWS, for instance, is designed to monitor and analyze various indicators that could signify impending conflicts. This system theoretically provides a powerful tool for preemptive action against potential crises by identifying signs of escalation like political tensions or social divisions, as was evident before the violence in the Central African Republic.

However, having a system in place is just the first step. The effectiveness of such a system hinges on its actual application and the subsequent actions taken based on the data and forecasts it provides. In many instances across Africa, despite the presence of early warning mechanisms, the response mechanisms are not robust or swift enough to act on the warnings. This delay or inaction can be attributed to several factors that have been addressed in Chapter 11, but they certainly merit passing mention here:

Lack of Political Will: There might be reluctance among political leaders to act on the warnings due to political reasons, fear of backlash, or because it may not align with their interests.

Resource Constraints: Effective response requires resources —financial, human, and technological. Often, there is a shortfall in the necessary resources to take timely action.

Coordination Challenges: Effective implementation of early warning signals often requires coordination between various national and regional bodies, which can be cumbersome and slow, particularly in high-stress situations.

b) Beyond Regulations:

The Importance of Implementation: Simply put, regulations and systems like CEWS are only as effective as their implementation. Without concrete actions following the alerts, the systems fail to fulfill their preventive role. This gap not only undermines the systems in place but also erodes trust in them over time, reducing their potential effectiveness even when they are properly followed. It is expected that the delivery framework of resolution 2719 will take onboard these realities.

- *Strategic Recommendations:*

Enhancing Responsiveness: It is crucial for the mechanisms that receive early warnings to have predefined action plans that can be triggered immediately once certain thresholds are met.

Building Capacity: Strengthening the capabilities of institutions responsible for responding to early warnings can ensure that these alerts are not just noted but acted upon effectively.

Political Commitment: Ensuring that there is a strong and unwavering political commitment to respect and act according to the frameworks established is essential. This might involve reforms to ensure greater transparency and accountability of leadership.

Regional Military Presence

The deployment of regional military forces during sensitive periods such as elections or transitions of power can provide a stabilizing effect. These forces, drawn from member states of regional organizations, operate under mandates to protect civilians and support the maintenance of order, thus reducing the reliance on national forces, which might be seen as biased or partisan. However, to ensure effective implementation of these strategies, states must be willing to cede some political sovereignty to regional and continental bodies and uphold judicial review to prevent abuses of power. After the contested presidential election in 2010, Ivory Coast experienced severe political turmoil and violence. A regional military presence by ECOWAS could have mitigated the conflict by providing a neutral force to maintain order and protect civilians. Such an intervention might have expedited the resolution of the crisis and prevented the large-scale violence that occurred.

Inclusive Governance

Africa requires the inclusion of women, minorities, and the economically disadvantaged in every leadership forum. Imagine a country where a new policy mandates that women and minorities must comprise at least 50% of all governmental advisory bodies. This policy would lead to more diverse viewpoints in decision-making processes, resulting in more equitable and comprehensive community development projects that enjoy broader support among the populace, thus stabilizing the political landscape.

Ensuring the participation of women, minorities, and economically disadvantaged groups in governance not only enriches the policy-making process but also reduces the likelihood of unrest that can lead to coups. Diverse perspectives are essential for creating well-rounded solutions to community challenges. In essence, the more women in politics, the less likelihood for usurpations, especially given that none of the many coups have been orchestrated by women. They have demonstrated more decorum in public office. It is vital to include the viewpoints of women, minorities, and the economically disadvantaged to ensure that our future leaders reflect the diversity of our nations. This inclusion is key to shaping products, policies, and infrastructure that serve everyone effectively. Historically, governance dominated by a homogenous group is more prone to challenges and less likely to address the broad spectrum of societal needs effectively. The diversity in leadership forums can lead to more comprehensive solutions to community challenges and ensure that future leaders reflect the diverse populations they serve.

Establishing an African Criminal Court (ACC) and Strengthening the African Court of Justice (ACJ)

The establishment of an African Criminal Court represents a pivotal advancement in ensuring that our leaders adhere to democratic principles and constitutional boundaries. This court could provide the necessary judicial mechanisms to address violations of governance that undermine stability and development across the continent. However, Branch (2019) notes that the ACC will only effectively contribute to emancipating politics if it is shaped by forward-thinking, democratic political forces. It is a possibility is supported by the court's integration within the AU and specific measures outlined in the Malabo Protocol. It explores the transformative potential of the ACC as outlined in the Malabo Protocol. It highlights several key aspects that enhance the court's effectiveness: firstly, the expansion of its jurisdiction to include a broader range of international crimes and a wider array of individuals and organizations; secondly, its integration within the African Union's regional peace and security architecture, which not only aligns it with continental policies and commitments but also boosts its symbolic power to enforce political claims. These elements collectively aim to make the ACC more accountable and responsive to the needs of African people, movements, and organizations, representing a significant step forward in the realm of international criminal tribunals.

It is fundamental to amend the Protocol on the Statute of the African Court of Justice and Human Rights to include specific provisions for handling election petitions. This amendment would need to clearly define the scope of the court's jurisdiction over election matters, ensuring it can adjudicate disputes arising from national elections across member states. The amendment process would require a consensus among member states, followed by ratifications according to the legal procedures in each country. This ensures that changes are made democratically and in line with the African Union's legal processes.

To establish the ACJHR's superior jurisdiction over national supreme courts, further amendments to the Protocol or a new legal instrument might be necessary. These amendments must outline that the ACJHR's decisions on election petitions are final and binding, superseding any national court decisions. An alternative arrangement is empowering regional courts like the ECOWAS Court of Justice and the East African Court of Justice to hear election petitions and maintain superior jurisdiction over national courts.

However, these steps could face significant resistance as it touches on national sovereignty and the independence of national judicial systems. First, the sovereignty vs. supranational authority issue will arise. It requires member states to relinquish some degree of sovereignty to allow a supranational body to enforce legal judgments within their territories, a significant challenge historically evident in the African Union's efforts to enhance continental judicial mechanisms. Secondly, the success of these courts heavily depends on the political will of the member states to enforce and adhere to the court's rulings, which requires broad support and recognition. Without this, enforcement of decisions could be problematic. Lastly, the establishment of effective and respected courts demands considerable financial investment and legal expertise. It is crucial to equip these courts with well-trained legal personnel and adequate resources to ensure their operational success and credibility.

Detailed negotiations and diplomatic discussions would be required to align all member states with this principle. This approach offers several significant benefits and can provide a robust framework for addressing electoral disputes in a manner that transcends national biases and limitations. Here are some of the key benefits of this arrangement:

- *Enhanced Neutrality and Impartiality:* Regional courts provide a more neutral setting than national courts, which may be influenced by local politics, thereby ensuring fairer resolution of election disputes.
- *Standardization of Electoral Justice:* They can standardize the handling of election petitions across countries, leading to consistent application of electoral laws.
- *Strengthening Rule of Law and Democracy:* This arrangement can boost public confidence in the electoral process and strengthen democratic governance by providing a dependable avenue for resolving electoral disputes.
- *Reducing Local Political Pressure:* Regional courts face less political pressure from local entities, which allows them to make decisions based more on legal merits rather than political influences.
- *Promoting Regional Integration and Unity:* Utilizing regional courts emphasizes regional

cooperation and supports a collective governance framework.

- *Deterring Electoral Fraud and Irregularities:* The oversight of a powerful regional court can act as a deterrent to electoral malpractice, knowing that such actions are subject to scrutiny beyond national borders.
- *Capacity Building and Resource Sharing:* Regional courts can pool resources and expertise from member states, enhancing the judicial capacity and efficiency of the region.

The creation of these courts is driven by the need for an independent judiciary capable of handling cases that are of significant importance to the integrity of governance in Africa. Currently, many of our nations rely on international bodies, such as the ICC, to prosecute cases involving major human rights violations and breaches of governance. Nonetheless, developing a functional domestic continental judicial system would eliminate concerns about the perceived bias against African states, which is often attributed to the ICC. These courts are envisioned to serve several critical functions within the African Union's legal framework, particularly in enhancing the rule of law and promoting justice across the continent. Here are the primary functions they could perform:

Functions and Impact

a. Upholding Democratic Principles

Mali experienced two coups within a year, creating significant political instability. In a situation where a regional court exists with competent jurisdiction, it could intervene to conduct a judicial review, holding the military accountable for breaches of constitutional order and emphasizing the importance of lawful governance. This court, composed of judges from neighboring ECOWAS countries, could prosecute the coup leaders and reinforce the consequences of unconstitutional changes in government. Judicial intervention would deter future coups, promote adherence to democratic processes, and restore faith in democratic institutions.

Expanding this scenario, the regional court could also prosecute dictators like Omar al-Bashir before uprisings topple them, addressing human rights violations and breaches of constitutional order proactively. Such actions by a regional court would demonstrate Africa's capacity to uphold justice within its own frameworks, preceding even the ICC.

This situation is not impossible, as it parallels the strong institutions and effective retributive and restorative justice systems in Europe. There, the strength of institutions ensures accountability and reinforces the rule of law, showing that with the right structures, such judicial interventions are both feasible and impactful in promoting stability and democratic governance.

b. Enforcing Constitutional Limits

By specifically focusing on constitutional violations by high-ranking officials, these courts could deter potential legal overreaches by sitting politicians. An example can be drawn from the situation in Guinea, where, in 2020, President Alpha Condé sought a third term in office, arguably in violation of the country's constitution, leading to political unrest and violence. The 2021 coup could have been averted if a regional court with a strong mandate was in operation, providing a forum for legally contesting this move before it resulted in a national crisis.

c. Enforcement of Human Rights

Both the ACC and the ACJ would play significant roles in enforcing human rights standards across the continent. This involves interpreting and applying the African Charter on Human and Peoples' Rights and other relevant human rights treaties to ensure that member states respect and protect the rights of their citizens. The August 10, 2022, protests in Sierra Leone, which were poorly handled by the government, leading to civilian deaths and arbitrary incarcerations, highlight the need for effective human rights enforcement. If an ACC and ACJ had proactively monitored the situation, issued warnings, and deployed observers, the tragedy might have been avoided. Swift judicial reviews and inquiries could have addressed the excessive use of force and arbitrary detentions, ensuring justice for victims and setting a precedent for the continent.

d. Resolving Disputes Between States

The ACJ would also have jurisdiction over disputes between member states of the African Union. This function is critical for maintaining peace and cooperation within the continent, providing a legal pathway to resolve inter-state conflicts peacefully and legally.

e. Inspiring Confidence in the Judicial Process

The presence of a credible, continent-wide judiciary would likely increase public trust in the legal system's ability to handle sensitive political issues fairly and without bias. This confidence can stabilize political landscapes and encourage greater public engagement in democratic processes.

f. Addressing Impunity

A central role of these courts would be to address the issue of impunity among high-ranking officials and to ensure that no individual is above the law. Africans like myself must be tired of fleeing our countries due to tyrants who are accountable to no one, not under national laws nor within the continental framework. The criteria for an ICC prosecution are typically stringent, and often, the grievous actions of our dictators do not reach the ICC's required threshold. By establishing a system to hold leaders accountable for their sub-ICC actions, our courts would bolster the rule of law throughout Africa.

g. Promoting Judicial Cooperation

By establishing common judicial standards and procedures, the courts would promote judicial cooperation among African countries. This includes facilitating extradition, mutual legal assistance, and the sharing of judicial practices and innovations. There will be no safe haven for deposed despots in Africa. The courts would inflict sanctions to any country that accommodates leaders fleeing justice in their country, not least those who were deposed because they refused to leave power after the expiration of their tenure.

In conclusion, establishing an African Criminal Court and

operationalizing the African Court of Justice represents a vital step forward in promoting governance and reinforcing democratic norms across Africa. Although there are hurdles, such as gaining political approval and securing sufficient resources, the ability of these institutions to create a more stable and equitable political landscape is substantial. These courts are essential for reshaping African politics, enhancing transparency, accountability, and justice, and are indeed the way to instill decorum in our body politic.

Addressing Historical Grievances

Allowing historical conflicts to go unresolved can exacerbate difficulties for regional organizations in managing coups. Rather than coercing individuals who harbor mutual animosity into sharing the same territory, efforts should be directed towards fostering continental unity. It may be simpler for countries like Nigeria and Cameroon to adopt a common currency than to expect minorities like the people of Southern Cameroon to relinquish their autonomy to a repressive regime. Oppression can only suppress dissent temporarily without extinguishing the desire for autonomy. Movements such as the Ambazonian Restoration Quest and various secessionist movements across Africa stem from state failure. The cultural heritage of these populations should be preserved as they engage in broader alliances. Forced integration of communities that feel excluded from decision-making processes is counterproductive. Minorities need to be convinced of the benefits and functionality of a larger union before they can genuinely commit to it.

I am minded to state that many of the historical conflicts in the continent require constitutional and legal solutions instead of a political settlement. Addressing the legal status or claims of both parties to the conflict and making a decision on such legalities has more lasting peace implications than addressing them based on who has the power or the upper hand. Many conflicts have festered since independence based on the latter approach, which only means a suppression of the will of a minority at all times. A vivid illustration of the workability of the legal approach to conflict resolution is the case between Nigeria and Cameroon over the Bakassi Peninsular.

The Bakassi Peninsula dispute was successfully resolved through international legal intervention by the International Court of Justice. In 2002, the ICJ ruled in favor of Cameroon regarding the sovereignty over Bakassi, based on colonial treaties and agreements between the parties. This legal resolution, rather than a political or military solution, provided a clear, binding outcome that both nations agreed to respect. The process included not only the ICJ's decision but also subsequent agreements between Nigeria and Cameroon to implement the decision peacefully, including the Greentree Agreement, which facilitated the transfer of authority and provided protections for the rights of local populations. This case underscores how legal mechanisms can provide clear resolutions to conflicts that have festered for ages, reducing the likelihood of future disputes and fostering stability in the region.

Drawing on the precedent of the Bakassi Peninsula case, a similar international legal body like the ICJ could be called upon to provide a binding resolution on the Ambazonian restoration claim based on historical and legal rights. However, this would require both parties' agreement to abide by such a decision. Also, given the challenges of reaching a purely internal settlement, international mediation may come in handy. Involving bodies like the African Union or the United Nations in mediating and arbitrating the dispute could help ensure neutrality and adherence to international legal standards.

The Sierra Leone Model of Mediated Dialogue

A new phenomenon has arisen within the political landscape of Africa, which I have termed the Sierra Leone Model. This concept captures a recent and intricate scenario that unfolded in Sierra Leone after the June 2023 elections. The sequence of events and the unique approach taken by the parties involved offer a compelling case study on conflict resolution and democratic negotiation in modern Africa.

- *Context and Initial Conflict*

After the June 2023 elections in Sierra Leone, controversy erupted when the Chief Electoral Commissioner announced incumbent President Julius Maada Bio as the winner. This swift declaration was criticized by both national and international observers for the lack of transparency in the tabulation process. The opposition leader and the All People's Congress opted against legal recourse for want of trust in the judiciary.

The APC's decision to avoid the courts led to organized civil protests, which escalated into a formal boycott of government functions by elected opposition MPs and councilors. The boycott created a governmental stalemate, highlighting a fundamental democratic principle that effective governance requires both ruling and opposition parties to functionally participate.

- *Mediated Dialogue*

The impasse compelled President Bio to initiate a call for a mediated dialogue to resolve the crisis. The dialogue was facilitated by major regional and international bodies, including the Commonwealth, the AU, and ECOWAS. It resulted in eight key resolutions aimed at ending the stalemate, with a particularly notable one being the establishment of a Tripartite Committee to investigate the electoral process.

- *The Tripartite Committee*

The Tripartite Committee is a significant innovation in this model. Composed of representatives from the Sierra Leone government, the APC, and the international community led by the United Nations, its purpose is to provide a balanced and transparent investigation into the electoral discrepancies. This committee is a critical test for international stakeholders like the UN, AU, ECOWAS, the US, Britain, and the EU, reflecting their commitment to reversing democratic backsliding. The model offers several important lessons for democratic governance and conflict resolution. First, it demonstrates the power of non-violent civil disobedience and political boycotts as tools for opposition parties, especially in contexts where the judiciary may not be trusted. Second, it underscores the effectiveness of international and regional bodies in facilitating dialogue and resolutions in national conflicts. Third, the model represents a novel approach to resolving electoral disputes through inclusive and transparent committees that incorporate both local and international stakeholders.

Lastly, the Sierra Leone Model serves as a potential blueprint for other African nations facing similar political crises. It offers a mechanism for opposition parties to assert their rights and challenge governance issues without resorting to violence, thereby promoting peace and democracy. This model, with its focus on mediation and inclusive dialogue, could indeed become a pivotal strategy for other countries experiencing similar democratic and electoral challenges.

Proactive Application of Transitional Justice Mechanisms

Reconciliation and transitional justice mechanisms can be proactively adapted to prevent future conflicts in Africa by incorporating strategies such as early warning systems, continuous dialogue, sustainable institutional reforms, inclusive political processes, and community-based approaches to justice. These measures, when effectively implemented, can address the root causes of conflicts and foster long-term stability.

Early Warning Systems and Conflict Prevention: Early warning systems are critical for detecting signs of potential conflicts before they escalate. These systems utilize data on political, social, and economic indicators to predict areas of potential instability. For example, the African Union's Continental Early Warning System aims to provide timely data to policymakers to prevent conflicts. It played a role during the 2015 political crisis in Burundi by identifying escalating tensions, although the effectiveness was somewhat limited by the lack of political action based on the warnings.

Continuous Dialogue and Peace Education: Ongoing dialogue between various community groups and peace education programs can mitigate underlying tensions. These initiatives promote understanding and tolerance among diverse groups. In Kenya, the Uwiano Platform for Peace, established after the 2007 post-election violence, facilitates dialogue and mediation between communities. This mechanism has been crucial in reducing tensions during elections, demonstrating the effectiveness of continuous dialogue in maintaining peace.

Sustainable Institutional Reforms: Proactive transitional justice should also include sustainable reforms in governance and security institutions to ensure they are inclusive and represent the diverse interests of the population. In Sierra Leone, post-civil war reforms of the judiciary and police were undertaken to make these institutions impartial and accessible, thereby reducing grievances that could potentially escalate into conflict.

Inclusive Political Processes: Ensuring that political processes include all societal groups, particularly marginalized and minority communities, can prevent disenfranchisement and exclusion. After the 2011 revolution in Tunisia, the transitional government included a broad range of political and social groups in the drafting of the new constitution. This inclusivity helped to prevent exclusionary practices that could lead to unrest.

Community-Based Approaches to Justice: Localized grievances can be effectively addressed through community-based approaches to justice and reconciliation, which involve local populations in the justice process. Rwanda's Gacaca courts, for example, provided a platform for justice post-genocide and actively involved local communities in the reconciliation process. This proactive approach has been instrumental in maintaining peace by resolving conflicts at their roots.

By leveraging these proactive strategies, African nations can not only respond to conflicts but also prevent them, utilizing reconciliation and transitional justice mechanisms to ensure lasting peace and democratic governance.

Regional Security Cooperation

Security initiatives that emphasize regional collaboration over national forces present a strategic approach to enhancing democratic consolidation and political stability in Africa. These initiatives can offer a more coordinated and adaptable response to violence, reducing the burden on national militaries and minimizing the potential for abuses. To forestall future violations of due process by ill-motivated leaders, the much touted regional peacekeeping force must be operationalized, with a strong presence during elections. Here's a deeper look into how such strategies can be implemented, along with instances illustrating their effectiveness:

a) Enhanced Regional Security Cooperation

Regional security initiatives allow countries to pool resources, share intelligence, and coordinate responses to cross-border threats, such as terrorism, insurgency, and organized crime. This collaborative approach can lead to more effective security measures that are less prone to manipulation by individual national leaders. The Multinational Joint Task Force (MNJTF) against Boko Haram, which includes forces from Nigeria, Niger, Chad, and Cameroon, is an example of regional cooperation. This task force has been crucial in curbing Boko Haram's activities across the Lake Chad Basin, demonstrating the effectiveness of collective regional efforts over isolated national actions.

For future arrangements, strategies such as enhanced intelligence sharing, joint training programs, common funding mechanisms, comprehensive legal frameworks, and community engagement are recommended. These strategies can standardize operations, improve funding stability, and foster local support, making regional security efforts more effective and sustainable. The success of the MNJTF provides a model that could be replicated in other regions facing similar security challenges.

b) Regional Peacekeeping Forces

Establishing regional peacekeeping forces that can intervene during crises, such as coups or violent elections, can help ensure stability and protect democratic processes. These forces can act as neutral parties that prevent escalations and safeguard civilian populations. ECOWAS has deployed military interventions in the past to restore order and uphold democratic principles in member states experiencing instability. The Gambian intervention in 2017 and the ECOMOG involvement in Sierra Leone in 1997 represent the most vivid illustration of proactive regional peacekeeping operations.

c) Diminishing Reliance on National Militaries

By reducing reliance on national forces, which may be deeply politicized or loyal to specific leaders rather than the state, regional initiatives can help diminish the military's role in politics and decrease the likelihood of military coups. The African Standby Force (ASF), an international, continent-wide peacekeeping force under the African Union, is designed to deal with various disturbances across Africa. It aims to reduce individual states' reliance on their national militaries for maintaining internal order, which can help prevent the military from seizing power.

To effectively deploy the African Standby Force (ASF) for future stability in Africa, it is essential to enhance cooperation through robust legal frameworks, ensure continuous training and joint exercises for operational readiness, and secure sustainable funding. Additionally, improving intelligence sharing, engaging with communities, and maintaining strong political commitment are crucial. Regular evaluation and adaptation of strategies will also help the ASF respond effectively to evolving security challenges.

d) Surrendering Sovereignty for Collective Security

The concept of ceding a degree of political sovereignty to regional bodies for security purposes involves significant trust and cooperation among states but can lead to greater overall stability and democratic integrity. The use of African Union peacekeeping missions, such as AMISOM in Somalia, shows how states can rely on regional entities to maintain peace. Such missions help stabilize environments for democratic governance and development by creating safer, more secure conditions less prone to unilateral military disruptions. For future arrangements, it's crucial to establish clear legal frameworks, build trust and transparency, enhance the capabilities of regional bodies, and balance national sovereignty with collective security benefits to ensure the success of such initiatives.

e) Operational Presence During Elections

Maintaining an operational presence of regional forces during elections in Africa can significantly enhance electoral integrity and prevent violence, thereby supporting democratic processes. This strategy reassures voters, deters potential aggressors, and supports local security forces, contributing to smoother and more credible elections. Examples include ECOWAS's role in Nigeria's 2015 and 2019 elections and the AU's support during Somali elections, both of which helped stabilize potentially volatile situations. Going forward, regional forces may conduct pre-election risk assessments, collaborate closely with local authorities, provide specialized training for electoral security, ensure transparency in their operations, and plan a strategic post-election withdrawal. It is a comprehensive approach that will effectively safeguard elections and strengthen democratic structures across the continent.

Democratizing Leadership Development through Mobile Technology

Democratizing leadership development is crucial for the growth and development of Africa as it fosters a diverse and inclusive range of leaders, driving innovation and inclusive policy-making. It involves making leadership training and opportunities accessible and equitable across all levels of society. Individuals from diverse backgrounds, including those from underprivileged or marginalized communities, are given access to the necessary resources and training to develop leadership skills. This approach leverages technology to reach wider audiences, ensures affordability, includes diverse groups in leadership programs, and adapts training to be culturally relevant. Programs like the Young African Leadership Initiative (YALI), established by the U.S. government and active across Sub-Saharan Africa, are aimed at nurturing the next generation of African leaders by providing them with training tools, technological support, and leadership opportunities. So far, it has been successful in creating a network of young leaders equipped to tackle challenges and drive change in their communities.

We need more of such programs to achieve economic growth through improved organizational performance and productivity. This concept is rooted in the idea that effective leadership shouldn't be restricted to individuals from certain socioeconomic backgrounds, educational levels, or specific geographic locations. By leveraging mobile platforms, leadership training, and development can be made accessible to a broader range of individuals across different societal levels, fostering inclusivity and equipping a diverse group of future leaders with the skills necessary for effective governance and societal advancement.

Insights on Leadership Development through Mobile Technology

- *Accessibility and Reach:* Mobile technology's extensive reach allows leadership development programs to be accessible to individuals in remote or underserved areas who might otherwise lack access to such resources. Mobile platforms can deliver educational content, interactive training, and connectivity with mentors and peers across vast distances.
- *Cost-Effectiveness:* Utilizing mobile technology can significantly reduce the costs associated with traditional leadership development methods. Digital platforms eliminate the need for physical infrastructure and can scale up quickly without a proportional increase in cost.
- *Personalization and Flexibility:* Mobile learning platforms can offer personalized learning experiences that cater to the individual needs of users. Users can engage with content that aligns with their specific interests or developmental gaps at their own pace and schedule.
- *Real-Time Feedback and Interaction:* Mobile technologies enable real-time feedback and interaction, which are crucial for effective learning and development. Learners can receive immediate feedback on assignments, participate in interactive

discussions, and engage in problem-solving activities with peers from diverse backgrounds.

Across Africa, mobile technology is significantly advancing leadership development through various innovative applications. In Kenya, mLearning projects like Eneza Education provide accessible leadership courses and professional development resources directly on mobile devices. Similarly, in Ghana, mobile mentoring programs such as Mentorship Spaces connect emerging leaders with experienced mentors in diverse fields, facilitating continuous learning. Additionally, platforms like Ushahidi in Kenya, initially developed for crisis response, are now adapted for broader uses, including community engagement in leadership activities. These platforms involve users in community mapping, problem identification, and solution development, effectively teaching practical leadership skills. Together, these initiatives showcase how mobile technology is democratizing leadership development, making it more accessible and interactive across the continent.

Future Considerations

To maximize the impact of mobile technology in leadership development, several strategies should be considered:

- *Inclusive Design:* Ensure that mobile platforms are inclusively designed to accommodate users with different levels of technological literacy and access. This might include options for low-data usage or interfaces that are easy to navigate.
- *Partnerships with Educational Institutions:* Collaborate with local universities and educational

institutions to develop content that is both academically rigorous and practically applicable.

- *Continuous Content Update and Localization:* Regularly update learning materials to reflect the latest leadership theories and practices and localize content to ensure cultural relevance and practical applicability.
- *Monitoring and Evaluation:* Implement robust monitoring and evaluation frameworks to assess the effectiveness of mobile leadership development initiatives and adapt strategies as necessary.

By harnessing mobile technology for leadership development, Africa can foster a new generation of leaders who are well-equipped to handle the continent's unique challenges and opportunities, thus contributing significantly to its future growth and stability.

Judicial Review

As I recount my journey as an asylee, it's crucial to delve into the significant role of judicial review in shaping the future stability of our continent. Amidst my experiences, I've observed firsthand the crucial impact a robust judiciary can have in maintaining the delicate balance of power and upholding democracy, especially in regions marred by political upheaval and corruption. In cases where it succeeds, such as when courts have annulled rigged elections or overturned unconstitutional laws, judicial review has reinforced transparency and integrity, fostering a culture of accountability. Kenya's 2010 Constitution significantly enhanced such powers, leading to a judiciary that has played an active role in checking the excesses of other government branches. Notably, the Supreme Court's intervention in the 2017 presidential election, where it nullified the election results due to irregularities, underscored its role in ensuring electoral integrity and political accountability.

In many parts of Africa, the consolidation of power, human rights abuse, and pervasive corruption pose serious risks not just to governance but to the very fabric of society. The role of judicial review in such contexts cannot be overstated—it is the linchpin that ensures governmental powers are not only checked but are exercised within the strict confines of the law. The Constitutional Court of South Africa has a long-standing reputation for exercising judicial review to overturn laws and executive decisions that violate the Constitution. This includes landmark rulings on various issues, including rights to housing, health, and social services, which have helped stabilize the political environment and ensure government accountability.

The concept is a cornerstone for the future stability of our continent. As we gaze into the horizon of what lies ahead, several key considerations come to the forefront in strengthening judicial review.

Firstly, the independence of the judiciary is paramount. This independence can be fortified by ensuring that judges have secure tenure, are adequately compensated, and are protected from arbitrary removal. Such measures would shield them from political influences that might otherwise sway their decisions and compromise their impartiality. In my own experiences in other countries, where the judiciary has remained uninfluenced by political powers, justice has not only been served but has been seen to be served.

Furthermore, the capacity of judicial systems must continually be enhanced to adeptly handle complex cases that involve significant government actions. This requires ongoing training and resource allocation, ensuring that the judiciary is equipped to effectively enforce its rulings. From my observations, where judicial capacities have been strengthened, there has been a notable improvement in the enforcement of law and order.

Raising public awareness about the role of judicial review in promoting accountability and protecting rights is also crucial. It empowers citizens to understand and utilize legal channels to address their grievances, fostering a culture of lawfulness and participation in the democratic process.

Lastly, regional cooperation plays a vital role. Institutions like the African Court on Human and Peoples' Rights exemplify how regional judicial bodies can provide an additional layer of scrutiny and help harmonize standards of justice across different countries. Such cooperation can enhance the consistency and fairness of judicial processes across borders, contributing to a more unified approach to upholding human rights and legal standards.

By focusing on these areas, we can further develop judicial review mechanisms in Africa, enhancing peace and stability. This process not only prevents potential abuses of power but also lays down a foundation of trust and accountability, elements that are crucial for the long-term stability and prosperity of the continent. Through my journey and experiences, I have come to realize the profound impact that a robust and respected judicial system can have on a nation's trajectory toward true democratic stability.

References

1. Aisen, A., & Veiga, F. J. (2013). How Does Political Instability Affect Economic Growth? European Journal of Political Economy.

2. Allen, J., & Mazurova, L. (2024). UNSCR 2719 and Its Implications for African Peace Operations. Journal of International Peacekeeping.

3. Allen, J. & Mazurova, N. (2024) African Union and United Nations Partnership Key to the Future of Peace Operations in Africa. African Center for Strategic Studies.

4. Andersson, R. (2022). The Political Economy of Extractive Industries in Africa. Journal of African Development.

5. Asiedu, E. (2002). On the Determinants of Foreign Direct Investment to Developing Countries: Is Africa Different? World Development.

6. Autesserre, S. (2010). The Trouble with the Congo: Local Violence and the Failure of International Peacebuilding. Cambridge University Press.

7. Branch, A. (2019). The African Criminal Court and its Transformative Potential. African Journal of International Law.

8. Chachavalpongpun, P. (2014). Thailand: The Politics of Despair. Journal of Democracy.

9. Chambers, P., & Waitoolkiat, N. (2016). Khaki Capital: The Political Economy of the Military in Southeast Asia. NIAS Press.

10. Collier, P. (2007). The Bottom Billion: Why the Poorest Countries are Failing and What Can Be Done About It. Oxford University Press.

11. Crocker, C. (2019). African Governance: Challenges and Their Implications. Hoover Institution.

12. ECOWAS (2017). Communiqué on The Gambia Presidential Crisis. ECOWAS Press Release.

13. Elowson, C., & Albuquerque, A. (2016). Challenges to Peace and Security in Eastern Africa: The Role of IGAD, EAC, and EASF. Studies in African Security.

14. Francis, D. J. (2005). Civil Militia: Africa's Intractable Security Menace? Ashgate Publishing.

15. Gallopin, J. B. (2021). Protest and Political Change in the Arab World. Routledge.

16. He, B. (2016). The Institutional Dynamics of China's Great Transformation. Cambridge University Press.

17. Human Rights Watch (2024). Uganda: Court Upholds Anti-Homosexuality Act. Human Rights Watch.

18. International Monetary Fund (IMF). (2019). Regional Economic Outlook: Sub-Saharan Africa. IMF Publications.

19. International Monetary Fund. (2022). Regional Economic Outlook: Sub-Saharan Africa. IMF Publications.

20. Johnson, D. H. (2016). South Sudan: A New History for a New Nation. Ohio University Press.

21. Kinzer, S. (2003). All the Shah's Men: An American Coup and the Roots of Middle East Terror. John Wiley & Sons.

22. Le Billon, P. (2001). The Political Ecology of War: Natural Resources and Armed Conflicts. Political Geography.

23. Magufuli, J. P. (2021). Nationalism and Foreign Investment: The Bagamoyo Port Project. Tanzania Development Review.

24. Marchal, R. (2015). Central African Republic:

Back to War Again? The World Today, 71(2), 22-24.

25. McGregor, A. (2020). Russia's Wagner Group in Libya: Real Influence or Illusion? Terrorism Monitor, 18(10).

26. Ndlovu-Gatsheni, S. J. (2009). Do 'Zimbabweans' Exist? Trajectories of Nationalism, National Identity Formation and Crisis in a Postcolonial State. Peter Lang.

27. Nest, M., Grignon, F., & Kisangani, E. F. (2006). The Democratic Republic of Congo: Economic Dimensions of War and Peace. Lynne Rienner Publishers.

28. Peou, S. (2009). International Democracy Assistance for Peacebuilding: Cambodia and Beyond. Palgrave Macmillan.

29. Ross, M. L. (2004). How Do Natural Resources Influence Civil War? Evidence from Thirteen Cases. International Organization.

30. Rossabi, M. (2005). Modern Mongolia: From Khans to Commissars to Capitalists. University of California Press.

31. Shambaugh, D. (2020). China's Future. Polity.

32. Suleiman, M., & Onapajo, H. (2022). African Democracies: Between Life and Death. African Studies Review.

33. Suleiman, M. & Onapajo, H. (2022) Why West Africa has had so many coups and how to prevent more. The Conversation.

34. Stubbs, R. (2005). Rethinking Asia's Economic Miracle: The Political Economy of War, Prosperity, and Crisis. Palgrave Macmillan.

35. Thompson, M. R. (1995). The Anti-Marcos Struggle: Personalistic Rule and Democratic Transition in the Philippines. Yale University Press.

36. United Nations Conference on Trade and Development (UNCTAD). (2020). World Investment Report 2020. UNCTAD.

37. United Nations Environment Programme (UNEP). (2015). Natural Resources and Conflict: A Guide for Mediation Practitioners. UNEP.

38. Vines, A. (2021). The New Era of Coups in Africa: What is Happening? Chatham House.

39. World Bank. (2021). Political Stability and Absence of Violence/Terrorism: Overview. World Bank.

FIFTEEN

AFRO-RENEWAL: A VISION FOR NEW BEGINNINGS

IN THE HEART OF THESE CHRONICLES, I PRESENT A VISION called Afro-Renewal, a canvas of hope and regeneration for Africa. This vision is not just a dream but a meticulously crafted catalogue of strategies and ideas designed to guide Africa towards a horizon of political stability and economic prosperity. As I unravel the journey of independence across various African countries, I realize that self-rule was achieved through motley means, depending on the region and the level of encroachment of the white masterclass. Nonetheless, involving the people directly in determining who gets to lead them was the common denominator of good for what ailed Africa. Afro-Renewal draws from this assumption of a democratic order. In its grand scheme, we can discern seven robust pillars that uphold this vision for Africa's resurgence. Each pillar presupposes our collective resolve to forge a future resplendent with opportunity and imbued with justice.

Pillar 1: Corporate Governance

This pillar embodies the principles of ethical leadership and managerial accountability, reinforcing the structure of businesses and public entities alike by demanding transparency and integrity in all corporate dealings. During the colonial period, many African economies were structured around corporate entities controlled by European powers. Companies such as the British South Africa Company in Zimbabwe, the Sierra Leone Company, and the Royal Niger Company in Nigeria were granted charters by their respective colonial governments, allowing them to operate both as business entities and quasi-governmental bodies (Fyfe, 1962; Hopkins, 1973).

Blending the extraction of wealth with the administration of territories, the Sierra Leone Company, for example, was pivotal in shaping the early colonial framework of Sierra Leone. The company managed not only trade but also set the foundations for what would become one of Britain's colonial administrations in Africa. Operating under charters granted by their imperial patrons, these companies often acted with the authority typically reserved for state institutions (Kup, 1961). They levied taxes, enacted laws, and administered justice, acting as de facto governments over vast territories. This period laid the groundwork for early corporate governance structures in Africa, though they were heavily skewed toward colonial interests (Anderson & Rathbone, 2000).

However, this blending of corporate and colonial governance was fraught with inherent conflicts of interest and accountability issues. The primary allegiance of these companies was to their shareholders and profitability rather than to the indigenous populations. The governance structures of these companies were primarily designed to benefit shareholders back in Europe, often at the expense of local populations (Acemoglu & Robinson, 2012). The result was a governance system that prioritized resource extraction over the welfare of local communities, leading to exploitation and significant social grievances.

Drawing a parallel to contemporary political parties in Africa, there lies a lesson in the structure and operation of these early corporate entities. Today's political parties can learn from the operational strength and adapt certain structural efficiencies from colonial companies with royal charter to administer territories, while fundamentally altering the ethical shortcomings, intent and inclusivity of governance attendant with them. This is against the backdrop that many of our political parties operate without the rigorous governance frameworks typical of corporations, which are accountable to their shareholders and bound by structured corporate governance principles. This lack of structure has led to grave inefficiencies and endemic corruption, much as the unchecked power of colonial companies led to exploitative practices.

The need of the hour for African political parties is to reimagine themselves along the lines of corporate entities, viewing the citizenry as shareholders who have a stake in the governance and outcomes of their administration. Just as a corporation is accountable to its shareholders, so too should political parties (not just ruling ones) be accountable to the voters. This transition would involve adopting clear governance structures, ensuring transparency in their operations, and holding leaders accountable for their actions. Such a transformation could enhance the viability of governments, making them more effective and responsive to the needs of their people.

In Africa, political parties are often the primary organizations responsible for forming democratic governments. The structure and strength of these parties are crucial to a nation's democratic trajectory and overall prosperity. Throughout the continent, there are instances where weakly structured political parties have led to fragile governance systems and ineffective public service delivery.

For example, in nations like the Democratic Republic of the Congo (DRC) and Zimbabwe, the political party systems have been characterized by fragmentation and lack of internal cohesion. This has resulted in unstable government coalitions, frequent shifts in policy direction, and an inability to effectively implement long-term development plans. In these countries, the weak party structures contribute directly to governance challenges, including corruption and limited accountability, which in turn affect economic stability and the quality of life for citizens.

Now, let us imagine African governments as viable corporations where every citizen is a shareholder entitled to transparency, accountability, and dividends in the form of social services and good governance. This corporate-like structure could significantly alter the landscape of political accountability in Africa, ensuring that leaders serve the interests of their constituents efficiently and ethically. It is a vision for political parties, that is not just an ideal but a practical blueprint for fostering sustainable governance structures that can drive the continent towards greater prosperity and stability in an era of Afro-Renewal.

Our political parties can learn valuable lessons from the structured governance, long-term planning, and management efficiencies practiced by corporate entities. Adopting a structured governance model with clearly defined roles and responsibilities can lead to more efficient decision-making and enhanced accountability. Emulating the long-term planning focus of companies, political parties could prioritize sustainable development goals, aligning their strategies with visions that surpass short-term electoral gains. Furthermore, by adopting management practices that emphasize operational efficiency and effective service delivery, political parties can ensure that government operations are streamlined and productive, reducing unnecessary bureaucracy and focusing on results. These adaptations, while drawing on corporate models, should fundamentally aim at promoting the public good and inclusive development.

Should existing political parties fail to adopt a corporate mindset, it is essential to open the political space to new parties that operate with a corporate approach, competing to govern the state akin to how colonial companies once did. However, in this modern context, it is the citizens who will act as shareholders, playing a critical role in guiding and benefiting from the governance of their country. Such parties are likely to implement business best practices like strategic planning and rigorous accountability mechanisms, leading to more effective administration and service delivery. They may also bring innovative problem-solving approaches, utilize data-driven decision-making, and attract diverse, skilled professionals who can offer new perspectives on policy issues.

Additionally, these parties could foster a focus on long-term sustainable development and improve public engagement, aligning governance more closely with citizen needs. The introduction of corporate-like parties could also increase competition in the political arena, prompting all parties to enhance their performance and governance standards. However, it's crucial to ensure that these entities prioritize public interest and uphold democratic values to maintain fairness and inclusiveness in governance.

Pillar 2: Democratic Resilience

Here lies the heart of governance, where democratic institutions are fortified—judiciaries, electoral bodies, and anti-corruption agencies—standing as sentinels of integrity and accountability. This pillar is dedicated to nurturing a system where laws govern, and rights are protected, ensuring that every African lives under the benevolent shade of justice and equality. Africa's democratic landscape is poised for significant transformation through the integration of advanced digital technologies and decentralized governance models, which collectively aim to enhance electoral integrity, boost citizen engagement, and empower local communities.

- *Digital Voting and Blockchain in Elections*: Digital voting technology allows votes to be cast electronically, which can streamline the voting process, reduce errors, and increase transparency. Few countries have adopted electronic voting systems to facilitate smoother and faster elections, ensuring that each vote is accurately recorded and swiftly counted. The adoption of blockchain technology in electoral processes is a crucial development. This technology offers a secure and transparent way to conduct elections, making each vote traceable and immutable. By securing the voting process against fraud, blockchain technology helps build trust in electoral outcomes. As each vote becomes a block in an unbreakable chain, nations like Sierra Leone, where electoral trust is the bedrock of peace, can cast aside the shadows of doubt. Here, blockchain is not just technology but a beacon of trust, ensuring that the echoes of the past

—fraught with disputes and disquiet—do not cloud the present.

- *Civic Tech Platforms:* The expansion of civic tech platforms is another significant innovation. These platforms enable more direct and continuous interaction between citizens and their governments. For example, tools like the open data portal adopted in Sierra Leone under the Open Government Initiative (OGI) supported by the World Bank program funded Open Government Partnership (OGP) was a success story in creating open channels of communication between government and the people. Such platforms, before they were abandoned by the less transparent government of Julius Maada Bio, were used to conduct virtual town halls and provide legislative updates, allowing citizens to express their opinions and concerns directly to their representatives. By adopting these strategies, African nations can leverage civic tech platforms to enhance democratic engagement, improve government transparency and accountability, and ultimately foster a more stable and democratic future. This approach not only brings government operations closer to the people but also empowers citizens to play an active role in shaping their governance structures.

- *Judicial Innovation:* To bolster their role in supporting democracy in Africa, judiciaries can implement several key innovations. Digital transformation, such as the introduction of e-filing and virtual courtrooms, can make judicial processes more efficient and accessible. Continuous training for judges on contemporary legal issues will ensure more informed and fair judgments, while public engagement programs can increase the judiciary's transparency and boost public trust. Promoting Alternative Dispute Resolution (ADR) methods can alleviate the caseload on courts and provide quicker resolutions. Establishing robust systems for monitoring judicial performance and ensuring the judiciary's financial and administrative independence will protect against external influences and enhance accountability. Moreover, fostering international collaborations can help African judiciaries to adopt best practices and effectively tackle transnational legal challenges. These steps will enhance the judiciary's responsiveness, transparency, and effectiveness, thereby strengthening its support for democratic governance across Africa.

- *Decentralized Decision-Making*: Down to the grassroots, where the heart of Africa beats strongest, decentralized decision-making empowers local communities. In few countries, decentralization has allowed communities to have more control over local decisions and resources, tailoring solutions to fit local needs and priorities. This approach not only improves government responsiveness but also increases public satisfaction with government services by making them more relevant and accessible to local populations.
- *E-Petitions*: Digital platforms enable citizens across the continent, from urban centers like Lagos to rural areas, to initiate and sign petitions online. These e-petitions allow individuals to rally support

for causes they care about, directly influencing policy and legislative decisions by demonstrating clear public support or dissent.

- *Public Consultations:* Tools such as online forums and survey platforms must be increasingly utilized for public consultations. In Kenya, the platform Ushahidi has been pivotal in allowing for real-time public feedback on various issues. It broadens participation by reaching a larger and more diverse group of individuals and also helps governments make informed decisions that reflect the will of the people.

- *Anti-Corruption Technologies:* The deployment of anti-corruption technologies like blockchain in Africa can significantly enhance economic prosperity by improving transparency and accountability in government operations. By creating immutable records of transactions, these technologies can reduce corruption, ensuring fair procurement and efficient resource allocation. Increased transparency attracts foreign investment, stabilizes the economy, and builds public trust by ensuring that funds reach their intended destinations. For example, Nigeria uses blockchain to ensure the proper distribution of government subsidies, enhancing efficiency and supporting local markets. Overall, integrating these technologies can lead to a more transparent, stable, and prosperous economic environment across Africa.

- *Legal Framework for Independent Candidacies:* Implementing legal frameworks to support independent candidacies in Africa can significantly enhance democracy by broadening electoral competition and providing an alternative to traditional party politics. This change can lead to increased accountability and reduced influence of money and corruption in politics, as independent candidates often operate with less financial backing. Moreover, these candidates can introduce innovative solutions to national issues and better represent marginalized groups, thereby increasing public satisfaction with the democratic process. It also promotes political stability by creating a more inclusive electoral environment. Overall, supporting independent candidacies can make African political systems more inclusive, responsive, and stable, benefiting countries with diverse societies like Kenya and South Africa.

As these methods deploy across the continent, a new democratic vista opens—wide and welcoming. Blockchain's integrity, combined with the connectivity of civic tech and the empowering embrace of decentralization, crafts a democracy robust and resilient. This kind of innovation harmonizes to ensure that Africa's democratic future is not only sound but also sings with the voices of all its people, a chorus of participation in a land where every vote is counted, every voice is heard, and every community shapes its destiny. This is the future—democratic, decentralized, digital—resonating with the promise of peace and prosperity.

Pillar 3: Enlightened Empowerment

This pillar illuminates our path with education and capacity building. It calls upon us to cultivate knowledge and skills, empowering our people to navigate the complexities of civic life and the convolutions of an evolving economy. Here, every citizen is both a learner and a contributor, equipped to drive change and thrive in a continent on the move. Education is central to this pillar, as it aims to illuminate the path forward for young Africans across the continent. From rural schools to urban universities, education acts as the foundation upon which individuals can build a better future for themselves and their communities. By investing in education, Africa can cultivate a generation of well-informed citizens who are prepared to take on roles as leaders, innovators, and thinkers.

Alongside formal education, capacity building through vocational training and skill development is equally important. Workshops and training programs provide practical skills that are directly applicable to the job market, enabling Africans to contribute effectively to their local economies. Whether it's through technology, agriculture, or entrepreneurship, these skills empower individuals to create, innovate, and drive economic growth. The empowered citizenry is better equipped to engage in civic activities, participate in democratic processes, and contribute to economic development. They become active players in governance, advocating for their rights and participating in decision-making processes that affect their lives.

To achieve enlightened empowerment, as envisioned in this concept, several practical interventions can be implemented across the continent. These interventions aim to educate, equip, and engage citizens, fostering a culture of continuous learning and active participation in civic life.

- *Community Learning Centers:* Establish community centers across both urban and rural areas that provide access to books, computers, and other educational resources. These centers would serve as hubs for learning and innovation, offering courses and workshops that cater to all age groups and skill levels.

- *Vocational Training Facilities:* Set up vocational training facilities that offer practical skills training in various trades and technologies. These workshops would focus on equipping young people with the skills needed for current and future job markets, encouraging entrepreneurship and self-employment.

- *Digital Infrastructure Expansion:* Expand digital infrastructure to ensure that all areas, especially underserved rural regions, have access to reliable internet. This would enable online learning and virtual participation in educational and civic activities, helping to bridge the digital divide.

- *Cultural and Artistic Hubs:* Develop cultural centers that promote local art and heritage while also serving as venues for community gatherings and discussions. These hubs would enhance cultural appreciation and encourage a deeper understanding of diverse African identities and histories.

- *Civic Engagement Platforms:* Create platforms such as an open data portal and other forums where citizens can engage in governance processes, such as town hall meetings and community discussions. These platforms would empower citizens to voice their opinions, participate in decision-making, and hold their leaders accountable.

This approach not only supports the educational and professional development of individuals but also strengthens democratic processes and enhances community cohesion. Through continuous learning, skill development, and active civic participation, the continent can move towards a more prosperous and stable future.

Pillar 4: Inclusive Governance:

Inclusive governance ensures that all voices are heard and integrated into the policymaking process, emphasizing that no one is left behind. Inclusive governance champions diversity, promoting policies that recognize and celebrate the unique cultural, ethnic, and social fabric of the continent.

It actively promotes gender equality, ensuring that women have equal opportunities in political, social, and economic spheres. It also focuses on empowering the youth and marginalized groups, providing them with platforms to participate actively in governance. Such empowerment helps transform these groups from passive observers of the political process to active contributors and decision-makers. Inclusive governance also prioritizes the building of bridges across various divides, be they ethnic, regional, or economic. By fostering a sense of unity and mutual respect, it encourages different groups to work together towards common goals, enhancing societal cohesion and stability.

This model of governance is not just about including diverse voices but also about ensuring transparency and accountability. It seeks to make the government more responsive to the needs and aspirations of all its citizens, reflecting a collective will that drives national development. Through such a governance structure, Africa can harness its diverse strengths, turning challenges into opportunities for growth and progress.

For Africa to truly benefit from inclusive governance, several interventions can be strategically implemented to ensure all segments of society are represented and have a voice in the governance processes. Here are some key interventions:

- *Constitutional and Legal Reforms*: Reform legal frameworks to ensure they mandate inclusivity in all government and public sector bodies. This could include implementing quotas for women, youth, and minorities in political positions and public service roles, ensuring these groups are fairly represented.
- *Youth Leadership Programs*: Develop and fund leadership and entrepreneurship programs targeted at the youth. These programs can help nurture a new generation of leaders who are committed to inclusivity and equipped to handle future challenges.
- *Gender-Sensitive Policies*: Implement policies that specifically address the barriers faced by women in political and public life. This could include measures to combat gender-based violence, ensure equal economic opportunities, and support women in leadership roles.
- *Inclusion in Economic Policies*: Design economic policies that ensure equal opportunities for all, including access to credit, land, and education, particularly for historically disadvantaged groups.
- *Decentralization of Power*: Strengthen local governance by decentralizing powers, which allows local communities more control over their resources and decisions. This approach can make governance more responsive and tailored to the unique needs of diverse communities.

- *Civic Education*: Expand civic education programs that not only educate citizens about their rights and responsibilities but also empower them to participate effectively in the governance process. This education should be accessible to all citizens, including marginalized communities.
- *Public Consultation Mechanisms*: Establish and enforce mechanisms for public consultation in the legislative process. This can include digital platforms that allow citizens to comment on proposed laws and policies, and public forums where community members can engage directly with their representatives.
- *Enhanced Representation in Political Parties*: Encourage political parties to adopt inclusivity in their ranks and leadership positions. Parties should be incentivized to diversify their candidate slates and leadership to better reflect the demographic makeup of their constituencies.
- *Transparency and Accountability Initiatives*: Implement technologies and policies that increase government transparency and accountability. This could involve open government data portals, live streaming of parliamentary sessions, and regular public reporting on government performance and spending.
- *Support for Civil Society Organizations*: Strengthen support for civil society organizations that advocate for minority rights and inclusivity. Such organizations can play a crucial role in holding governments accountable and pushing for more inclusive policies.

These interventions can help pave the way for a more inclusive governance structure in Africa, ensuring that the continent's governance evolves in a way that genuinely reflects and benefits its diverse populations. It builds bridges across divides, fostering a society where diversity is our strength and every voice can say its truth.

Pillar 5: Economic Renaissance

For too long, Africa has relied heavily on its natural resources, but now, we envision a new future—one that is diverse, sustainable, and innovative. In this new chapter, agriculture takes center stage. No longer just a means of survival, farming becomes a symbol of progress. Farmers use modern technology to turn dry lands into thriving fields, growing enough food to feed not just local communities, but entire countries. This sustainable approach ensures that the land remains fertile and productive for generations to come.

Before leaving my country, I had a vision to transform agriculture, promote agri-business, and bring about food security. I communicated this vision to the Home-Grown School Feeding Feasibility Studies run in partnership with the Ministry of Education. I envisioned building an information ecosystem that supports sustainability and precision in farming while we assess farmers' adoption of new crop varieties and identify the barriers they face. By utilizing existing networks, we will have a "network of networks." This initiative will include a fee-based network of rural agents, the development of seed catalogues and protocols for nationwide distribution, and a strategy to prevent the use of poor-quality seeds.

We will also leverage post-harvest technologies for distribution and organize training sessions on machine learning to enhance farmers' knowledge and productivity. To ensure efficient delivery, we will establish grain corridors that connect schools and utilize last-mile delivery logistics, including drones, to reach remote areas quickly and effectively.

Through a collaborative network of policymakers, farmers, schools, and community stakeholders, we will create a comprehensive feedback loop. This involves linking scientific research to data, building insights into decision support tools, and using these tools to guide farmers while continuously monitoring their activities. This data-driven approach will feed back into the network, ensuring continuous improvement. Recognizing that farming is knowledge-intensive, we will engage farmers in understanding the interactions between climate, topography, and soil to optimize their practices.

Technology also plays a crucial role in this economic renaissance. Young innovators across the continent are harnessing the power of the digital age, creating new businesses and solutions that connect remote villages to bustling cities. Their creativity and determination are transforming Africa into a hub of technological advancement, where ideas flourish and opportunities abound.

Manufacturing, once a dormant sector, is coming to life with renewed vigor. Factories produce goods that are not only high-quality but also environmentally friendly. Such sustainable manufacturing ensures that Africa's growth does not come at the expense of its natural beauty. Products bearing the mark of Africa become symbols of craftsmanship and innovation, respected worldwide.

This renaissance is more than just economic growth; it is about building a sustainable future. By focusing on renewable energy sources like wind and solar power, Africa can protect its environment while powering its development. Conservation efforts restore forests and waterways, ensuring that natural resources are preserved for future generations.

As someone living far from home, I long to see this transformation. Although I am disheartened by the challenges Africa faces, I hold onto the hope that one day, I will witness this economic renaissance. My heart remains connected to my homeland, and I dream of a time when Africa stands strong and prosperous, a beacon of hope and innovation on the global stage.

As an asylee that cannot return to my country now based on my views, this is my vision for Africa's future— a diverse and sustainable economy driven by agriculture, technology, and manufacturing. It is a future where growth and environmental stewardship go hand in hand, ensuring that the continent thrives today and for many generations to come. This economic renaissance is the key to unlocking Africa's full potential and securing a brighter, more prosperous future for all its people.

Pillar 6: Peer Review by African Leaders: A Path to Africa's Democratic Future

There lies a promise of a future where democracy flourishes, and good governance is the norm. This vision is nurtured by the collective wisdom and mutual accountability of African leaders through a peer review mechanism. Regional and continental bodies must look at their metrics and engage in name calling.

The APRM, a unique instrument born from the aspirations of the African Union, stood as a beacon of hope, until it ran out of steam. It was a testament to Africa's commitment to uphold the principles of democracy, human rights, and sustainable development. Through this platform, African nations voluntarily submit to self-assessment and external review by their peers, fostering a culture of transparency and accountability.

Peer review by African leaders is ideal for Africa's democratic future because it is rooted in shared experiences and common goals. Leaders, bound by the collective history and future of the continent, are uniquely positioned to offer insights, constructive criticism, and support. They understand the complexities and nuances of governing in Africa, making their reviews relevant and impactful.

However, to complement the shortcomings of the APRM and make democracy and good governance work for Africa, we must take a few key steps:

- *Strengthening Institutional Capacity*: The APRM must be empowered with greater resources and expertise. Building a robust secretariat with skilled professionals can enhance the quality and depth of the reviews. Continuous training and development for those involved in the process will ensure that the mechanism evolves with the changing political landscape.
- *Enhancing Participation and Inclusivity*: For the peer review process to be truly effective, it must involve a wide range of stakeholders, including civil society, academia, and the private sector. Their voices and perspectives can provide a holistic view of the challenges and opportunities within each country, leading to more comprehensive and actionable recommendations.
- *Ensuring Follow-Up and Implementation*: Recommendations from the peer review process should not gather dust on shelves. Establishing a robust follow-up mechanism to monitor the implementation of these recommendations is crucial. Regular progress reports and reviews can keep the momentum going and hold leaders accountable for making tangible changes.

- *Promoting Cross-Border Learning and Collaboration*: African nations can learn a great deal from each other's experiences. Facilitating exchanges and collaboration between countries can help spread best practices and innovative solutions. Regional workshops, conferences, and study tours can foster a spirit of cooperation and collective advancement.
- *Utilizing Technology and Data*: In this digital age, technology can be a powerful ally. Leveraging data analytics and digital platforms can enhance the peer review process, making it more efficient and transparent. Real-time data can provide accurate insights and enable timely interventions.
- *Encouraging Political Will and Commitment*: Ultimately, the success of the APRM hinges on the political will of African leaders. A renewed commitment to the principles of democracy and good governance, backed by genuine action, can inspire confidence and drive progress.

Through these steps, we can transform the APRM into a dynamic and effective tool for promoting democracy and good governance across Africa. As the sun sets on the old ways and rises on a new era of accountability and transparency, Africa will stand poised to fulfill its democratic promise. In this journey, peer review by African leaders is not just an ideal but a necessity. It is a testament to our collective strength, wisdom, and determination to shape a future where every African can thrive in a just and democratic society. Together, we can build a continent where the dreams of today become the realities of tomorrow.

Pillar 7: Looking Outward

Africa must actively engage with the world to ensure its voice is heard and its interests protected. I envision a new Africa that will take a proactive stance on geopolitical developments, recognizing that global conflicts often significantly impact our continent. By participating in international forums and advocating for justice and stability, Africa can influence global governance while maintaining its sovereignty and values. For instance, South Africa brought a case against Israel at the International Court of Justice, accusing it of genocide for the bombing of innocent civilians in Gaza. As it demonstrates our potential to uphold international justice and assert our moral stance on global issues, this action underscores the importance of addressing injustices beyond our borders and sets a precedent for other African nations. By following South Africa's lead, countries across the continent can collectively enhance Africa's influence on the global stage, advocating for human rights and justice.

This ambitious vision requires courage, unity, and a relentless pursuit of justice, ensuring Africa's voice shapes global change and secures a prosperous and harmonious future.

- *Geopolitical Awareness and Engagement*

Africa must be acutely aware of the indirect effects of geopolitical developments on our continent. Global conflicts, economic policies, and environmental issues often have far-reaching consequences that exacerbate our challenges. Thus, our engagement must be proactive, ensuring that our interests are safeguarded and our perspectives are integrated into global decisions.

For too long, Africa has been reactive to global events, often bearing the brunt of disruptions without having a say in their resolution. This must change. Our leaders should actively participate in international forums, advocating for policies that promote stability, equitable trade, and sustainable development. By doing so, we not only protect our interests but also contribute to a more balanced and fair global order.

- *A Collective Effort*

This vision for Africa's outward engagement is not just about governments; it is a collective effort involving civil society, businesses, and the broader citizenry. African academics, activists, and entrepreneurs must also be present in global discussions, bringing diverse perspectives and innovative solutions. A collective voice will amplify our presence and ensure that Africa is not just a participant but a leader in shaping global agendas.

- *Competing Globally*

Positioning ourselves on the world stage is crucial for Africa to be taken seriously and to compete globally. It involves not only political and diplomatic efforts but also economic and cultural exchanges. African nations must seek strategic partnerships that enhance our technological capabilities, boost our economies, and promote our rich cultural heritage. Imagine an Africa where our technological innovations lead global advancements, where our economies are resilient and thriving, and where our cultural influence is celebrated worldwide. This is a future where Africa is a key player, respected, and valued for its contributions to global progress.

References

1. Acemoglu, D., & Robinson, J. A. (2012). Why Nations Fail: The Origins of Power, Prosperity, and Poverty. Crown Business.

2. Adebajo, A. (2010). The Curse of Berlin: Africa after the Cold War. Hurst & Company.

3. African Union. (2020). African Peer Review Mechanism (APRM).

4. African Union. (2020). African Union Strategy for Mainstreaming Geopolitics into African Foreign Policy.

5. Anderson, D. M., & Rathbone, R. (2000). Africa's Urban Past. James Currey Publishers.

6. APRM Secretariat. (2009). African Peer Review Mechanism Annual Report.

7. Autesserre, S. (2010). The Trouble with the Congo: Local Violence and the Failure of International Peacebuilding. Cambridge University Press.

8. Bond, P. (2006). Looting Africa: The Economics of Exploitation. Zed Books.

9. Boone, C. (2003). Political Topographies of the African State: Territorial Authority and Institutional Choice. Cambridge University Press.

10. British Broadcasting Corporation (BBC). (2020). #EndSARS Protests: A Timeline of the Movement in Nigeria. BBC News.

11. Bush, R. (2007). Poverty and Neoliberalism: Persistence and Reproduction in the Global South. Pluto Press.

12. Chigora, P., & Chisi, T. (2009). South-South Cooperation: The Case for Africa's Involvement in Global Governance. Journal of International Affairs.

13. Cilliers, J., & Sisk, T. (2013). Assessing Long-Term State Fragility in Africa: Prospects for the African Union's Peer Review Mechanism. African Futures Paper, Institute for Security Studies.

14. Cohen, J. (2022). Macron's Pivot to Africa: France's New Diplomatic Strategy. Foreign Policy.

15. Council on Foreign Relations. (2022). Africa in the World: Implications for Global Stability and Prosperity.

16. Crocker, C. (2019). African Governance: Challenges and Their Implications. Hoover Institution.

17. Davidson, B. (1992). The Black Man's Burden: Africa and the Curse of the Nation-State. Times Books.

18. Farah, I., Kiamba, S., & Mazongo, K. (2011). Major Challenges Facing Africa in the 21st Century: A Few Provocative Remarks. International Journal of African Renaissance Studies, 6(2), 171-194.

19. Fyfe, C. (1962). A History of Sierra Leone. Oxford University Press.

20. Herbert, R., & Gruzd, S. (2008). The African Peer Review Mechanism: Lessons from the Pioneers. South African Institute of International Affairs.

21. Hopkins, A. G. (1973). An Economic History of West Africa. Longman.

22. Human Rights Watch. (2024). Uganda: Court Upholds Anti-Homosexuality Act. Human Rights Watch.

23. International Monetary Fund (IMF). (2019). Regional Economic Outlook: Sub-Saharan Africa.

24. Johnson, H. F. (2011). Waging Peace in Sudan: The Inside Story of the Negotiations That Ended Africa's Longest Civil War. Sussex Academic Press.

25. Kagwanja, P., & Kondlo, K. (2009). State of the Nation: South Africa 2008. HSRC Press.

26. Kaplan, R. D. (1994). The Coming Anarchy: How Scarcity, Crime, Overpopulation, and Disease Are Rapidly Destroying the Social Fabric of Our Planet. The Atlantic Monthly.

27. Khadiagala, G. M. (2001). African Foreign Policies: Power and Process. Lynne Rienner Publishers.

28. Kup, P. (1961). A History of Sierra Leone, 1400-1787. Cambridge University Press.

29. Landsberg, C. (2004). The Quiet Diplomacy of Liberation: International Politics and South Africa's Transition. Jacana Media.

30. Le Billon, P. (2001). The Political Ecology of War: Natural Resources and Armed Conflicts. Political Geography.

31. Makinda, S. M., & Okumu, F. W. (2007). The African Union: Challenges of Globalization, Security, and Governance. Routledge.

32. Maru, M. T. (2013). The Role of Africa in the Geopolitical Shifts of the 21st Century. Strategic Review for Southern Africa.

33. Masterson, G. (2005). Defining Civil Society in the Context of the African Peer Review Mechanism (APRM). Electoral Institute for Sustainable Democracy in Africa (EISA).

34. Mazrui, A. A. (1986). The Africans: A Triple Heritage. BBC Publications.

35. Mbeki, T. (2003). The African Union and Peer Review Mechanism. South African Journal of International Affairs, 10(2), 1-8.

36. Mills, L. (2022). Narrow Framing of Democracy in Africa. Democracy in Africa Blog.

37. Mutume, G. (2002). African Peer Review Process on Track. Africa Recovery.

38. Nganje, F. (2013). The African Peer Review Mechanism and the Promotion of Human Security in Africa: A Critical Reflection. African Security Review.

39. Nest, M., Grignon, F., & Kisangani, E. F. (2006). The Democratic Republic of Congo: Economic Dimensions of War and Peace. Lynne Rienner Publishers.

40. Pape, R. (1997). Why Economic Sanctions Do Not Work. MIT Press Direct.

41. Rodney, W. (1972). How Europe Underdeveloped Africa. Bogle-L'Ouverture Publications.

42. Ross, M. L. (2004). How Do Natural Resources Influence Civil War? Evidence from Thirteen Cases. International Organization.

43. Sachs, J. D. (2005). The End of Poverty: Economic Possibilities for Our Time. Penguin Press.

44. South African Institute of International Affairs. (2021). South Africa and the International Criminal Court: The Challenge of a Coherent Foreign Policy.

45. Swaniker, F. (2016). Great Leaders Aren't Born – They're Made. And Africa is Showing Us How. World Economic Forum.

46. Turianskyi, Y. (2012). The APRM: A Case Study in Democratic Institution Building?. The Centre for Policy Studies (CPS).

47. United Nations Conference on Trade and Development (UNCTAD). (2020). World Investment Report 2020.

48. United Nations Economic Commission for Africa. (2017). Africa's Engagement with the International Community: Strategies for the 21st Century.

49. United Nations Environment Programme (UNEP). (2015). Natural Resources and Conflict: A Guide for Mediation Practitioners.

50. World Bank. (2021). Political Stability and Absence of Violence/Terrorism: Overview.

51. Zartman, I. W. (1995). Collapsed States: The Disintegration and Restoration of Legitimate Authority. Lynne Rienner Publishers.

AFTERWORD

As my reflections unfurl, each page of the last two chapters is a step towards a future where Africa's stability is unshakeable, its growth inclusive, and its place on the world stage, indomitable. This is not just a renewal but a profound transformation—a renaissance of a continent ready to claim its destiny with both hands.

The journey chronicled in "Resurgence of Coups in Africa: Reflections from the Diaspora" is not merely a personal narrative but a testament to the struggles and aspirations of millions of Africans. Forced to flee my homeland, I now find myself in exile, yearning for the day when my return will signify not just personal closure but a triumph of good governance and democracy in Africa.

The migration crisis in Europe and America is an ever-growing concern, a living, breathing narrative of the African soul yearning for the promise of a brighter tomorrow. This crisis calls for introspection and action, for the realization that true change must come from within. It beckons leaders to rise above self-interest and embrace the collective good, to transform governance and foster environments where dreams can flourish. The root of this mass exodus lies in the systemic failures of leadership across the continent, where political instability, economic mismanagement, and corruption force people to seek refuge in distant lands.

By the time this book is published, Sierra Leone's elections will be decided by an out-of-court investigation committee. This committee, born out of necessity, underscores the judiciary's loss of credibility and the urgent need for electoral justice. Sierra Leone stands as a microcosm of the broader African experience, where compromised institutions and disenfranchised populations cry out for justice and reform.

The people of Sierra Leone need electoral justice; the English-speaking people of Southern Cameroon need a permanent solution to their conflict with Paul Biya. The endless cycles of amendments allowing autocrats to extend their terms must be abolished. France's role in Africa must be critically reviewed to ensure it does not perpetuate the very instability it claims to combat. Our business relationships with China must be grounded in mutual respect for human rights and democratic values.

It is time for Western governments and institutions to end the lip service to democracy in Africa. Real change requires more than rhetoric; it demands action that supports the establishment of democratic guardrails and the promotion of good governance. The international community must trace the root of the problem to its source: bad leadership. Without addressing this fundamental issue, any efforts to stem the tide of migration will be futile.

Africans themselves must recognize their agency in fixing the problems of Africa. The recent surge of coups is a reflection of deeper, systemic issues that must be addressed. Allowing these problems to fester only means allowing the spate of unconstitutional changes of government to continue. The continent needs comprehensive interventions to forestall good governance and reverse democratic backsliding.

This book is a call to action for all stakeholders—Africans, international partners, and global institutions. We must collectively strive for a future where Africa's potential is fully realized, where governance is transparent and accountable, and where every citizen can live in peace and prosperity. The last surge of coups is but a reflection of these underlying problems. It is time for a new era of Afro-Renewal, where Africa's renaissance is not just a dream but a tangible reality. Together, we can build a continent that stands proud and strong on the global stage, a beacon of hope and resilience for all.

ACKNOWLEDGEMENTS

I am profoundly grateful to those who have stood by me on this journey of pouring out my reflections about power grabs and leadership in Africa. First and foremost, to my dear mother, Mrs. Isatu Kamara, your unwavering support and boundless love have been the cornerstone of my strength. Your encouragement has been a beacon of light guiding me through the darkest times. To my beloved grandmother, Mrs. Zainab Fullah, your prayers are a constant stream of blessings, nurturing my spirit and fortifying my resolve. Your faith in me has been a source of relentless motivation.

My heartfelt thanks go to my elder sister, Mrs. Nenneh-Binta Kamara in Columbus, Ohio, and my stepmother, Ms. Fatmata Fonti Kanu in Springfield, Virginia. Your generosity in offering me a sanctuary in your homes provided me with the peace and space to reflect and pour out my ideas. Your kindness has been immeasurable.

I am also deeply appreciative of the incredible team at Spines. Alejandra Restrepo, your patience and willingness to answer every question, no matter how trivial, have been invaluable. Andres Herrera, my Project Manager, your editorial expertise and unwavering support have been extraordinary. I could not have wished for a better team to bring this project to life.

To all of you who, for want of space, cannot be mentioned

here, may Allah bless you abundantly. As you read these lines you can be sure that I am referring to you. Your contributions towards my journey this far have been pivotal, and I carry immense gratitude in my heart for each one of you. Thank you.